COLLECTED WORKS OF HARRY G. JOHNSON

MONEY, TRADE AND ECONOMIC GROWTH

MONEY, TRADE AND ECONOMIC GROWTH

Survey Lectures in Economic Theory

HARRY G. JOHNSON

Volume 2

Routledge
Taylor & Francis Group
LONDON AND NEW YORK

First published in 1962
Second edition published in 1964

This edition first published in 2013
by Routledge
2 Park Square, Milton Park, Abingdon, Oxon, OX14 4RN

Simultaneously published in the USA and Canada
by Routledge
605 Third Avenue, New York, NY 10017

First issued in paperback 2022

Routledge is an imprint of the Taylor & Francis Group, an informa business

British Library Cataloguing in Publication Data
A catalogue record for this book is available from the British Library

ISBN 13: 978-0-415-82549-8 (Set) (hbk)
ISBN 13: 978-0-203-49713-5 (Set) (ebk)
ISBN 13: 978-1-03-202946-7 (Volume 2) (pbk)
ISBN 13: 978-0-415-83173-4 (Volume 2) (hbk)
ISBN 13: 978-0-203-64021-0 (Volume 2) (ebk)

DOI: 10.4324/9780203640210

Publisher's Note
The publisher has gone to great lengths to ensure the quality of this reprint but points out that some imperfections in the original copies may be apparent.

Disclaimer
The publisher has made every effort to trace copyright holders and would welcome correspondence from those they have been unable to trace.

HARRY G. JOHNSON

MONEY, TRADE AND ECONOMIC GROWTH

SURVEY LECTURES IN ECONOMIC THEORY

London
UNWIN UNIVERSITY BOOKS

FIRST PUBLISHED IN 1962

SECOND EDITION 1964

UNWIN UNIVERSITY BOOKS
40 Museum Street
London, W.C.1

PRINTED IN GREAT BRITAIN

in 10 point Times Roman

BY SIMSON SHAND LTD.

LONDON, HERTFORD AND HARLOW

TO RAGNAR

PREFACE

This book originated in the Pakistan Refresher Course for Economists, conducted in Karachi in July 1956 under the joint auspices of the International Economic Association and the Pakistan Economic Association, for which Professor Carl Kaysen and I attempted to survey modern developments in economic theory in five lectures each. My lectures, but regrettably not Professor Kaysen's, were later prepared from a tape-recording for publication in the *Pakistan Economic Journal.* Colleagues who have used them for teaching have found them helpful and encouraged me to make them available to a wider audience. Four of them are reproduced in this book (Chapters I, II, V and VII); the fifth, on 'Banking and Monetary Policy', proved on re-reading to be too sadly dated by the Radcliffe Report and the Report of the Commission on Money and Credit to be worth salvaging. In preparing them for re-publication, I have revised them only as much as was required to clarify the argument, and have added references to the books and articles on which I drew in giving the lectures.

I have also included two lectures (Chapters III and IV) delivered to the more extended Pakistan Refresher Course of 1958, conducted at Murree under the same auspices as the previous Course. To the first I have appended a geometrical analysis of customs union, a revised version of two short articles published in the *Indian Journal of Economics.* The second appears in a revised version prepared as a two-lecture series which I was invited to deliver in Copenhagen in the spring of 1959; since this lecture follows the outline of my own previous work more closely than the others, I have appended a bibliography of recent work on trade and growth prepared for me by Herbert F. Wass, in lieu of extensive bibliographical notes to the text itself.

Finally, I have included three recent papers (Chapters VI, VIII and IX). The commemorative lecture on *The General Theory* was delivered at the invitation of the American Economic Association to its December 1960 meetings at St Louis; it has been revised to include some extra material and the bibliographical references that time and the space limitations of the *Papers and Proceedings* forced me to sacrifice. *The Political Economy of Opulence* was read to the June 1960 meetings of the Canadian Economics and Political Science Association at Kingston; it puts in final form ideas previously tested on various university audiences in England. *The Social Policy of an Opulent Society*, a sequel to it, was the opening address to the Forty-first Annual Conference of the Canadian Welfare Council, held in Ottawa in May 1961.

I have described the contents of this book as survey lectures to indicate that they aim at reviewing a broad subject in a short space. Their purpose is to call attention to the prominent features of the terrain, rather than to provide a detailed map of it. Such an endeavour is necessarily impressionistic, and closely governed by personal judgments respecting relevance and significance. I trust that these limitations will be appreciated by my readers.

Technically speaking, the two chapters on opulence are not lectures; nor are they as concerned as the other chapters with the exposition of existing knowledge. But they have in common with the others that they were written for oral presentation, and that they attempt to survey a broad range of ideas. They both, though in different ways, are concerned with the formulation of an economic theory relevant to the problems of what Galbraith has labelled indelibly as 'the affluent society',[1] a society which has successfully attained sustained economic growth. The intrusion of an economist into the field of social welfare work and policy may seem strange to North American (though not to British) readers; nevertheless, I am convinced that this will become an increasingly important field for interesting and fruitful applications of economic analysis.

I should like to make the usual acknowledgments to the editors of the *Pakistan Economic Journal*, *The Indian Journal of Economics*, *Nationaløkonomisk Tidsskrift*, *The Canadian Journal of Economics and Political Science*, and the *Papers and Proceedings of the American Economic Association*, for permission to reproduce material previously published in their pages.

Institute for Economic Research,
Queen's University,
Kingston, Ontario.

July 1961

[1] My reasons for preferring 'opulence' to 'affluence' are given in Chap. VIII. Since this lecture reached its final form I have discovered that Galbraith has used the same term in a more restricted context. Chap. VIII, 101–14 of his *American Capitalism* (Boston: Houghton Mifflin, 1952), which is largely concerned with advertising, is entitled 'The Unseemly Economics of Opulence'.

CONTENTS

PART ONE: TRADE AND GROWTH

I

THE BALANCE OF PAYMENTS*

In the past twenty years, there has been a great deal of change in the theoretical approach to balance-of-payments problems and the mechanism of adjustment. This has been associated, on the one hand, with the Keynesian revolution, which led to the formulation of theories in terms of disequilibrium rather than equilibrium and, on the other hand, with the prevalence of balance-of-payments problems particularly in the post-war period. Very briefly, the change has been from the idea of a mechanism of adjustment to the idea of the balance of payments as a policy problem.

In the classical theories, the analysis of balance-of-payments problems ran in terms of automatic systems of adjustment towards balance-of-payments equilibrium. The two cases considered were: one, the pure gold standard, where adjustment came through automatic and free gold flows raising interest rates in one country and lowering them in the other, thus reducing and increasing the demand and price levels so as to bring about equilibrium; and, two, the other extreme of an inconvertible paper currency, where adjustment came through exchange rate changes which cleared the exchange market. In both systems, the decisions and actions of monetary and economic authorities were treated as a part of the system. The actions which monetary authorities took under the gold standard, for example, were included in the automatic mechanism of adjustment. In the past twenty years we have moved away from that view of an automatic and free system of adjustment towards viewing the balance of payments as a policy problem, and setting up an analysis in which we construct models designed to display continuing disequilibrium, a circumstance which permits us to study alternative ways of rectifying the balance-of-payments disequilibrium. These models have been set

* *Pakistan Economic Journal*, VIII, no. 2, June 1958, 16–28.

up to promote and permit study of balance-of-payments problems in both under-employment and full-employment conditions.

The change-over from the automatic system to the policy problem approach was not an immediate result of the Keynesian revolution. The application of the Keynesian ideas to international trade theory in the period immediately after the Keynesian revolution was conducted largely within the old framework of the mechanism of adjustment. The theory of the foreign trade multiplier, for example, was developed in order to see how far the Keynesian mechanism of variations in income and employment would work to restore equilibrium in the balance of payments, once that equilibrium had been disturbed. Similarly, other extensive Keynesian analyses of the nineteen-thirties, such as that of Mrs Robinson,[1] were concerned with the rôle of income and employment variations in the classical mechanism of adjustment framework.

The development of policy-orientated models has been a post-war development, a development which is due particularly to Professors Meade and Tinbergen. (I do not mean to imply that other writers have not contributed importantly to the subject; but these two writers have written books specifically concerned with this problem, whereas other writers have mainly confined themselves to articles.) Meade, in *The Balance of Payments*,[2] was primarily concerned with the conflict between the requirements of full employment and balance-of-payments equilibrium, and the means of reconciling them. Tinbergen, on the other hand, in his book *On the Theory of Economic Policy*,[3] was concerned with the more general problem of achieving a number of policy objectives with a variety of policy instruments. The general point of importance for economic policy which emerges from the work of both writers, incidentally, is that for each policy objective a separate policy instrument is required. For example, to achieve both full employment and balance-of-payments equilibrium—in Meade's terminology, to preserve both internal and external balance—a country must employ *both* some means of control over its aggregate expenditure *and* some means of control (the exchange rate or trade restrictions) over its international trade. I shall develop this point later on; here I merely want to indicate the general theoretical point involved, that for each policy objective you need a policy instrument.

[1] Joan Robinson, 'The Foreign Exchanges', in *Essays in the Theory of Employment* (London: Macmillan & Co., 1937), 183–209.

[2] J. E. Meade, *The Theory of International Economic Policy*, Volume I: *The Balance of Payments* (London: Oxford University Press, 1951).

[3] J. Tinbergen, *On the Theory of Economic Policy* (Amsterdam: North Holland Publishing Co., 1952).

In the course of his analysis, Meade develops an approach to balance-of-payments problems which is much more suitable to post-war conditions of full employment than the Keynesian analysis previously available. Unfortunately, the most useful aspects of this approach tend to be hidden by Meade's habit of assuming the pursuit of appropriate internal control policies by the Government, without investigating what happens if the Government is not successful in maintaining knife-edge full employment with stable prices. The approach and its implications are more fully developed in Sidney Alexander's article 'The Effects of a Devaluation on a Trade Balance'.[4] Alexander's method of analysis, which has come to be known as 'the absorption approach', has recently been severely criticized by Professor Fritz Machlup, who defends the older 'elasticity approach' to devaluation.[5] My own view of the matter is that the absorption approach is of much more general usefulness for balance-of-payments problems than appears from this particular debate—especially when Meade's work is looked at in the same context. In what follows I shall try to synthesize a general treatment of balance-of-payments problems in terms of this approach, laying particular emphasis on the policy problems.

To start with, it is useful to recall that the existence of a balance-of-payments problem assumes the presence of a monetary authority which intervenes in the foreign exchange market to peg the rate of exchange, using official reserves of gold or foreign exchange to do so. This permits a divergence to arise between the demands of the rest of the country (excluding the monetary authority) for foreign exchange to pay for purchases abroad, and the supply of foreign exchange in return for domestic currency to pay for sales abroad.

The usual approach to the balance of payments is to consider it as the difference between receipts from and payments to foreigners by the residents of the country, excluding the monetary authority. In symbols, the balance of payments is defined as $B = R_f - P_f$. But it is fruitful to define the balance in another way, by using the fact that receipts by residents from residents are identical with payments by residents to residents. By adding these receipts to and subtracting these payments from the balance of payments, the latter is transformed into the difference between total receipts by residents and total payments by residents (again excluding the monetary authorities). In symbols, $B = R - P$. This is the starting point of the absorp-

[4] S. Alexander, 'The Effects of a Devaluation on a Trade Balance', *International Monetary Fund Staff Papers*, II, no. 2, April 1952, 263–78.

[5] F. Machlup, 'The Analysis of Devaluation', *American Economic Review*, XLV, no. 3, June 1955, 255–78.

tion approach to balance-of-payments problems. In discussing these problems, I shall deal throughout with the case of a balance-of-payments deficit, that is, an excess of payments over receipts by residents.

Before I go on to discuss the policy problems, I think it is worth while to investigate briefly the monetary implications of a balance-of-payments deficit. A deficit means that payments by residents exceed receipts by residents, and this implies either one of two things. The first possibility is that residents are running down their cash balances, so that there is an increase in the velocity of circulation of money. With a deficit financed by running down of cash balances, the balance-of-payments deficit would obviously be self-correcting in time, because eventually residents would reduce their cash balances towards zero, and in the process of doing so the rate of interest will rise, demand will be restricted, possibly the supply of goods for export will increase and a variety of factors will set to work which will tend to correct the situation. But nowadays it is very unlikely that monetary authorities will be able to give the economy time to work out the correction of the disequilibrium, because the excess of payments over receipts has to be financed in foreign currency and the monetary authority may well have insufficient reserves to allow the balance-of-payments deficit to go on until it corrects itself. The second possibility is that the monetary authority replaces the cash which is being abstracted by the balance-of-payments deficit, through offsetting internal monetary operations. This will happen automatically if the monetary authority follows a policy of stabilizing interest rates. In this case, the deficit will not be self-correcting: it will be corrected only when the policy of the monetary authority is changed.

To sum up on this point, a balance-of-payments problem implies either that the domestic currency supply is insufficiently backed by a reserve of gold or foreign exchange or that the authorities of the country concerned are pursuing a policy which entails a balance-of-payments problem. In either case, it is evident that a balance-of-payments problem is monetary in nature and that it is fundamentally related to the fact that the banking system can create credit. Both where a country has insufficient international reserves to back its domestic currency and where the monetary authorities replace reserves by other internal assets, credit creation is involved.

That balance-of-payments problems are fundamentally monetary phenomena is an important proposition that must always be borne in mind; it is an obvious proposition, but one which is often overlooked. It has become a habit in writings on policy to discuss 'structural' disequilibrium and other concepts as if exchange rates and other governmental policies had nothing to do with balance-of-payments difficulties. Such concepts may have some usefulness in sorting out primary causative factors or types of solution; but they cannot constitute rigidly separate classes of balance-of-payments problems. Balance-of-payments problems are always fundamentally monetary. This does not, however, mean either that they can always be ascribed to monetary mismanagement, or that monetary policy is either the most appropriate policy to employ or the policy instrument most likely to be effective in correcting a balance-of-payments problem. To put the same point another way, no matter what problems a country may have, their manifestation as a balance-of-payments problem is always a consequence of governmental policy; though it must be recognized that in many cases a balance-of-payments problem is easier to endure than the alternative problems the country could have.

Let me now turn to the policy problem posed by a balance-of-payments deficit. To simplify the argument, I shall exclude international capital transactions (other than those necessary for the financing of the deficit); this, together with the fact that intermediate transactions can be cancelled out, permits us to measure the balance of payments as the difference between total domestic output and domestic expenditure. In symbols, $B=Y-E$; to avoid certain difficulties, it is convenient to conceive output and expenditure in real rather than monetary terms.

A balance-of-payments deficit, on these various assumptions, entails an excess of expenditure over output or income. To correct it, expenditure and income must be brought into equality. The policies which may be employed to produce this result may be divided into two types: policies of expenditure reduction and policies of expenditure switching. A policy of expenditure reduction, or reduction of aggregate demand, implemented for example by higher taxes or interest rates, affects both expenditure and output. Expenditure is directly affected, and part of the reduction in expenditure falls on domestic production, in turn setting up multiplier effects which reduce expenditure and output still further. Thus an expenditure-reducing policy has two effects on the balance of payments, in terms of the equation: the first is the direct effect of the expenditure reduction, which is favourable; the second is the induced effect through lower output and consequently lower expenditure, which will be unfavourable so long as a reduction in income reduces expenditure by a smaller amount—that is, so long as the marginal propensity to spend is less than one. The unfavourable effect will be smaller, the more the initial reduction in expenditure falls on imports; and so long as the marginal propensity to spend is less than one, the net effect of an expenditure-reducing policy must be an improvement in the balance of paymerts.

Two further points should be made before we leave expenditure-reducing policies. One is that the reduction in expenditure and output may reduce the domestic price level, so giving rise to switches of expenditure between foreign and domestic goods; I shall discuss this type of effect in a moment. The second is that the reduction in expenditure, by reducing the country's imports, will bring about multiplier reductions in incomes abroad, which in turn will reduce foreign expenditure on this country's output. The analysis of these 'foreign repercussions' is familiar,[6] and I shall not go into it here; so long as the marginal propensity to spend is less than one in all countries, the foreign repercussions will simply reduce the extent of the favourable effect of expenditure reduction, but will not make it unfavourable.

Let us now consider the other type of policy, that of switching expenditure towards home-produced and away from foreign-produced goods. Such switches of expenditure will increase domestic output, and so long as the marginal propensity to spend is less than one (so that expenditure rises less than income) will improve the country's balance of payments. Two types of expenditure-switching policies can be distinguished. One is devaluation, which by making the country's goods relatively cheaper compared with foreign goods will tend to switch both domestic and foreign expenditure towards domestically-produced goods. The other is the use of controls. These are usually applied to restrict imports, in which case there will be a tendency for frustrated domestic consumers to purchase domestic substitutes and for domestic producers to seek to produce substitutes for imports no longer available. Thus the use of import restrictions tends to switch domestic expenditure towards domestic goods—though sometimes import restrictions are described very naïvely, as if preventing people from buying imports led them automatically to save the money they would have spent. Controls may also be applied in order to stimulate exports; in this case, the aim is to induce the foreigners to switch their expenditure towards domestic output.

In the case of both types of expenditure-switching policy, the aim is to increase the demand for domestic output. This raises the question of where the extra output required to meet this additional demand comes from. In this connection, we have to consider three possible cases for analysis.

The first is that in which there is widespread unemployment. In

[6] F. Machlup, *International Trade and the National Income Multiplier* (Philadelphia: The Blakiston Co., 1943).

this case the switch of demand towards domestic output will give rise to increased domestic output and income by increasing the utilization of unemployed resources. The second case is that in which the country has conditions of full employment but the policy of switching expenditure is backed by a complementary policy of reducing domestic demand—a combination of an expenditure-switching and an expenditure-reducing policy. In this case the switch policy can be regarded as a trimming device designed to ensure that balance-of-payments equilibrium is attained without sacrificing full employment;[7] a policy of deflating demand by itself would tend to lead to unemployment because expenditure would have to be cut sufficiently to reduce demand for imports enough to rectify the deficit, implying reduction in demand for domestic output; so the switch policy is used as a means of directing the reduction in expenditure entirely on to imports. In order to achieve the two objectives of policy, internal and external balance, it is necessary to use two policy instruments, control of aggregate demand and some sort of switch instrument. The third case is that in which a switch policy is employed under conditions of full employment, but is not reinforced by an expenditure-reducing policy. In this case the switch of demand to domestic output will tend to promote inflationary developments. This is the case analysed by Alexander, who has shown how the inflationary consequences may cure the initial excess of expenditure over income, by reducing effective demand in real terms. I am not going to discuss all the ways in which this may happen, only the more important ones, though I should mention that the argument was designed for European conditions and may be inapplicable to underdeveloped countries.

One possibility is that as income rises in monetary terms the real burden of taxation will become higher and higher. In so far as the Government does not spend the extra tax revenue but accumulates it in a budget surplus, there is a deflationary effect through increased leakages into taxation. A second possibility is that price rises may lead to a redistribution of income to profits, and if we can assume—which may not always be reasonable—that businesses do not in consequence increase their investment, there will be an increase in real savings and a deflationary effect on expenditure. Because investment is influenced by the level of profits, it is debatable how far this factor will work in a favourable direction. A third possibility related to the second is that there may be a redistribution of income to wage-and-profit earners on the one hand from fixed-income groups on the other; this may or may not reduce aggregate consumption, depending

[7] R. F. Harrod, 'Currency Depreciation as an Anti-Inflationary Device: Comment', *Quarterly Journal of Economics*, LXVI, no. 1, February 1952, 102–16.

on the relative sizes of the marginal propensities to consume of the groups concerned, and the way in which the redistribution is shared between wages and profits. Finally—a possibility to which Alexander devotes considerable attention—there is the effect of higher prices in reducing the real value of monetary assets and so inducing the public to spend less and save more. This effect depends on there being a stock of cash, or of Government debt which is regarded as an asset by its holders but not, effectively, as a liability by the tax-paying public, so that a rise in the price level makes some asset-holders feel poorer without making anyone else feel richer. For ordinary private debts, nothing much can be deduced about the effects of rising prices, since while the creditor becomes poorer the debtor becomes richer in real terms, and the net effect on spending might go either way.

There is one further point I want to make at this stage of the argument, and that is that the use of import restrictions, in addition to a switching effect, may have a direct expenditure-reducing effect. For various reasons—the structure of the economy, or governmental controls—it may be difficult to provide domestic substitutes for imports, so that, instead of buying more remote substitutes, people simply save the money they are not allowed to spend on imports. I do not think, though, that this is a very important possibility, if we assume that the restrictions on imports are expected to last indefinitely; but it may be that people will save money temporarily, in the expectation that a little later domestic substitutes will become available at lower prices.

To summarize the argument so far: I have been dealing with the balance of payments, looked at as the difference between expenditure and income, and discussing two different types of policy for correcting a deficit, one aimed at reducing aggregate domestic expenditure and the other at switching domestic and foreign expenditure away from foreign towards domestic goods. I now want to discuss some special aspects of devaluation and the use of restrictions on trade, which I have glossed over in outlining the general framework of balance-of-payments theory.

To begin with the problems of devaluation, you are no doubt familiar with at least some of the analyses which have been made of the factors which determine whether or not devaluation will be successful in switching expenditure from foreign goods to home goods.[8] A great deal of effort has been expended on analysing the effect of devaluation on the trade balance, or, as it is sometimes called, the problem of exchange stability. There are in fact two different ap-

[8] Joan Robinson, *op. cit.*, and L. A. Metzler, 'The Theory of International Trade', Chap. V in H. S. Ellis (ed.), *A Survey of Contemporary Economics* (Philadelphia: The Blakiston Co., 1948), especially 225–8.

proaches to this problem. One is the Marshallian or partial equilibrium approach, which analyses the effects of devaluation in terms of the elasticities of demand and supply of exports and imports. The general formula is quite complicated, but the necessary condition for the balance of trade to be worsened by devaluation is that the sum of the elasticities of demand for imports be less than one. If supplies are inelastic, this has the general effect of restricting the responsiveness of trade to exchange-rate changes, thereby reducing the effects whether favourable or unfavourable; this is the reason why, if supplies are inelastic, devaluation may improve the balance even if the sum of the demand elasticities is less than one.

The Marshallian approach, however, depends upon two sorts of questionable assumptions. The first is that any cross-relations between exports and importable goods through demand and supply can be ignored, so that the export and import sectors of the economy can be dealt with in isolation from one another. The second is that international changes affect the country's aggregate expenditure only through altering its trade balance and hence its level of output. In recent years a considerable amount of work has been done in modifying these assumptions and approaching the problem in a more general way which includes the determination of the level of income along with the balance of payments, and takes into account both the interconnections between demands for different goods and the possible direct effects of changes in the terms of trade on the level of expenditure from a given income. The stability criterion that emerges from this work is that the sum of the elasticities of demand for imports should be greater, not than one, but than one plus the sum (for the domestic economy and the rest of the world) of certain complex factors embodying the direct effect of a change in the terms of trade on expenditure. These factors are each equal to the proportion of the change in real income due to the terms of trade which is reflected in a change in saving, multiplied by the ratio of the marginal propensity to import to the marginal propensity to save. Various approximations to these factors have been derived, which suggest that the elasticity requirement for stability is both higher than the Marshallian one and varies with the circumstances.[9]

The possibility of exchange instability, however, does not seem to me a very realistic problem, at least if one takes a sufficiently long-run view to ignore the problem of short-run speculation, and excludes

[9] See Harry G. Johnson, 'The Transfer Problem and Exchange Stability', *Journal of Political Economy*, LXIV, no. 3, June 1956, 212–25 [reprinted as Chap. VII of *ibid.*, *International Trade and Economic Growth* (London: Allen and Unwin, 1958)] especially Sec. III, for a survey of the literature.

cases of inflationary conditions in which devaluation is not an appropriate policy. In this connection, I should like to refer you to an article by E. V. Morgan in the June 1955 issue of *The American Economic Review*, in which it is shown that exchange instability requires instability of the market for some commodity or group of commodities.[10] If you believe that the exchange market is unstable, you must believe that the market for some commodity or commodities is unstable. The point can be illustrated by means of our earlier formula, $B=Y-E$. Assuming E constant, B will improve if a reduction in the exchange rate increases the demand for the national product and so increases Y; exchange instability implies that a reduction in the price of the country's output, relative to the price of the output of the rest of the world, will reduce the quantity of the country's output demanded.

The much more important practical problem concerns the possibility that devaluation will worsen the devaluing country's terms of trade. This raises the question of the effect of devaluation on the terms of trade; in theory, the effect may be either a worsening or an improvement, depending on the relative magnitudes of the elasticities of demand and supply for exports and imports. Some attempts have been made to deduce a general presumption that the term of trade will turn against the devaluing country from such considerations as that a country is likely to be more important in the market for its exports than in the market for its imports, but such arguments are obviously not very satisfactory.[11]

The proposition that devaluation will involve an adverse movement of the terms of trade underlies much of the argument that has been advanced for preferring controls of various kinds to devaluation. The argument about control *versus* devaluation I shall consider shortly; at this point, I should merely like to warn against two fallacies commonly perpetrated in putting the case for controls. In the first place, a deficit entails an excess of expenditure over income, and to correct it the country must forgo the enjoyment of resources obtained on credit, either imported foreign goods, or domestic goods which must now be exported instead of consumed at home. This is true whether devaluation or controls are used, though exponents of controls sometimes imply that only devaluation entails this loss. Secondly, in circumstances in which the terms of trade are likely to turn adverse, controls also are likely to involve a substantial loss to the country through the inability of residents to obtain the goods they prefer. This

[10] E. V. Morgan, 'The Theory of Flexible Exchange Rates', *American Economic Review*, XLV, no. 3, June 1955, 279–95.

[11] See, for example, Joan Robinson, *op. cit.*, 197–8.

is so because a severe adverse movement of the terms of trade implies that the country cannot readily do without imported goods or substitute exportable goods for them. It is of course often argued in favour of controls that they permit a country to maintain the inflow of 'essential' goods while keeping out 'luxury' goods; but this is a 'second best' argument, since there is no obvious reason why 'unnecessary' consumption should not be tackled directly, and in any case control of such consumption through import controls may not in fact be effectively workable.

We now come to controls on trade. There are a great variety of such controls, but it is possible to classify them under two heads, financial controls and commercial controls.[12] Financial controls operate through control over the use of money, by restricting the freedom of use of domestic money either through regulation of certain uses or (as in the case of multiple exchange rates) by making some uses of money more expensive than others. Commercial controls, on the other hand, operate on the goods side of transactions by preventing people from buying certain goods or forcing them to buy others, or providing financial incentives (tariffs, subsidies) for certain kinds of sales or purchases. Whether financial or commercial, and whether applied to imports or exports, the effect of controls is to create a divergence between the internal and the external values of commodities: the restriction of exports makes the internal value of goods less than the external value; and the restriction of imports makes the external value of the goods less than the internal value. The divergence in turn implies an abnormal profit from foreign trade; this profit may be either absorbed by the State (through tariffs or export duties, State trading profits, or possibly the profits from the sale of trade licences) or left to be reaped by private citizens (the consumer, the domestic trader, or the foreign trader, depending on the system of trade control). The existence of an abnormal profit on trade also creates an incentive to evade the controls, and a need for policing the controls to ensure that they are effective. Because controls of any form have the same effect of creating a divergence between the external and internal value of goods, they can all be treated as equivalent to a combination of export or import duties and a redistribution of income of some kind.

Controls on trade, as compared with the 'price-system' method of devaluation, raise two important problems. The first is the effectiveness of controls, as against devaluation, in increasing net foreign exchange earnings. Roughly, we can think of devaluation as being

[12] For a more extended discussion, on which this brief account is based, see J. E. Meade, *op. cit.*, Chaps. XX and XXI.

the equivalent of an import duty and an export subsidy;[13] and an import duty is bound to save foreign exchange, whereas an export subsidy will save foreign exchange or not according to whether the elasticity of demand for the country's exports is greater or less than one. Thus an import duty by itself will only save foreign exchange to a greater extent than devaluation if an export subsidy would actually reduce the country's earnings from exports, that is if the foreign elasticity of demand for exports were less than unity. If the elasticity of demand for exports were less than unity, the country should of course restrict rather than encourage exports. An export subsidy by itself would always be worse than a devaluation, since it would fail to obtain the necessarily favourable effect of devaluation in reducing the amount spent on imports. All of this argument, it should be noted, treats exports and imports as aggregates; for the maximum improvement in the balance of payments, it would obviously be desirable to distinguish between different export and import commodities according to their elasticities of demand or supply.

The second problem concerns the welfare aspects of the choice between trade controls and devaluation. Considering the welfare of the country concerned by itself, this choice depends on the relation between the existing degree of controls and the optimum degree of trade restriction, given the country's trading position. If the country possesses unexploited monopoly or monopsony powei then it stands to gain by exploiting this power by further trade restriction; on the other hand, if its trade is restricted beyond the optimum level, it will benefit by relaxing its trade restrictions and devaluing still more than it would have to, if it left its trade restrictions at the existing level.[14]

Fundamentally, the optimum degree of trade restrictions depends on real considerations, and is not conditional on the state of the balance of payments. The balance-of-payments position provides only a second-best argument for trade restriction, that the optimum degree of restriction cannot be legislated without a balance-of-payments crisis. To this point there is one exception, which depends on

[13] The equivalence is only rough because an import duty yields additional tax revenue and an export subsidy requires the imposition of taxes to finance it. These income effects can be assumed to cancel when the two are applied together (and the percentage rate is the same), but they should really be taken into account when comparing either alone with devaluation. The following argument ignores this complication; for a more accurate analysis, see J. E. Meade, *op. cit.*, Chap. XXIII, and Harry G. Johnson, *International Trade and Economic Growth* (London: Allen and Unwin, 1958), Chap. VII, Sec. IV, 190–5.

[14] See S. Alexander, 'Devaluation versus Import Restriction as an Instrument for Improving Foreign Trade Balance', *International Monetary Fund Staff Papers*, I, no. 3, April 1951, 379–96.

confusion on the part of other nations—it may only be possible to get away with monopolistic trade restriction without invoking retaliation from other nations if a balance-of-payments deficit can be offered as an excuse for this behaviour.

There is one final point I should like to make about the optimum degree of trade restriction. The argument for seeking to achieve it assumes either that other countries will not retaliate, or that there is no possibility of reaching any international agreement on trade policy. Retaliation is too difficult a matter to discuss here; so far as agreement is concerned, it is obvious that it will never pay two countries to have trade barriers against each other. Such barriers could always be cleared down to a barrier on the part of one country only, to the benefit of both, and possibly they could be completely eliminated. If international income transfers were possible, freedom of trade could always be more beneficial than the preservation of barriers.[15]

[15] See J. M. Fleming, 'On Making the Best of Balance of Payments Restrictions on Imports', *Economic Journal,* LXI, no. 241, March 1951, 48–71, and J. E. Meade, *op. cit.*, Chap. XXIV.

II

COMPARATIVE COSTS AND COMMERCIAL POLICY*

'Comparative costs and commercial policy' is a general title, designed to comprise the 'real' side of the theory of international trade. I shall divide my discussion of it into three parts. The first section will be on the theory of international trade as it has come to be expounded in international economics in recent years. This will deal with comparative costs, and with the causes of trade and the effects of international trade on prices of goods and factors of production. The second section will be concerned with the theory of commercial policy, that is, of tariffs and other kinds of trade barriers like quantitative restrictions. The third section will be concerned very briefly with what I regard as the major new development in international trade theory, the theory of customs unions and preferential groups, a theory which has been developed practically entirely since the war.

Let me begin with the pure theory of international trade and the law of comparative costs. It is convenient to start with a brief statement of comparative-costs doctrine in its neo-classical form, as it has been elaborated by Ohlin and a number of other writers.[1] Such a statement would run as follows: First, international trade takes

* *Pakistan Economic Journal*, VIII, no. 2, June 1958, 29–43.

[1] B. Ohlin, *Interregional and International Trade* (Cambridge, Mass.: Harvard University Press, 1933);

W. W. Leontief, 'The Use of Indifference Curves in the Analysis of Foreign Trade', *Quarterly Journal of Economics*, XLVII, no. 2, May 1933, 493–503, reprinted in American Economic Association, *Readings in the Theory of International Trade* (London: Allen and Unwin, Philadelphia: The Blakiston Co., 1949), Chap. 10, 229–38;

W. F. Stolper and P. A. Samuelson, 'Protection and Real Wages', *Review of Economic Studies*, IX(1), no. 1, November 1941, 58–73, reprinted in American Economic Association, *Readings in the Theory of International Trade* (London: Allen and Unwin, Philadelphia: The Blakiston Co., 1949), Chap. 15, 333–57.

place, and countries derive benefit from it, because different countries possess different comparative advantages in the production of different goods, or have different comparative costs of production. Secondly, these cost differences are largely to be associated with differences in the relative availability of different factors of production, as reflected in their prices. Thirdly, the effect of international trade (ignoring the influence of transport costs and other trade barriers) is to tend to equalize prices of commodities in different countries, to permit specialization of countries on the production of those goods in which they have comparative advantages, and to tend to equalize the prices of factors of production as between the different countries.

This is a statement of general principles; I have framed it to cover a wider range of topics than is usually included under comparative costs, to indicate how the theory hangs together. It is a very loose statement, but it contains a number of specific propositions. Much recent work on the theory of trade has been devoted to clarifying the meaning of comparative costs and related propositions and several recent articles have been devoted to showing that these propositions are not generally valid or that they depend upon some very specific assumptions, more specific than have been given in the statement which I have just made. Let me just recapitulate that statement briefly: different initial endowments of factors of production give rise to differences in comparative costs, which in turn give rise to trade; trade gives rise to the equalization of commodity and factor prices, levelling out the scarcity of different factors in different countries in the process of equalization of commodity prices. The first part of my exposition will be concerned with these successive notions.

To begin with, I want to clarify the nature of the concept of comparative costs by an exposition and application of the techniques of analysis which have come to be used in modern international trade theory. These techniques are designed to give the simplest possible general equilibrium system required for investigation of 'real' trade problems. They make a number of simplifying assumptions, specifically that the world can be represented by two economies, each of which has given tastes and given quantities of factors and has available to it the same techniques of production; that two goods are produced and that their production requires the use of two factors of production—labour and capital; and that production is subject to constant returns to scale. This last is an important assumption because it implies that the marginal cost of production is equal to the average cost of production, which in turn implies that private and social costs are equal and that factor prices depend solely on the ratios in which factors are employed in industry, without reference to the scale of production. Finally it is assumed that perfect competitive conditions prevail in all markets.

On this assumption we can summarize the data of each economy with two techniques—one corresponding to the conditions of demand and the other corresponding to the conditions of supply. On the supply side, we can represent the given techniques of production and given quantities of factors by a curve showing the maximum amount of one commodity that can be produced, given a specified amount of the other to be produced. This curve, known as the transformation curve, is shown in Fig. II.1. With constant returns to scale it will be

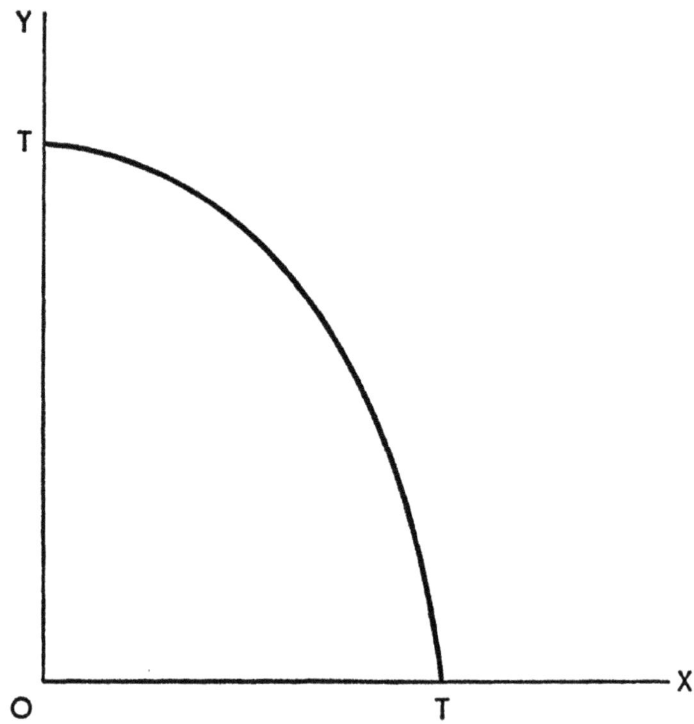

Fig. II.1

concave to the origin, or in the limit a straight line. The transformation curve is derived from the production functions and given factor supplies which provide the economy with its production alternatives. These may be represented by a *contract box* as in Fig. II.2: the quantities of factors are measured along the sides, and the contours of the production functions for the goods are entered in the box from opposite corners. Any point in the box represents a possible distribution of factors between industries; but only those points will be efficient, which correspond to the tangency of production contours for the two goods. The 'efficient' points define the transformation curve. Before going on, I should point out that in drawing the box I have assumed X to be labour-intensive and Y capital-intensive (the slope from the X-origin to any point on the contract curve is steeper

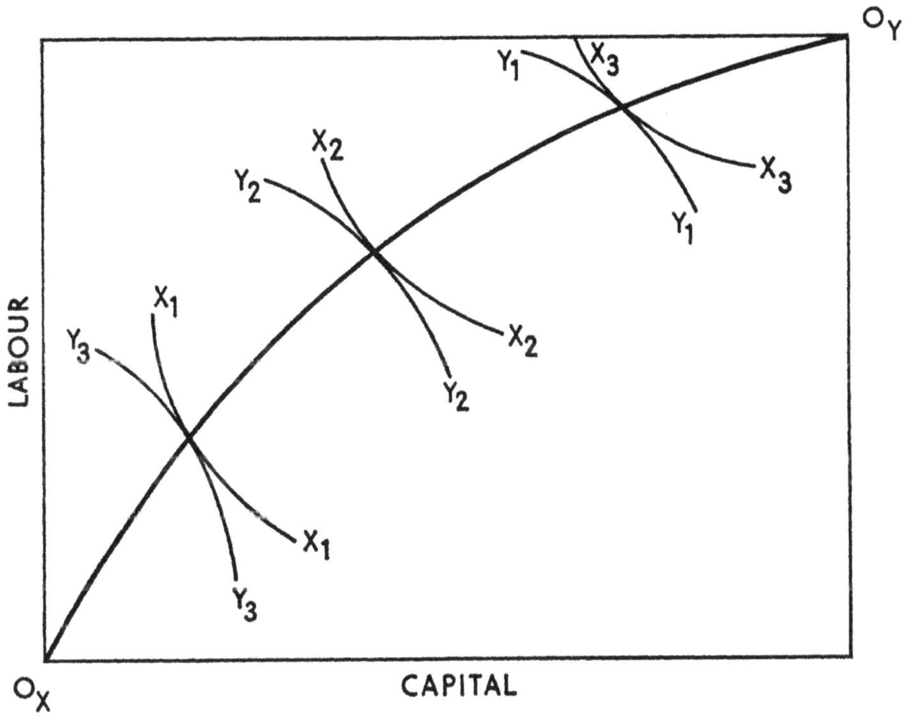

Fig. II.2

than the slope from that point to the Y-origin; and these slopes represent the labour-to-capital ratios in the two industries.)

On the demand side, the economy can be represented by a set of community indifference curves (Fig. II.3). The procedure, however, conceals a number of difficulties, which can only be evaded by making one or other of a number of restrictive assumptions, designed to make the preferences of the community independent of the point on the transformation curve at which it may be. We can assume for example that the State has its own preference system, or we can assume that the State follows some social welfare policy which specifies the distribution of real income amongst the citizens. The problem here is that if we assume a free-enterprise economy, with income distributed according to factor-ownership, then (unless ownership shares and individual tastes are identical) any change in production will, by altering factor prices, shift the weights given to the different people's preferences in adding up the social preference system.

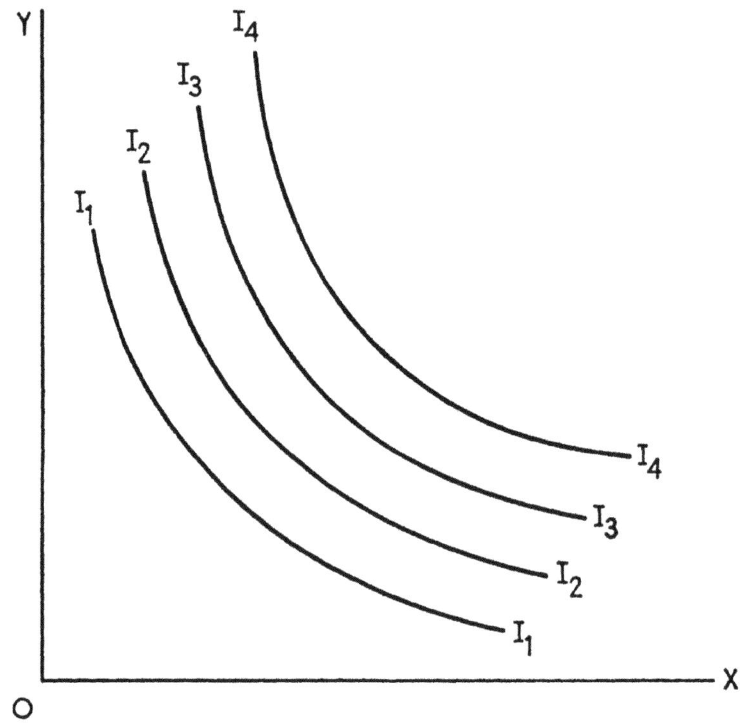

Fig. II.3

The objections to the use of community indifference curves, however, are not important for the purposes of international trade theory. In the first place, all that we may want to do is to represent the characteristics of an equilibrium position in international trade, and then we can say that the community indifference curves we use relate to this equilibrium situation. Usually, we want to go farther and say something about the effects of international trade on social welfare. If we use the curves for that purpose and say that a move to a higher curve is a welfare improvement, we are in fact using a version of the Hicks criterion for a welfare improvement. This criterion has certain well-known defects.[2] However, we can show that the results that we get through this technique will not be different from the results we get from a more reliable concept, and specifically that certain changes in international trade brought about by changes in tariffs and so on will lead to an increase in welfare in the only sense in which we can possibly discuss economic welfare, and that is in the sense of a potential increase of welfare.

The literature of welfare economics is of course voluminous, and I have no time to discuss its intricacies; but as I understand it the only way in which welfare conclusions can be drawn these days is to say that certain kinds of changes will constitute an improvement if social-welfare-maximizing income-distribution policies are pursued, both before and after the circumstances change. We can never say that a certain change by itself will actually make people better off. What we can say is that if the right steps are taken along with it, then people can be made better off. It is in this sense that the changes in welfare indicated by the community indifference curve technique should be interpreted.

By putting the diagrams representing the two sides of the economy —demand and supply—together, the equilibrium that would exist in a closed economy can be determined. It will be characterized by the tangency of a community indifference curve with the transformation curve, and equality of the rates of substitution between commodities in production and consumption, expressing the maximization of social welfare (given the community's production opportunities). The closed economy equilibrium is represented by the point P in Fig. II.4, the price-and-marginal-cost ratio between the goods being represented by the slope of the line PP.

Now, let us introduce the possibility of international trade; we can do this by supposing that the economy has a chance to exchange goods at a different price ratio than the closed economy price ratio. We can assume that this different price ratio corresponds to the marginal cost ratio of the world; and we can represent this international price ratio by a slope either steeper or less steep than PP, for example, by PP_1 in Fig. II.4.

[2] T. de Scitovszky, 'A Reconsideration of the Theory of Tariffs', *Review of Economic Studies*, IX, no. 2, Summer 1942, 89–110, reprinted in American Economic Association, *Readings in the Theory of International Trade* (London: Allen and Unwin, Philadelphia: The Blakiston Co., 1949), Chap. 16, 358–89;

I. M. D. Little, 'Welfare and Tariffs', *Review of Economic Studies*, XVI(2), no. 40, 1948–49, 65–70;

J. de V. Graaff, 'On Optimum Tariff Structures', *The Review of Economic Studies*, XVII(1), no. 42, 1949–50, 47–59, incorporated as Chap. IX of *ibid.*, *Theoretical Welfare Economics* (Cambridge: Cambridge University Press, 1957).

comparative marginal cost of production would be different in the country concerned, as compared with the rest of the world, *in the absence of trade*. One of the effects of trade is to tend to equalize prices, and therefore to eliminate differences in comparative costs. This assumes that the trade is free and there are no transport costs; and also (this is important) that both the country and the rest of the world continue to produce both goods.

Let us now consider the effect of trade on factor prices, on the assumption that specialization is not complete. The production of commodity Y expands and of X contracts. In terms of Fig. II.2, there is a shift along the contract curve towards the X corner. It is clear that the effect of trade will be to increase the labour-to-capital ratio in both industries. Now the relative prices of labour and capital, by the assumption of constant returns, depend on the ratio in which they are used. If the labour-to-capital ratio rises in both industries, the price of labour must fall. To put this more simply, if we shift production from X to Y, we release more labour than can be absorbed at the initial price of labour, since X is more labour-intensive than Y; hence, to reabsorb this labour, the price of labour must fall.

To summarize, a country will export those goods which, in the absence of trade, would be relatively cheap compared with their values in other countries. The price of the factor which is used relatively more in the production of these cheap goods will also rise. This leads us to two related problems: can we associate cheapness of a good with cheapness of the factor it mainly uses, and will the rise in the price of the latter resulting from trade mean that factor prices tend to be equalized as between countries?

These questions contain the same problem, whether there is a unique relationship between prices of goods and prices of factors. Specifically, is there a one-to-one relationship between the price of a factor and the price of the good in which it is important? If so, equalization of the prices of the goods will equalize factor prices.

Before considering this question, I should like to say something about the relationship between 'cheapness' and 'advantage'. Obviously, we can always say that the comparative advantage lies with the country which produces the goods cheaply; but there is a deeper meaning to 'advantage' than that, one that runs in terms of factors of production and supply. We are assuming that the technique of production is the same throughout. If the prices of goods were the same in the two countries, then we could say that the country which would produce a higher ratio of a particular commodity than the other country at those prices has an advantage over the other country in producing that good. This is illustrated in Fig. II.6.

Here, country A produces a higher ratio of Y goods, and country B produces a higher ratio of X goods, or country A has an advantage over country B in the production of Y goods and B has an advantage over A in producing X goods. But will Y goods be cheaper in country A and X goods be cheaper in country B? Not necessarily. X might be expensive in country B if a lot of it is consumed in B, and similarly with Y in country A. This case might arise if tastes in the two countries were very different, or if incomes differed and the one good was a luxury and the other a necessity. For example, if the level of income

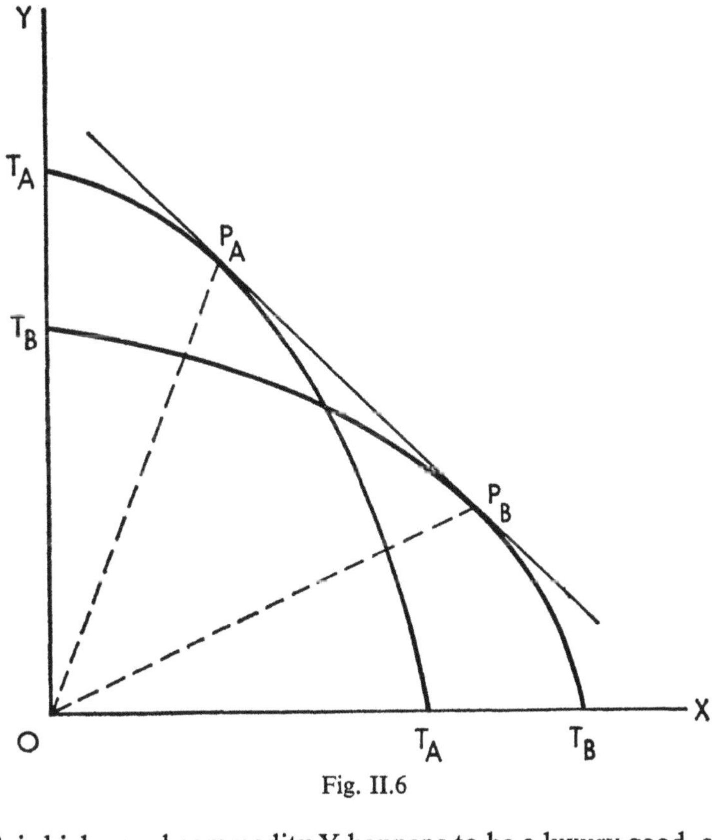

Fig. II.6

in A is higher and commodity Y happens to be a luxury good, and if B happens to be a poor country and commodity X a necessity, then A would consume relatively more Y and B relatively more X at the same prices of the two goods and therefore each country might want to import the good in which it has a production advantage. In short, cheapness and advantage do not necessarily go together.

Now let us return to the problem of the relationship between factor prices and goods prices. In an article published in *The Economic*

Journal in 1948, Samuelson attempted to establish that equalization of goods prices means equalization of factor prices; from this he jumped to some rather startling policy conclusions.[3] His analysis has since been challenged by a number of writers, who have emphasized the dependence of his conclusions on a factual assumption about the nature of the production functions for traded goods.[4]

I think the simplest way of understanding the nature of the problem is the following. Suppose we choose an initial factor price ratio (which implies a certain commodity price ratio) and that at this factor price ratio X is labour-intensive and Y capital-intensive. Now let us raise the price of labour; the price of X must then rise more than the price of Y, that is, the relative price of X rises. As the price of labour rises, capital will be substituted for labour in both industries and the capital-to-labour ratio will rise in both. But so long as X remains relatively labour-intensive, the relative price of X will rise as the price of labour rises. There are two possibilities which depend entirely on the nature of productive techniques. One is that, no matter what the price of labour, X is always labour-intensive; in that case, we have the situation shown in Fig. II.7a, with a one-to-one relation between commodity and factor prices. The other is that substitution of labour for capital (and *vice versa*) is easier in X than in Y, so that eventually X switches from being labour-intensive to being capital-intensive; after the switch-over point is reached, further increases in the price of labour *reduce* the relative price of X, until another switch-over point is reached. This situation is represented in Fig. II.7b.

In the first case, it is clear that the cheap good must use the cheap factor, and commodity-price equalization must imply factor-price equalization. In the second case, neither of these propositions is true. Suppose, for example, that countries A and B, in the absence of trade, would be at the equilibrium points shown. Then A would export Y, the commodity which uses more of the relatively expensive factor, in exchange for imports from B of X, the commodity which uses rela-

[3] P. A. Samuelson, 'International Trade and The Equalization of Factor Prices', *Economic Journal*, LVIII, no. 230, June 1948, 163–84.

[4] S. F. James and I. F. Pearce, 'The Factor Price Equalization Myth', *Review of Economic Studies*, XIX(2), no. 49, 1951–52, 111–20;

Romney Robinson, 'Factor Proportions and Comparative Advantage: Part I', *Quarterly Journal of Economics*, LXX, no. 2, May 1956, 169–92;

R. W. Jones, 'Factor Proportions and the Heckscher-Ohlin Theorem', *Review of Economic Studies*, XXIV(1), no. 63, 1956–7, 1–10.

See also P. A. Samuelson, 'International Factor Price Equalization Once Again', *Economic Journal*, LIX, no. 234, June 1949, 181–97, especially 188, where the empirical assumption on which the conclusion of the earlier article depends is recognized.

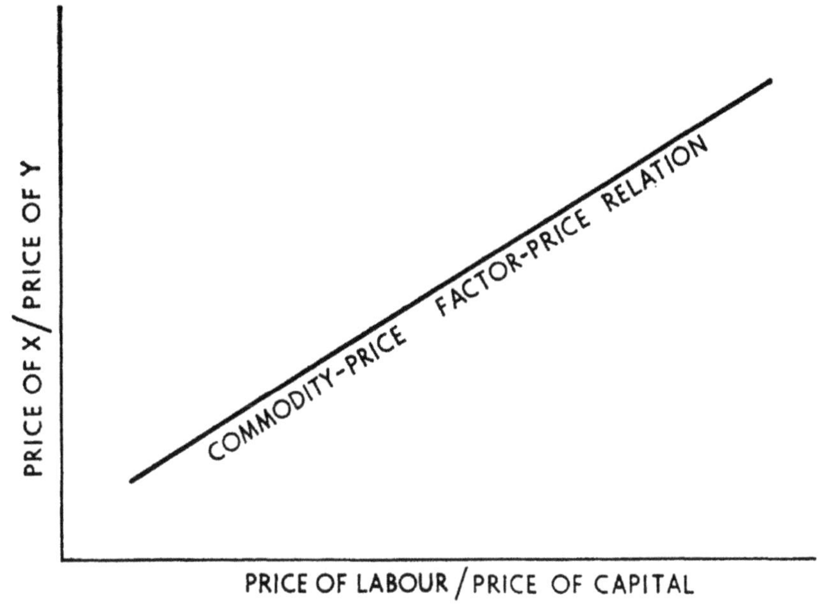

Fig. II.7a

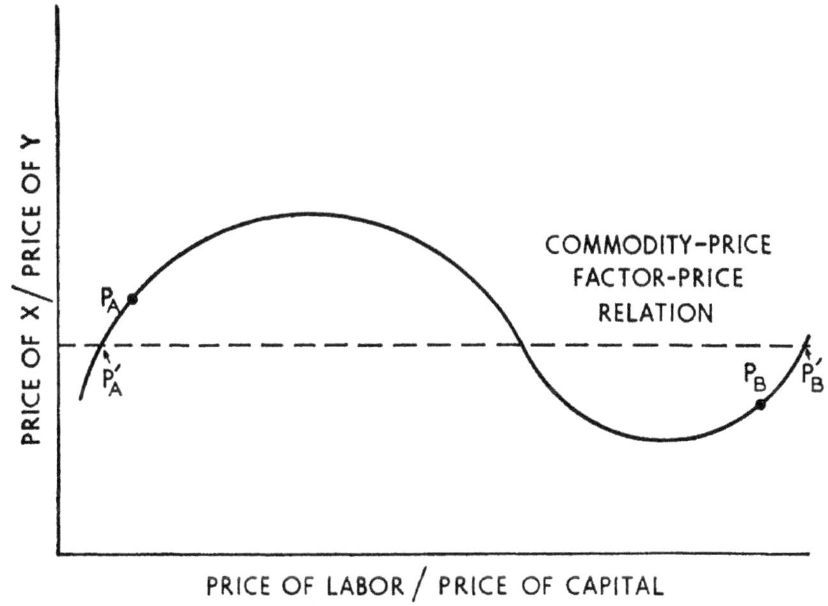

Fig. II.7b

tively more of A's cheap and B's expensive factor; and the equalization of commodity-prices would drive factor-prices still farther apart.

It is important to note, however, that the movement to a higher relative price of labour always implies a higher capital-to-labour ratio in both industries, which in turn assumes a higher average capital endowment; that is, economies can only be in different segments of the curve in Fig. II.7b if they have different factor endowments.

This means that we can restate Samuelson's factor-price equalization proposition as follows: assuming that both countries continue to produce both goods, equalization of commodity-prices through trade ensures equalization of factor prices only if *either* technology is such that one good is labour-intensive and the other capital-intensive at *all* factor prices, *or* factor endowments are similar enough to confine both countries to a range of production possibilities within which there is the same one-to-one relation between factor and goods prices. It is clear that both of these conditions are empirical requirements whose presence cannot be established *a priori*, and that in their absence we cannot relate production advantage to factor endowment, even with all the assumptions of similarity of production functions and factors we have already made.

I shall now leave the pure theory of comparative costs, and turn to the theory of trade intervention. What I shall do here is to survey the various arguments that have been advanced by various writers as to why a free trade policy can be improved on. My general theme is the necessity of making two kinds of distinction: (1) between cases in which intervention is required to make the market work, and cases in which it is required to prevent the market from working; and (2) cases in which intervention should take place through the medium of international trade policy, and those in which it should not—quite often, an argument for, say, a tariff is really an argument for some other policy which the writer is not prepared to espouse, or thinks would be less readily accepted.

We can distinguish five kinds of arguments for trade intervention. The first of these is concerned with cases in which market prices do not reflect social costs or benefits. There are two sub-cases of this. The first sub-case is where the market is imperfectly competitive or where there is a monopoly or something of that kind, and in that case the obvious conclusion would be to try to make price determination more competitive. A special and important case here is the Manoilescu argument for tariffs.[5] Assume the economy to be divided into two

[5] M. Manoilescu, *The Theory of Protection and International Trade* (London: P. S. King & Son, 1931).

sectors—an industrial sector and an agricultural sector. In the agricultural sector, in a peasant economy, the level of real income enjoyed by labour will reflect not the marginal productivity of labour but the average productivity of labour. The marginal productivity of labour may be zero but nevertheless labour will get an income in agriculture, whereas in industry labour must be paid its marginal productivity. Consequently, industry will be underexpanded compared with agriculture. Social and private costs are unequal because labour is paid according to its marginal productivity in industry and its average productivity in agriculture. There is a case here for intervention; but whether intervention should take the form of a tariff is another question. Also there is a limitation of the argument which has been recognized: if land is owned by landlords and let out to tenants, as a result of competition the earnings of agricultural labour will reflect the marginal productivity of labour on the land.[6]

The second sub-case is where competitive prices do not reflect social costs. One of these is the case of increasing returns in industry—the infant industry argument. Here there are two questions—the factual importance of the case, and the question whether a subsidy would not be better than a tariff. A second case is the terms of trade argument for protection. If export or import prices are sensitive to volume, the marginal social benefit from exports will fall short of their prices, or the marginal social cost of imports will exceed their prices. These considerations provide a case for exploiting whatever monopoly or monopsony power the country has. The possibility of retaliation must of course be taken into account, though it is not always true that it destroys the possibility of gain.[7]

The second group of arguments centres around the question of unemployment, which is often argued to provide a case for trade intervention to divert demand from foreign to home goods. Actually, there is no reason to tie commercial policy and employment policy together; unemployment provides an argument for a full-employment policy, not for sacrificing the advantages of specialization and division of labour.

The third kind of argument centres on the question of income distribution. This also is a 'second best' kind of argument because

[6] Compare W. A. Lewis, 'Economic Development with Unlimited Supplies of Labour', *The Manchester School of Economic and Social Studies*, XXII, no. 2, May 1954, 139–91, especially 149; Lewis argues that the rent will be set to allow a conventional minimum of subsistence, but this is not inconsistent with the equality of wage and marginal product.

[7] Harry G. Johnson, 'Optimum Tariffs and Retaliation', *Review of Economic Studies*, XXI(2), no. 55, 1953–54, 142–53, reprinted as Chap. II in *ibid.*, *International Trade and Economic Growth* (London: Allen and Unwin, 1958), 31–61.

there is no reason why you should link up the desirable distribution of income with a policy of making prices different from those which would reflect the country's trade opportunities. This may be the only way that the income distribution can be changed, but the limitations on alternative policies should be explicitly recognized.

The fourth kind of case concerns an argument from the dynamics of economic growth. It is alleged that there is a difference between agriculture and trade on the one hand and industry on the other. Trade and agriculture, it is alleged, dispose of any surpluses of income in non-productive ways; as occupations they are biased against expansion and towards non-productive expenditure. In contrast, it is alleged, industry tends to plough any profit back; as an occupation, it favours expansion and has greater growing capacity. If you like, industry is a kind of productive system which extracts taxes which are used for investment, whereas trade and agriculture are a productive system which extracts taxes and uses them in non-productive expenditure.[8] How far these are characteristic of the different occupations is, I think, an important factual question. In so far as they differ in this way, and in so far as the Government wants economic growth, there is a case for intervention.

The fifth group of arguments comprises arguments for intervention to improve the balance of payments. These arguments are generally based on a second-best view of things, in that they assume that the country must maintain a fixed exchange rate, price level, volume of effective demand, and so on.[9]

To summarize, most of the arguments for intervention in international trade are second-best arguments for achieving results which would better be achieved by more direct means. Further, where there is a case for intervention in international trade, there is often a choice between intervention by trade restrictions or tariffs and intervention by subsidies; and the latter are often to be preferred.

I shall finish by commenting very briefly on the major development in international trade theory that has emerged during the past few years, the theory of customs unions and preferential groups. This subject is of particular interest to a country like Pakistan which is a member of a preferential payments and trading area—the Sterling Area—and which may at some stage be considering a closer union with neighbouring countries. The theory was first outlined by Jacob

[8] Cf., W. A. Lewis, *op. cit.*, especially 169–170. Lewis is there concerned with the development effects of inflation; but the same empirical proposition has been used on various occasions by Nicholas Kaldor as an argument for protection.

[9] For a fuller discussion, see Chap. I.

Viner, in his book on *The Customs Union Issue*; it has been greatly elaborated by James Meade, whose work builds on an important article by Marcus Fleming.[10] The subject is especially interesting theoretically because it involves a comparison between sub-optimum situations.

The theory of choices between sub-optimal situations has come to be known as 'the theory of second-best'.[11] Its central theorem can be formulated in the following way. If a number of the marginal conditions for a welfare optimum are not fulfilled, and another violation of these conditions is imposed, you cannot tell in which direction economic welfare will change. Similarly, if a number of the marginal conditions are violated and one of these violations is eliminated, you cannot be sure that this will make any improvement in welfare. This theorem can be applied to customs unions or to the unilateral reduction of customs tariffs. For example, it has been shown by Ozga[12] that if the United States were to reduce its tariffs this might not lead to an improvement from the world point of view. In the same manner you can show that the debate which has been going on in the theory of public finance as to whether an income tax is more efficient than an excise tax is necessarily inconclusive; so is the argument as to whether a public utility should price its output at marginal cost or not, if other industries are not perfectly competitive.[13]

Let me sketch briefly the nature of the customs union problem. It starts from a desire of some countries to form a union; these countries decide to abolish tariffs against each other's goods while retaining tariffs against the rest of the world. The question is whether this is beneficial to them or not and whether it is beneficial to the world or not. On the one hand, trade is free in the area; on the other hand, the union discriminates against the goods of the outside world. This entails an analysis in terms of two concepts, trade creation and trade diversion, which were introduced by Jacob Viner.

If, instead of producing goods themselves, these countries now get

[10] J. Viner, *The Customs Union Issue* (Princeton: Carnegie Endowment for International Peace, 1950);

J. M. Fleming, 'On Making the Best of Balance of Payments Restrictions on Imports', *Economic Journal*, LXI, no. 241, March 1951, 48–71;

J. E. Meade, *The Theory of International Economic Policy, Volume II: Trade and Welfare* (London: Oxford University Press, 1955) and *The Theory of Customs Unions* (Amsterdam: North Holland Publishing Co., 1956).

For a fuller bibliography and more extended exposition, see Chap. III.

[11] R. G. Lipsey and K. Lancaster, 'The General Theory of Second Best', *Review of Economic Studies*, XXIV(1), no. 63, 1956–57, 11–33.

[12] S. A. Ozga, 'An Essay in the Theory of Tariffs', *Journal of Political Economy*, LXIII, no. 6, December 1955, 489–99.

[13] See Lipsey and Lancaster, *op. cit.*, and references there cited.

their goods from sources elsewhere in the area (trade creation) this will improve welfare because the source of the goods will be a cheaper source than the home sources previously relied on. If, on the other hand, all that happens is that a country gets goods from a country inside the union instead of from a country outside it (trade diversion), having switched from the one source to the other owing to the union, there will be a deterioration in welfare because the country has switched to a higher cost source of supply.

Viner concluded from his analysis, which was concerned only with the location of production, that a customs union is more likely to benefit the countries involved if they are initially similar than if they are initially different. This terminology is liable to cause confusion; if one takes a commonsense view, it might appear that a customs union is a good idea if the countries are different in structure. But the proposition has gradually been clarified; a more accurate statement of it is that a customs union is likely to be beneficial if the countries are alike at the start but can become different. The more alike they are the more scope there is for them to become complementary to each other by specializing; the scope for such complementary specialization is small when the countries already produce completely different goods. Countries entering a union, in Dennis Robertson's phrase, should be 'actually highly competitive but potentially highly complementary'.[14] For example, a union between France, Germany and England would probably be highly beneficial because they are very alike in the kinds of things they produce and they could derive considerable benefit by specializing on (say) some kinds of steel production in Germany, other kinds in France and still other kinds in England.

James Meade has greatly elaborated on Viner's analysis by extending Marcus Fleming's technique so as to derive from it some concrete propositions about the effects of a customs union. Fleming's analysis starts from the fact that the effect of trade restrictions of any kind is to create a difference between the internal and external values of goods. What Fleming does is to use this difference to measure the possible gain or loss from a change in trade restrictions under conditions of restricted trade. Say, for instance, that the value of a motor car is $3,000 in Pakistan and its cost outside is $2,000; then the gain to the economy from importing one car would be $1,000 and expansion of motor imports would be worth this much to the country. This is a simple idea but one can use it to analyse this sort of problem because one can relate the possible benefit or loss from a change in

[14] D. H. Robertson, *Britain in the World Economy* (London: Allen and Unwin, 1954), Chap. IV, 78; a fuller exposition of the principle is given on 73–4.

trade policy to the extent of restriction on trade. For example, even if production in two uniting countries does not change, the countries may gain because they can consume more of the goods they like; so (contrary to Viner) the benefit of union does not depend on changing the location of production. Also, the higher the level of restrictions against non-members before the union, the less is gain likely, and the lower these restrictions, the more is gain likely; alternatively the gain is likely to be greater, the lower the initial level of restrictions on trade with outside countries. And finally—and this is a most interesting conclusion—a partial union is likely to be more beneficial than a complete customs union. The reasoning here is that the more the restrictions on trade from within the area are reduced, the less is the remaining divergence between the internal and external value of goods traded and the less the probable gain from further freedom of trade with the rest of the area. On the other hand, the divergence between the internal and external values of goods imported from the outside world remains the same; so that while the possible gain from trade creation measured in this way diminishes, the possible loss from diversion of trade away from outside sources towards inside sources does not diminish as barriers to intra-union trade are lowered. The conclusion from this reasoning, it should be observed, runs counter to the accepted international rules for commercial policy, which frown on preferential trading areas like the Sterling Area but approve of customs unions.

country better off than would its non-fulfilment. The achievement of the maximum *attainable* welfare will generally require violation of the conditions for maximum welfare; and the effect on welfare of a movement towards fulfilment of one of the optimum conditions will depend on the precise circumstances of the case.

Before proceeding to the customs union problem let me illustrate the difference between traditional optimum theory and second-best

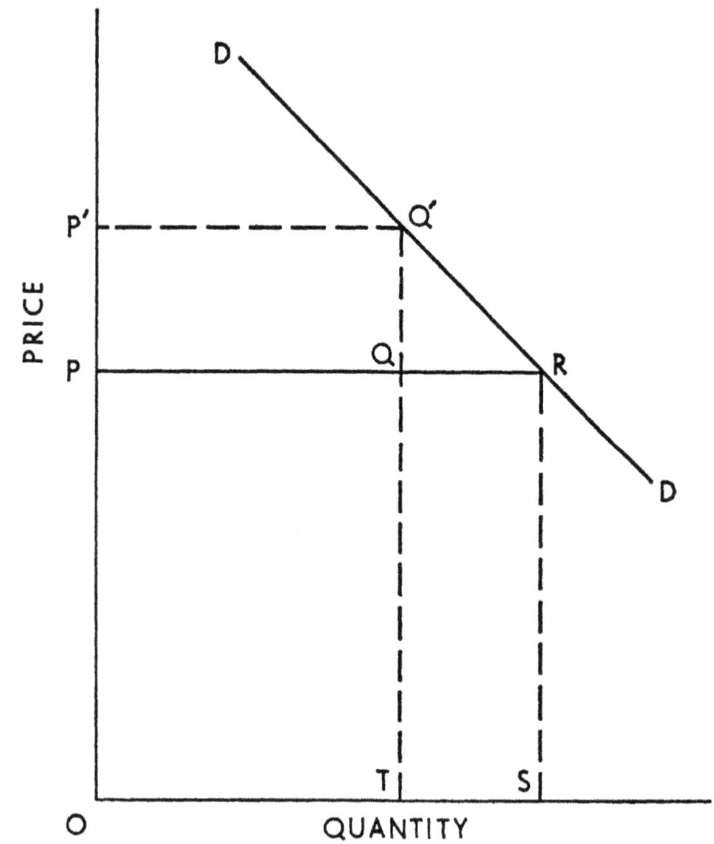

Fig. III.1

theory by reference to the familiar proposition that a tax on a specific commodity imposes an excess burden. In so doing I assume (what is not always so) that money prices and costs represent real social values and costs; and I employ Marshallian consumers' surplus analysis, even though in its crude form this entails certain well-known difficulties associated with changes in the marginal utility of income. For simplicity, I also assume constant costs in production.

The traditional argument is illustrated in Fig. III.1, where DD is the demand curve, PQR the constant-cost supply curve, and P′Q′ the supply curve including the tax. The tax shifts the equilibrium point from R to Q′, imposing a loss of consumer surplus P′Q′RP, of which P′Q′QP is balanced by tax revenue accruing to the government, leaving Q′QR as the net loss of consumers' surplus due to the taxation of the commodity, or the 'excess burden' of the tax; so that if the tax were removed and replaced by, for example, a lump sum tax, there would be a gain Q′QR of consumers' surplus.

This analysis rests on the assumption that value to consumers is equal to production cost at the margin elsewhere in the economy.[7] But value may exceed cost for other commodities, either because of imperfections in the markets for these commodities, or, as I shall assume, because they also bear taxes. The analysis of the effects on welfare of replacing the specific tax on the original commodity by a lump sum tax in this case can be carried out on two alternative lines, depending on whether the Government is assumed to maintain tax rates unchanged, or to adjust the amount of lump sum taxation so as to maintain an unchanged total revenue.[8]

On the first assumption, in order to expand consumption from OT to OS, consumers must reduce expenditure on other goods by QTSR. To the extent that other goods are taxed, reduction of expenditure on them releases resources which were not required to produce consumer satisfaction but instead were being used by the Government for its own purposes; the corresponding reduction in the amount of Government tax revenue and activity must be counted as a loss, against the gain in consumers' surplus on the commodity freed from taxation. This loss is illustrated in Fig. III.2, where AB is the constant-cost supply curve of other commodities (treated as an aggregate for convenience), A′B″B′ is the supply curve including taxes, dd is the demand curve when the original commodity is taxed, and d′d′ the demand curve when the tax on the original commodity is replaced by a lump sum tax.[9] The replacement of the tax on the original commodity

[7] The assumption is implicit in the cancellation of the production cost QRST against the corresponding part of the marginal utility Q′RST of the difference in consumption TS between the taxed and untaxed situations to arrive at the net loss Q′QR; this procedure assumes that resources worth QRST would produce QRST worth of utility in other industries.

[8] It is assumed that the location of DD is not affected by the difference between the two assumptions. This, as well as the implicit assumption of the ensuing analysis that changes in Government revenue can be cancelled against consumers' surplus, implies that the level of Government expenditure is optimal and that changes in it can be treated as small.

[9] Movement from dd to d′d′ involves no loss of consumers' surplus; all changes in consumers' surplus are already taken into account in Fig. III.1.

reduces expenditure on other commodities by B′DD′B″ (equal to QTSR in Fig. III.1) but of this amount, only CDD′C′ was required to produce the initial quantity of other commodities consumed, B′CC′B″ going to the Government as tax revenue financing Governmental services. In diverting expenditure from other commodities to the commodity on which the tax is replaced, the community must sacrifice not only the consumption of other commodities, but also the consumption of the Governmental services previously financed

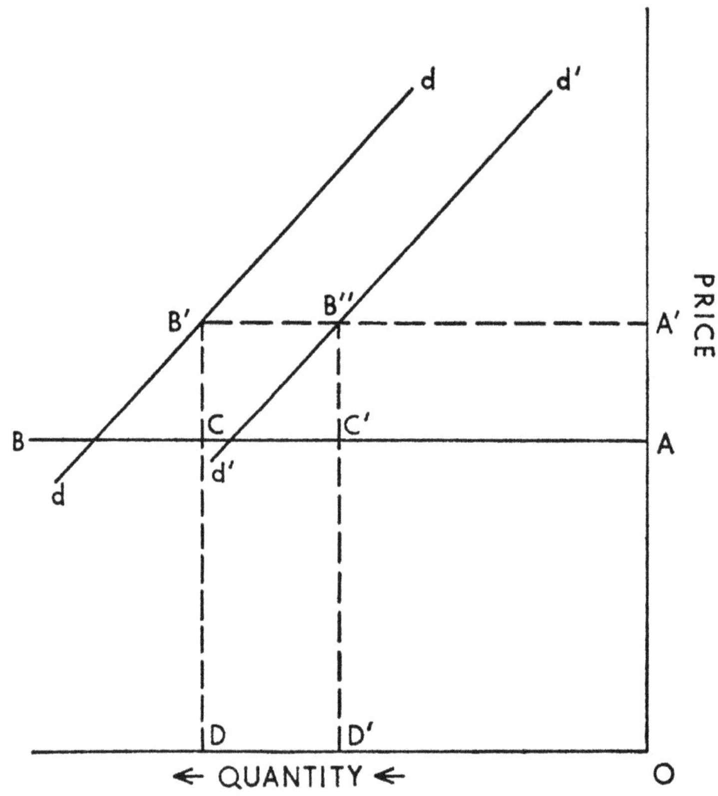

Fig. III.2

by taxes levied on the sacrificed consumption. There is a net gain only if this latter sacrifice is less than the gain in consumers' surplus on the increased consumption of the tax-freed commodity, that is, if Q′QR in Fig. III.1 exceeds B′CC′B″ in Fig. III.2.

On the second assumption, for production of the tax-freed commodity to increase from OT to OS resources to the value QTSR must shift out of other lines of production. To the extent that other lines of production bear taxes, expenditure on other goods must fall by more than the value of the resources required to expand production of the tax-freed commodity, the excess corresponding to the additional lump sum taxes required to compensate the Government for the loss of tax revenue due to reduced consumption of these other goods; the corresponding reduction in total consumer expenditure on commodities is a loss which must be counted against the gain in consumers' surplus on the commodity freed from taxation. This loss can also be illustrated by Fig. III.2, if the definitions of its construction are slightly modified, so as to equate CDD′C′, the reduction in the quantity of resources employed in other industries due to the tax replacement, with QTSR in Fig. III.1. The diversion of resources to production of the tax-freed commodity entails a reduction of expenditure on other commodities of B′DD′B″, a net reduction of expenditure of B′CC′B″ which corresponds to the increase in lump sum taxes required to compensate the Government for the loss of tax revenue B′CC′B″. There will be a net gain only if the reduction of consumer expenditure is less than the gain in consumers' surplus on the tax-freed commodity, that is, if QQ′R in Fig. III.1 exceeds B′CC′B″ in Fig. III.2.

The two alternative lines of analysis I have just expounded correspond to two ways of looking at the excess of value to consumers over cost of production of the other commodities than the one freed of tax. The first emphasizes the fact that it costs less to produce a given amount of (marginal) satisfaction in the taxed than in the untaxed industry, so that to maintain satisfaction unchanged while switching consumption to the latter industry it is necessary to obtain additional resources by reducing Government activity. The second emphasizes the fact that a given amount of resources produces more (marginal) satisfaction in the taxed than in the untaxed industry, so that a reallocation of production towards the untaxed industry must reduce the total of consumers' satisfaction obtained.

There is a further, important complication to the analysis. The foregoing argument assumes that other commodities than the tax-freed good can be treated as an aggregate, subject to a common rate of taxation, expenditure on which is simply diverted to the commodity on which the tax is replaced. In fact, some of these commodities will be substitutional, and others complementary, with the good on which the tax is replaced; and they will bear taxes at different rates. The effect of the replacement of the tax on a particular commodity by a lump sum tax will be to divert expenditures from the substitutes for that commodity to its complements, as well as to the commodity itself; insofar as the complements are subject to higher taxes than the substitutes, this diversion will involve a gain (which may be reckoned in either of the two ways discussed previously) additional to the increase in consumers' surplus on the tax-freed good; and conversely, insofar as complements are subject to lower taxes than substitutes, there will be an additional loss. There will be a net gain or loss to the economy from the replacement of the tax by a lump sum subsidy, according as the net reduction in the amount of taxes collected on other commodities is less or greater than the increase in consumers' surplus on the commodity on which the tax is replaced.

Let us now turn to the application of this kind of analysis to the problem of tariffs and commercial policy. To avoid the problem of welfare changes associated with the re-shuffling of internal production between goods bearing different tax rates, let us assume that there are no taxes on domestically produced goods;[10] and to avoid the complications arising from the fact that in practice the rate of tariff on an imported good often depends on the particular country from which it comes, let us assume that the tariff does not discriminate between imports of the same commodity according to their country of origin.

The effect of tariffs is to foster production of domestic goods which meet the consumers' demands at a higher real cost than would imports from abroad. This is because the consumer chooses between domestic and imported goods on the basis of their price inside the country: in the case of a domestically-produced good this price is equal to cost at the margin, whereas in the case of an import this price is above cost by the amount of the tariff collected on the good. The higher cost of want-satisfaction brought about by tariffs has two aspects: on the one hand, it takes the form of higher-cost domestic production of goods identical with those that would otherwise be imported; on the other hand, it takes the form of domestic production of other goods which meet the same need as imports would, but which cost more to produce. In both ways, the tariff promotes the choice of more expensive domestic as compared with cheaper foreign means of satisfying demand. But as between alternative sources of foreign goods, the tariff does not interfere with the choice of the cheaper source: because the tariff rate on imports is (by assumption) the same whatever their source, the import from the cheapest source will have the lowest price after the tariff has been paid and the commodity landed in the importing country.

A customs union involves eliminating the tariff on imports from some foreign sources ('the partner country' for short) but not from

[10] We also abstract from divergences between price and marginal cost due to imperfect competition.

others ('the foreign country' for short). One effect of this is to promote a shift from consumption of higher-cost domestic products to consumption of lower-cost foreign products originating in the partner country. This shift has two aspects, paralleling the two aspects of the effects of tariffs just discussed: domestic production of goods identical with those produced abroad is reduced or eliminated, the good now being imported from the partner country; and there is increased consumption of partner-country substitutes for domestic goods which formerly satisfied the need at a higher cost. In short, the demand for imports increases for two reasons: the replacement of domestic by partner production of the same goods—'the production effect'—and increased consumption of partner substitutes for domestic goods—'the consumption effect'; the production effect and the consumption effect together constitute 'the trade creation effect' of the customs union.[11] Corresponding to its two components, trade creation entails an economic gain of two sorts; the saving on the real cost of goods previously produced domestically and now imported from the partner country; and the gain in consumers' surplus from the substitution of lower-cost for higher-cost means of satisfying wants.

The gain from trade creation is illustrated diagrammatically in Fig. III.3. In the diagram, DD is the domestic demand curve for a commodity, SS its domestic supply curve, PQR the partner supply curve (assumed to be constant-cost) and P′Q′R′ the partner supply curve with the tariff added to the partner price. With the tariff, the country consumes OS′ of which OT′ is supplied by domestic production and T′S′ imported. When the tariff is eliminated, domestic production falls to OT and consumption rises to OS. The saving of cost on domestic production replaced by imports is QQ′M, and the gain in consumers' surplus from substitution of imports for other goods previously domestically produced is R′NR, so that the total gain from trade creation is the sum of these two areas, approximately equal to half the product of the change in the quantity of imports (TT′ plus S′S) and the money amount of the tariff per unit of imports (PP′). (The area P′PQQ′ represents a transfer of producers' surplus to consumers, and the area Q′MNR′ a transfer of tax proceeds to

[11] It should be noted that the use of the concept of trade creation in this lecture and the Appendix to it differs from that of other writers (such as Meade and Lipsey) who, following Viner, use it (and the corresponding concept of trade diversion) to refer solely to changes in the location of production, dealing with consumption changes in a rather different fashion, as part of the problem of optimizing trade. The present usage, which lumps production and consumption effects together in the categories of trade creation and trade diversion, seems more easily manageable, particularly when (as below and in the Appendix) imperfectly elastic supplies and incomplete specialization are considered.

consumers' surplus, both of which cancel for the country as a whole.)

In addition to the trade creation effect, however, the elimination of the tariff on imports from partner but not from foreign sources has the effect of promoting shifts in the source of imports from lower-cost foreign to higher-cost partner sources. As before, such shifts have two aspects: an increase in the cost of identical goods owing to the shift

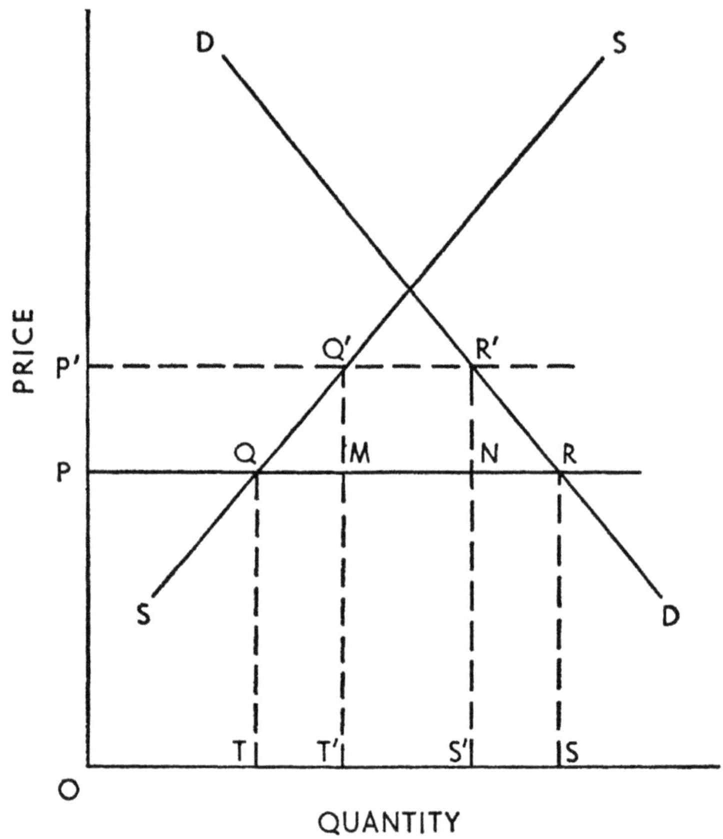

Fig. III.3

from foreign to partner sources; and substitution of higher-cost partner goods for lower-cost foreign goods of a different description but suitable for satisfying the same needs. Such shifts constitute 'the trade diversion effect' of customs union. The loss to the country from this source is measured by the difference in cost between the two sources of imports multiplied by the amount of trade diverted.

The loss from trade diversion is illustrated diagrammatically in

Fig. III.4. DD is the demand curve, PT and πR the foreign and partner supply curves (assumed to be constant-cost) and P′Q′ and π′Q″ these curves after the tariff. These supply curves can be thought of either as relating to physically identical products, or as relating to the quantities of different products required to produce the same consumer satisfaction. With the tariff applied to both sources of

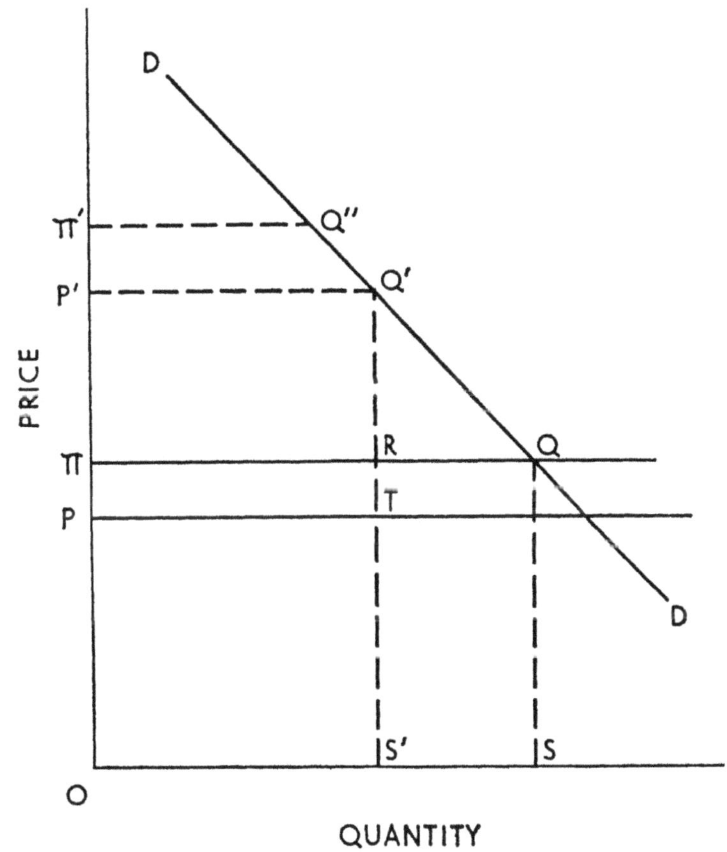

Fig. III.4

imports, the country imports OS′ from the foreign country at a total cost of OPTS′. When the tariff on partner imports is eliminated, the country shifts to importing OS from the partner country; for its previous consumption OS′ it now pays a total cost OπRS′, representing an increase in cost (a loss) of πRTP. This loss must be weighed against the gain from trade creation (increased total consumption) of Q′RQ.

The foregoing argument assumes perfect foreign and partner elasticity of supply of importable goods. If supplies are not perfectly elastic, the trade diversion effect has two further consequences.[12] In the first place, as trade is diverted from foreign to partner sources the foreign supply price falls. In consequence, the country enjoys a terms-of-trade gain on any trade with the foreign country which survives the formation of the customs union. In addition, any such survival of trade with the foreign country reduces the amount of, and loss from, trade diversion. This has an important implication: the greater the exploitation of the foreigner through a favourable movement of the terms of trade, the less the loss from trade diversion. This implication is to be contrasted with the argument often put forward in favour of customs union by protectionists, that a customs union is a means of favouring the partner country at the expense of the foreigner (rather than of domestic industry)—to the extent that imports from the partner expand at the expense of the foreigner, it is the domestic consumer who loses. The second consequence of imperfectly elastic supplies is that the partner supply price rises as trade is diverted. This means that the loss to the country per unit of trade diverted is greater than it would have been with constant costs; on the other hand, it implies that part of this loss is not a net loss to the domestic and partner economies taken together, but simply a transfer from domestic consumers' surplus to partner producers' surplus.

In addition to the consequences of customs union previously analysed, there may also be various secondary repercussions. For example, if some particular foreign goods are complementary to imports from partner country sources, the trade creation effect of elimination of tariffs on partner imports will also create trade with the foreign country, thereby resulting in additional gains. Similarly, if the country's exports to the partner country which are stimulated by the customs union are substitutes in domestic consumption for foreign goods, the country may increase its imports from the foreign country and so enjoy a gain measured by the tariff revenue on the increased imports. Conversely, complementarity-substitutionary relations between goods might accentuate the country's loss from trade diversion.

Similar gains and losses to those discussed above would result from the elimination of partner duties on the country's exports resulting from customs union. Most of these would accrue to the partner country; but insofar as domestic supply of exports was in-

[12] A formal analysis of the effects of discriminatory tariff elimination when partner and foreign supplies are imperfectly elastic is appended to this lecture.

elastic, the country would enjoy a terms of trade gain from elimination of the partner country's import duties.

A full analysis of the factors which determine the gains and losses from the formation of a customs union accruing to the individual members would require more time than is available.[13] But the foregoing analysis does indicate certain general principles relevant to this question. In the first place, a country is more likely to gain from the creation of trade resulting from a customs union the higher the initial level of its tariffs, and the more elastic the domestic demand for and supply of goods which the partner country is capable of producing. In the second place, a country is less likely to lose from trade diversion the smaller are the initial differences in cost between the partner and the foreign sources of supply for goods which both can produce, the more elastic is the partner supply of such goods, and the less elastic is the foreign supply of them; also, the less the degree of substitutability in consumption between goods from partner and from foreign sources. Thirdly, the country is more likely to gain on its terms of trade with the foreign country the more inelastic is the foreign supply of imports to it, and the more inelastic the foreign demand for its exports. Further, since a customs union usually involves some change in the level of the tariff on imports from foreign sources, the loss from trade diversion will tend to be less, and the possibility of gains on the terms of trade with foreign sources also less, the lower the tariff on foreign sources after the formation of the customs union as compared with the level of that tariff before the formation of the union.

These general principles can be summarized, very roughly, in the form of a statement about the relation between the natures of the countries embarking on a customs union and the probable gains from such a union. Statements of this kind, however, must be recognized as dangerous, since a general description of the nature of a country is not an adequate substitute for detailed analysis of the probabilities of trade creation, trade diversion and terms of trade effects. With that qualification, it can be said that a country is more likely to reap a gain from entering on a customs union, the more it and its partner country (countries) are initially similar in the products they produce but different in the pattern of relative prices at which they produce them. This is especially true if the products both produce are things which are consumed in rapidly increasing quantities as the standard of living rises, since in this case the income-raising effect of trade creation is self-reinforcing. Further, members are more likely to gain the more different they are from the rest of the world, since this

[13] For a full discussion, see J. E. Meade, *op. cit.*

implies that the possibility of losses from trade diversion is less; and the more dependent the rest of the world is on member countries for the import of products in inelastic supply in the rest of the world or the export of products in inelastic demand in the rest of the world, since these imply the possibility of gains on the terms of trade with the rest of the world. (There is some conflict between these last two criteria since exploitation of the foreigner through a favourable movement of the terms of trade requires the possibility of some diversion of imports or exports away from the foreigner towards members of the union.)

This general statement implies that a customs union between heavily protected manufacturing countries, such as the European Common Market, is likely to lead to considerable gain, especially if each has been using some of the income derived from its manufacturing skill to protect its agriculture from foreign competition. Similarly, agricultural areas of a similar kind each bent on industrialization are likely to gain from entering a customs union.

To reverse the statement, a country is less likely to gain from entering a customs union, the more different it is from its partners, the more the partners produce close substitutes for goods produced in foreign countries, and the greater the difference in real costs between foreign and partner supplies of such products; also the more elastic is the foreign supply of such products, and the more the country concerned is a producer for the world market rather than for the market of one or more of the partner countries. An example of a country unlikely to gain from participation in a customs union is an economy with strong advantages in agricultural production uniting with a manufacturing region. The usual objection to such a union is that an agricultural region is unlikely to industrialize without substantial protective tariffs on manufactures. This argument is not particularly cogent, because the comparative advantage of the economy may well lie in agricultural production and the effect of tariffs be to reduce its real income; the fundamental objection in this case is that the customs union renders it subject to exploitation by the inefficient manufacturing partner country, so that it loses its comparative advantages without compensation. This may have been the case, for example, with the maritime and western provinces of Canada in the past, when both could compete on a world market for their products but through their participation in Confederation were forced to buy manufactures from central Canadian manufacturing industry.

The argument so far has been concerned with possible gains and losses from the effects of customs union on the efficiency of specialization and division of labour within the customs union and between it and the outside world. There are other economic aspects of customs union which may also be important. In particular, the enlargement of the internal market brought about by customs union may bring economic advantages besides those of more efficient allocation of production and consumption between countries on the basis of costs

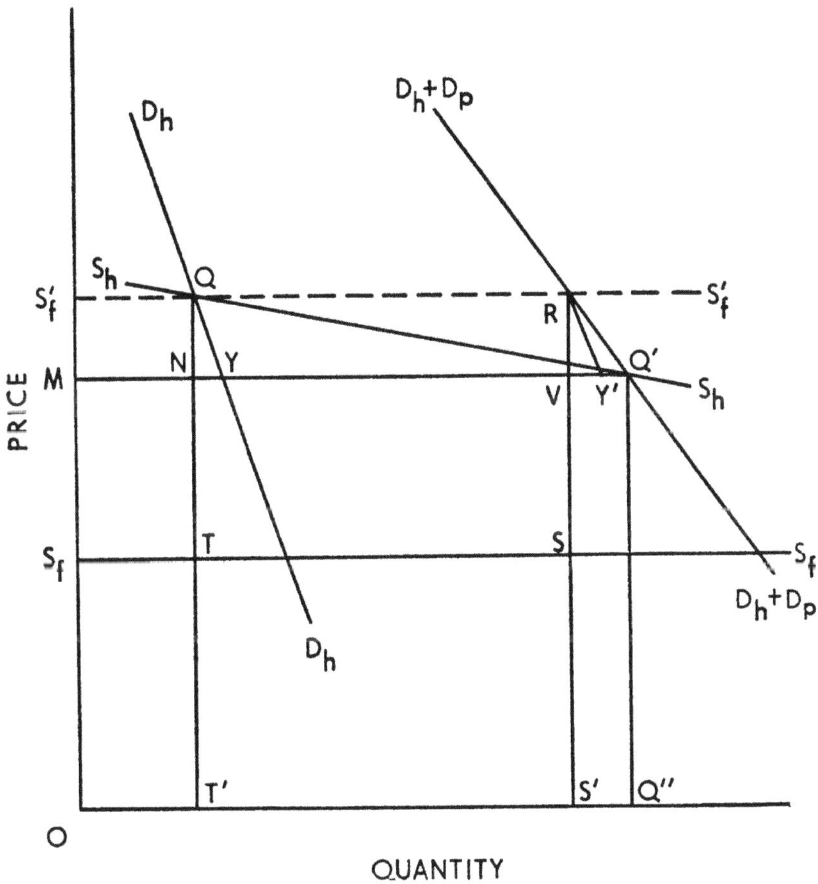

Fig. III.5

of production of commodities before the formation of customs union. For one thing, formation of a customs union may bring about more widespread and effective competition between firms and industries, with a consequent elimination of monopolistic distortions of the economy. In the argument presented so far, it has been assumed that competition prevailed within national markets, so that prices conformed to the minimum real costs technically attainable; if tbis is untrue, increased competition brought about by customs union may have significant effects in increasing the efficiency of production, apart from specializing production on producers with the lowest real production costs in the pre-union situation. Second, and possibly of greatest long run importance, formation of a customs union may increase the average rate of growth of the member economies, since the larger size of the internal market available to individual industries may both make it safer for the individual firm to invest resources and effort in the introduction of innovations and the deliberate pursuit of expansion, and put increased competitive pressure on individual firms to exploit whatever opportunities they have for expanding their share of the market and their absolute level of sales.[14] Third, formation of a customs union may permit individual firms, and also industries, to exploit the possibilities of economies of scale in production. The possibility of exploiting economies of scale does not, however, necessarily mean that each partner, or all members together, will be better off with the customs union than without; for even though such economies reduce cost of production inside the union that cost may still be higher than the cost of supplies formerly imported from outside the union.

This point is illustrated in Fig. III.5. In the diagram S_hS_h is the long-run Marshallian supply curve of domestic output in the home country, and D_hD_h the home demand curve; S_fS_f is the foreign supply curve, and $S'_fS'_f$ that supply curve with the tariff initially levied by the home and partner countries; D_h+D_p D_h+D_p is the demand curve of the home and partner countries together. Before union, the home country consumes OT′ of domestically-produced output at a total cost of OT′QS′$_f$; while the partner country consumes T′S′ of imports, at a cost of T′S′ST.[15] With the formation of the customs union, partner consumption is diverted to home-country supply, which expands and in so doing lowers cost, the final equilibrium entailing production and consumption in the market as a whole of OQ″ at a cost of OQ″Q′M. The two countries together enjoy a gain of consumers' surplus from expanded consumption of RVQ′, of which RVY′ (=QNY) accrues to the home country; on its previous level of consumption the home country enjoys a reduc-

[14] This point is stressed by Tibor Scitovsky in relation to European integration; see his *Economic Theory and Western European Integration* (London: Allen and Unwin, Stanford: Stanford University Press, 1958), especially Chap. I, Sec. A, par. 2, 19–48, and Chap. III, 110–35.

[15] For diagrammatic simplicity it is assumed that the home tariff rate is just sufficient to protect domestic output from foreign competition, i.e. the difference between the cost at which domestic demand can be satisfied and the foreign cost is just equal to the tariff rate.

tion of the real cost in the amount $MNQS'_t$; the partner country, however, suffers an increase in the real cost of its previous consumption in the amount TSVN, which may outweigh its gain of consumers' surplus from expanded consumption RY'Q' and may be large enough to outweigh the home country's gains from lower real cost and expanded consumption as well—as shown by the magnitudes in the diagram. This case, it should be noted, requires that the partner country previously met its wants by imports: if both previously met their wants from protected domestic production, concentration of production in one country where it was subject to economies of scale would necessarily be beneficial to both.

The three possible favourable effects of the enlargement of the market brought about by customs union just discussed all assume that the enlargement of the market will be of the right type to promote such favourable effects. Whether this will be so or not depends on the nature of the existing markets in the member countries and the effects of enlargement through customs union on the nature of the resulting market. If the separate markets of the various members are divided by serious geographical barriers which require high transport costs to overcome them, the enlargement of the market may be more apparent than real; similarly, cultural differences may preserve the separation of member markets despite the removal of tariffs. Again, the Canadian case, at least in its early stages, offers an example of the limitations of removal of taxation barriers in the presence of important physical and cultural barriers to a mass market. This problem is obviously even more acute in the case of Pakistan.

Let me conclude by turning from the economic theory of customs union to some of the problems which arise in the negotiation of them. In discussing these, I shall draw in a general way on the recent experience of the Common Market and Free Trade Area negotiations. The motivation towards the formation of a customs union is often political rather than economic; the economic urge may spring either from a desire for more effective protection, or from a desire for the advantages of greater freedom of trade. In the latter case, the formation of a customs union appears to offer a way around the difficulties of bargaining for mutual tariff reductions within the framework of the most-favoured-nation clause, a framework which impedes progress after a certain point because much of the benefit of a tariff concession goes to third countries, and even more because commodity-by-commodity bargaining accentuates the influence of vested interests in protection in the bargaining countries. The vested interests in protection, however, keep reasserting themselves in the negotiations. The central problem of establishing a customs union is to determine the height and the pattern of the common tariff. Both offer scope for conflict between the protectionist interests of various countries, as well as between protectionists and free traders. One problem which has been important in the Common Market negotiations concerns the treatment of components and materials, where there is a conflict between countries which rely on imports and find their comparative advantage in the processing and advanced stages of production, and those which protect domestic production of such things from imported substitutes; the fixing of the common tariff level determines the distribution of loss between the materials-using industries of the former group and the materials-producing industries of the latter group. Needless to say, the straight averaging of rates which is sometimes resorted to to solve such problems, and is also often taken as a standard ensuring that the degree of protection against outside countries is not increased, has no simple economic rationale—as can be readily inferred from the foregoing analysis of welfare effects.

Two problems which may be of considerable practical importance, particularly for customs unions among underdeveloped countries, are the division of the revenue from the common tariff—especially difficult if certain ports carry on entrepôt activity—and the replacement of lost tariff revenue by other taxes, which may easily have equivalent protective effects. Again, the practical rules of thumb which tend to suggest themselves are often difficult to rationalize in terms of the theory of the welfare effects of customs union and of taxation.

Finally, since freedom of trade between countries both increases the risks of competitive enterprise and reduces the autonomy of domestic economic policy, negotiations for establishment of a customs union (or a free trade area, for that matter) tend to encounter demands for the co-ordination of national economic policies and in particular for the 'harmonization' of laws, regulations and other practices affecting the competitive position in the common market area of producers in different countries. Such demands, particularly those for 'harmonization', can generally be shown to rest on fallacious arguments stemming from ignorance of the principle of comparative cost, or from an implicit assumption that domestic wage-price levels and the exchange rate are both absolutely rigid; but they may nevertheless cause misunderstanding and bedevil negotiations.

APPENDIX

A MARSHALLIAN ANALYSIS OF CUSTOMS UNION*

For simplicity of exposition, the formal part of the analysis of customs union presented in the lecture concentrated on the effects on the welfare of an importing country of granting a discriminatory elimination of its tariff on imports from the partner country, while retaining its tariff on imports from the foreign country; it also assumed perfect elasticity of supply of imports from the partner and foreign country. This Appendix presents a more elaborate analysis of the effects of discriminatory tariff elimination on the economic welfare of the three 'countries' concerned—the home country, the partner country, and the foreign country—and of the world as a whole, on the assumption that supplies of goods from their various sources are sufficiently inelastic for discriminatory tariff elimination not to alter the structure of production and trade in the world economy, but only the relative quantities produced and traded.

This analysis may appear to cover only one aspect of the effects of a customs union on a participating country—the effects of discriminatory removal of its own duties on imports from other participants—and neglect the other—the effects of discriminatory removal of duties levied on its exports by other participants—but in fact it includes both aspects, since the latter effects may be obtained from the former simply by interchanging the identities of the home and partner countries.

On the other hand, it is not a full analysis of the effects of mutual tariff elimination under a customs union, even within its own frame of reference, since it is confined to cases in which foreign suppliers compete with partner suppliers in the markets of participating countries, and if the foreign country exports to the customs union, it must also import from it. Thus tariff elimination in a customs union may apply to goods imported solely from the partner country, which the partner also exports to foreign markets, the foreigner appearing as a competing demander rather than a competing supplier in relation to the customs union. Such tariff elimination, it should be noticed, need not be discriminatory, since by assumption the partner supplier already undersells foreign competitors in the home country market; but it has effects on the welfare of the countries concerned similar to those of discriminatory tariff reduction. If foreign countries impose tariffs on imports from the partner supplier, elimination of the home country tariff does in fact amount to a kind of discrimination, though it is one introduced by differences between national tariffs rather than within them, and it involves discrimination between demanders rather than between suppliers. This case is analysed briefly in the second part of the Appendix. For symmetry with the main case, the analysis assumes that the home country exports to both the partner and the foreign

* *Indian Journal of Economics*, XXVIII, no. 148, July 1957, 39–48, and XXXIX, no. 153, October 1958, 177–81.

country, and benefits by the elimination of the former's tariff on its exports; but as in the main case the identities of home and partner countries can be interchanged to yield an analysis of both aspects of the effects of customs union on a participating country.

The analysis in both cases employs the familiar concepts of Marshallian consumers' and producers' surplus. These concepts are admittedly defective tools in various respects, especially when applied to the analysis of international trade problems; but they have the advantage of simplicity and familiarity, and their application can be justified as an approximation resting on the *ceteris paribus* conditions of partial equilibrium analysis. Two significant qualifications on the results obtained from the present application should be noted. First, the Marshallian technique ignores interrelations between demands and supplies of different goods; while the analysis below can be interpreted as applying either to an individual commodity or to the aggregate of commodities traded, the results on the former interpretation cannot be simply added together to obtain an aggregate result. Second, in adding together changes in surpluses in different countries to approximate the change in their joint welfare as is done below, it must be assumed *either* that the welfare of each counts equally for purposes of evaluation, *or* that compensations are actually levied and paid.

For simplicity of geometrical analysis, it is assumed that the various demand and supply curves are straight lines and that tariffs take the form of specific duties; these assumptions permit various results to be derived simply and in an exact form, which otherwise would have to be derived as approximations, by a cumbrous geometrical argument. To simplify the economic analysis, countries are assumed to produce only for export or consume only from imports, except for the home country in the first case, which is assumed to produce some of its imported goods domestically; the extensions of the argument required when countries consume some of the goods they export or produce some of the goods they import can easily be derived from the analysis of the home country in the first case.

1. *Discriminatory Tariff Elimination: Imports from the Foreign Country*

In Fig. III.6, D is the home demand curve for the commodity, S_h the domestic supply curve, $S_h+S'_f$ the sum of the domestic supply curve and the supply curve from the foreign country, *inclusive* of the tariff, and $S_h+S'_f+S'_p$ the sum of these two and the supply curve of the 'partner' country, also *inclusive* of tariff. S_h+S_f is the sum of the domestic supply curve and the foreign curve *exclusive* of tariff, and $S_h+S'_f+S_p$ the sum of the domestic supply curve, the foreign supply curve *inclusive* of tariff, and the partner supply curve *exclusive* of tariff.

In equilibrium with the non-discriminatory tariff, the domestic price of the commodity is 0A, consumption AP_1, domestic production AH_1, foreign production H_1F_1, partner production F_1P_1. Domestic producers' surplus is the area below AH_1 to the left of the domestic supply curve, domestic consumers' surplus the area above AP_1 to the left of the demand

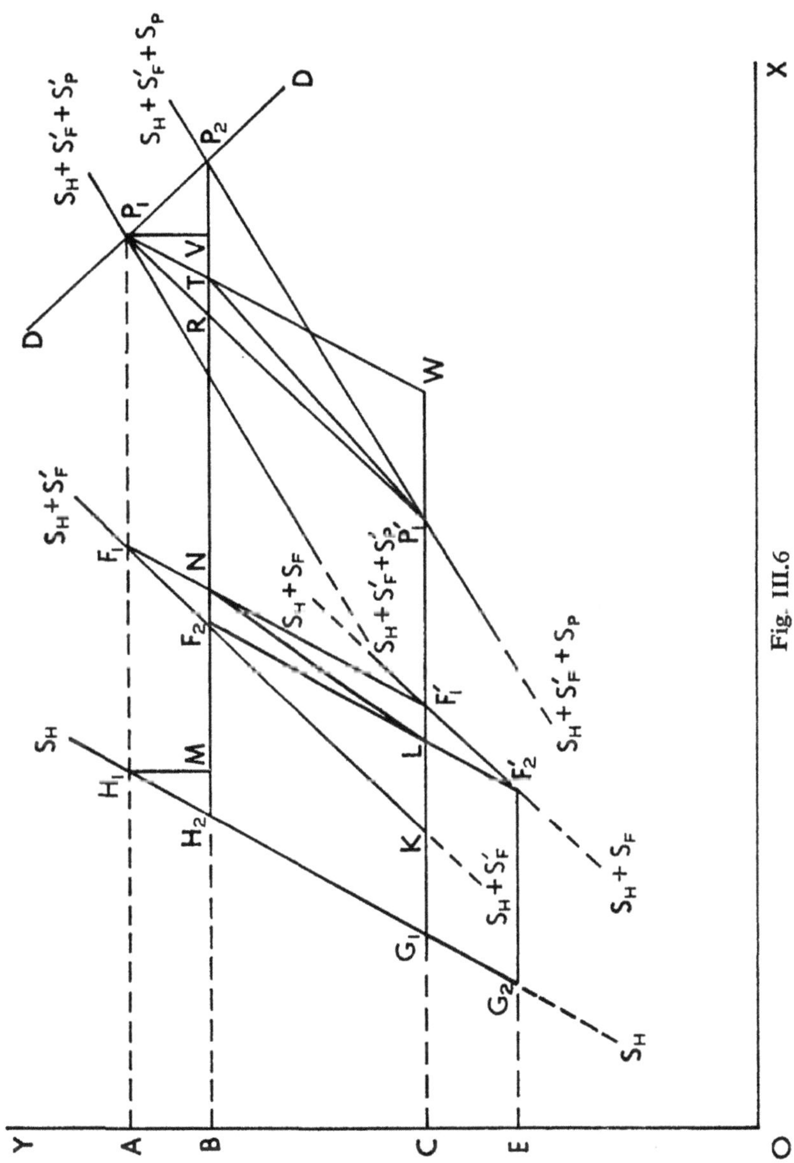
Y
A
B
C
E
O
X
D
D
P_1
P_2
P_1'
R
T
V
W
N
M
L
K
F_1
F_2
F_1'
F_2'
H_1
H_2
G_1
G_2
S_H
S_H
$S_H + S_F'$
$S_H + S_F'$
$S_H + S_F$
$S_H + S_F$
$S_H + S_F' + S_P'$
$S_H + S_F' + S_P'$
$S_H + S_F' + S_P$
$S_H + S_F' + S_P$

Fig. III.6

curve. In addition, the country enjoys $H_1G_1F'_1F_1$ tariff proceeds on its trade with the foreign country, and $F_1KP'_1P_1$ tariff proceeds on its trade with the partner country, $F_1F'_1$ being drawn parallel to S_h and $P_1P'_1$ parallel to $S_h+S'_f$. If P_1W is drawn parallel to S_h intersecting $G_1P'_1$ extended at W, then the total domestic gain from trade is the area bounded on the right by the domestic supply curve to G_1, G_1W, WP_1, and the demand curve, and on the left by the Y-axis. The foreign country's gain from trade, in the form of producers' surplus, is the area between S_h and S_h+S_f below $G_1F'_1$, and the partner country's gain, also producers' surplus, the area between $S_h+S'_f$ and $S_h+S'_f+S_p$ below KP'_1.

The effect of the elimination of the tariff on trade with the partner country, along with its retention on trade with the foreign country, is to shift international trade equilibrium from P_1 to P_2. Consumption increases from AP_1 (=BV) to BP_2, an increase of VP_2. Domestic production contracts from AH_1 to BH_2, a contraction of H_2M=TV. Thus the discriminatory tariff reduction increases imports by the amount TP_2 (=TV+VP_2); this is the 'trade-creation' effect, made up of the consumption-increasing effect (VP_2) and the output-reducing effect (TV) of the tariff reduction. Foreign production of imports contracts from H_1F_1 (=H_2N) to H_2F_2, a decrease of F_2N which is replaced by increased partner production of RT; F_2N=RT represents the 'trade-diversion' effect of the tariff reduction. Partner production of imports increases from F_1P_1 to F_2P_2, an increase of RP_2 (=RT+TV+VP_2=F_2N+H_2M+VP_2), which is the sum of the trade-diversion and trade-creation effects of the change in the tariff.

The domestic producers' surplus is now the area below BH_2 to the left of S_h, the consumers' surplus the area above BP_2 to the left of the demand curve, and the tariff proceeds on trade with the foreign country $H_2G_2F'_2F_2$. The total domestic gain from trade is now shown by the area bounded on the left by OY and on the right by the domestic supply curve to G_2, $G_2F'_2$, F'_2F_2, F_2P_2, and the demand curve; and it may be greater or less than the gain in the previous situation. The foreign country's gain from trade is reduced by the loss of producers' surplus $G_1G_2F'_2F'_1$ while the partner's gain from trade increases by the gain of producers' surplus $F_2KP'_1P_2$. Thus the home country may gain or lose from the elimination of the tariff on trade with the partner country, the partner country necessarily gains, and the foreign country necessarily loses.

The change in the tariff has two sorts of effects on the domestic gain from trade: a redistribution of gain from domestic producers' surplus and tariff proceeds to consumers' surplus, resulting from the reduction in the domestic price level due to the change; and a change in the total gain from trade. The redistributive effect is represented by the area $ABTP_1$, consisting of the transfer to domestic consumers' surplus of domestic producers' surplus ABH_2H_1, foreign tariff proceeds $H_1H_2NF_1$, and partner tariff proceeds $F_1F_2RP_1$ (=F_1NTP_1). The change in the total domestic gain from trade may be decomposed into the following parts:

H.1. The gain in consumers' surplus due to the expansion of consumption, measured by the area P_1VP_2.

H.2. The gain from the saving in cost on marginal domestic production through its replacement by imports, measured by the area P_1 VT.

These two elements of improvement may be lumped together as 'the gain from trade creation', measured by the area P_1TP_2. This gain will be greater the greater the amount of trade creation and the greater the reduction in the domestic price of the commodity following the tariff change. The area $P_1TP_2 = \frac{1}{2}.P_1V.TP_2$, i.e. half the product of the domestic price reduction and the amount of trade creation.

H.3. The gain from the reduction in the cost of the surviving imports from the foreigner due to the effect of trade diversion on their supply price, measured by the area $G_1G_2F'_2L$. This gain, which may be described as 'the gain on the foreign terms of trade', will be greater the greater the surviving volume of trade with the foreigner and the greater the reduction in the domestic (and foreign) price of the commodity; it is equal to the product of the surviving foreign trade volume and the domestic price reduction.

H.4. The loss from the increased cost of imports formerly bought from the foreigner and now purchased from the partner country ('the loss from trade diversion'), measured by $F_2LF'_1N$. This loss is greater the greater the amount of trade diversion and the greater the increase in the price of the commodity in the partner country; it is equal to the product of the amount of trade diversion and the partner price increase.

H.5. The loss from the increase in the cost of the former volume of imports from the partner country, due to the effect of expansion of trade with the partner (as a result of trade creation and diversion) on the supply price of partner imports, measured by the area $F_2KP'_1R = NF'_1WT$. This loss, which may be described as 'the loss on the partner terms of trade', will be greater the greater the initial volume of trade with the partner and the greater the increase in the price of the commodity in the partner country; it is equal to the product of the initial partner trade volume and the partner price increase.

The loss from trade diversion and the loss on the partner terms of trade may be lumped together as 'the loss from tariff reduction', measured by F_2LWT and equal to the product of the difference between total initial imports and surviving foreign imports, and the increase in the average cost of these imports. It is less than the loss of tariff receipts on international trade by the amount of the transfer from tariff proceeds to consumers' surplus.

The foreign country's loss of producers' surplus is composed of two parts:

F.1. The reduction in the value of surviving exports to the home country, measured by $G_1G_2F'_2L$ and equal to the home country's gain (H.3). As explained above, this loss is equal to the product of the surviving trade volume and the domestic price reduction.

F.2. The loss of producers' surplus on goods whose production is discontinued in consequence of trade diversion, measured by $LF'_2F'_1$. This loss is greater, the greater the amount of trade diversion and the greater the reduction in the price of the goods, and is equal to half the product of the amount of trade diversion and the domestic price reduction.

The partner country's gain of producers' surplus is also composed of two parts:

P.1. The increase in the value of the initial volume of exports to the home country, measured by $F_2KP'_1R=NF'_1WT$ and equal to the home country's loss (H.5). As already explained, this loss is equal to the product of the initial partner trade volume and the partner price increase.

P.2. The gain of producers' surplus on the increased production of exports to meet the demand arising from trade diversion and trade creation, measured by RP'_1P_2. This gain will be greater the greater the amount of trade creation and trade diversion, and the greater the increase in the price in the partner country; it is equal to half the product of the amount of trade creation and diversion, and the partner price increase.[1]

From the standpoint of the home country, elimination of the tariff on imports from the partner country will be beneficial or not according to whether H.1+H.2+H.3−H.4−H.5 is positive or negative—that is, according to whether the gain from trade creation (P_1TP_2) and the gain on the foreign terms of trade ($G_1G_2F'_2L$) together outweigh the loss from tariff reduction (F_2LWT). It is clear that a net gain is more likely, the greater the amount of trade creation, the less the amount of trade diversion, the greater the initial trade with the foreigner and the less the initial trade with the partner, and the greater the reduction in the domestic price of the

[1] In symbols, let t be the amount of the tariff, and p the reduction in the domestic price when the tariff on partner imports is removed; then (t−p) is the increase in the partner price. Let M_f and M_p be the initial volumes of imports from foreign and partner countries, M_c and M_d the amounts of trade created and diverted by the change. Then the various gains and losses are as follows:

$$\text{H.1}+\text{H.2}=\tfrac{1}{2}p\,M_c$$
$$\text{H.3}=\text{F.1}=p\,(M_f-M_d)$$
$$\text{H.4}=(t-p)M_d$$
$$\text{H.5}=\text{P.1}=(t-p)M_p$$
$$\text{F.2}=\tfrac{1}{2}p\,M_d$$
$$\text{P.2}=\tfrac{1}{2}\,(t-p)\,(M_d+M_c).$$

It can easily be shown that

$$p=\frac{s_p\,t}{d+s_h+s_f+s_p}$$
$$M_c=(d+s_h)p$$
$$M_d=s_fp,$$

where d is the slope of the demand curve (defined to have a positive sign), s_h, s_f, s_p are the slopes of the domestic, foreign, and partner supply curves respectively, and $d+s_h$ is the slope of the home country's demand curve for imports (defined to have a positive sign)—all slopes being referred to the OY (price) axis.

commodity (the less the rise in the partner price) relative to the size of the tariff.[2]

From the combined standpoint of the home country and the partner country, the loss on the partner terms of trade to the former (H.5) is cancelled out by the gain in producers' surplus on the initial volume of trade to the latter (P.1), and there is also an additional gain of partner producers' surplus on the expansion of trade to be reckoned in. The net result is beneficial or not according to whether H.1+H.2+H.3−H.4−H.5+P.1+P.2=H.1+H.2+H.3−H.4+P.2 is positive or negative—that is, according to whether the domestic gain from trade creation (P_1TP_2) and the gain on the foreign terms of trade ($G_1G_2F'_2L$) together with the partner country's gain from trade expansion (RP'_1P_2) collectively outweigh the loss from trade diversion ($F_2LF'_1N$). The two countries gain or lose according to whether the combined area of $P_1TRP'_1P_2$ and $G_1G_2F'_2L$ exceeds or falls short of the area of $F_2LF'_1N$. By subtraction of RP'_1T LF'_1N from, and addition of $LF'_2F'_1=F_1F_2N$ to each of these, the total gain or loss becomes equal to $G_1G_2F'_2L+LF'_2F'_1+P_1TP'_1P_2-F_1F_2LN=H_2F_2.AB+\frac{1}{2}F_2N.AB+\frac{1}{2}(TP_2-F_2N).AC$. The first term is the gain on the foreign terms of trade; the second the loss of foreign producers' surplus; the third and fourth together amount to half the product of the tariff and the difference between the amount of trade creation and the amount of trade diversion.

The net effect must be a gain so long as trade creation exceeds trade diversion, though there may be a gain even in the opposite case. The gain will be greater or the loss less, the more trade is created, the less trade is diverted, the larger the initial trade with the foreign country, and the greater the reduction in the domestic price of the commodity. If trade creation exceeds trade diversion the gain will be greater the higher the tariff; but in the opposite case the magnitude of the gain or loss does not depend simply on the height of the tariff.[3]

[2] In terms of the symbols of the previous footnote, the home country's gain or loss is

$$\begin{aligned} H.1+H.2+H.3-H.4-H.5 &= \tfrac{1}{2}p\ M_c+p\ (M_f-M_d)-(t-p)\ (M_d+M_p)\\ &= \tfrac{1}{2}p\ M_c+p\ (M_f+M_p)-t(M_d+M_p)\\ &= \tfrac{1}{2}p\ M_c+pM_f-tM_d-(t-p)\ M_p. \end{aligned}$$

[3] The combined domestic and partner gain or loss is

$$\begin{aligned} H.1+H.2+H.3-H.4+P.2 &= \tfrac{1}{2}pM_c+p(M_f-M_d)-(t-p)M_d\\ &\quad +\tfrac{1}{2}(t-p)\ (M_d+M_c)\\ &= \tfrac{1}{2}tM_c+pM_f-tM_d+\tfrac{1}{2}(t-p)M_d\\ &= \tfrac{1}{2}t\ (M_c-M_d)+pM_f-\tfrac{1}{2}pM_d\\ &= \tfrac{1}{2}t\ (M_c-M_d)+p(M_f-M_d)+\tfrac{1}{2}pM_d. \end{aligned}$$

By substituting for M_c and M_d from footnote 1, this can be rewritten as $G=\frac{1}{2}k[(d+s_h-s_f-s_fk)t^2+2M_ft]$, where $k=p/t$ is a constant. Differentiating,

$$\begin{aligned} \frac{dG}{dt} &= k[(d+s_h-s_f)t+M_f-ks_ft]\\ &= (M_c-M_d)+k\ (M_f-M_d). \end{aligned}$$

Since (M_f-M_d) is positive by assumption, if (M_c-M_d) is positive, the gain must increase as t increases; but if (M_c-M_d) is negative, the gain or loss may

From the standpoint of the world as a whole, the gain on the foreign terms of trade (H.3) is cancelled by the loss in foreign producers' surplus on the surviving volume of the foreign country's exports (F.1); and loss of foreign producers' surplus owing to trade diversion (F.2) must be added in. The world as a whole will gain or lose according as

$$H.1+H.2+H.3-H.4+P.2-F.1-F.2=H.1+H.2+P.2-H.4-F.2$$

is positive or negative—that is, according to whether the domestic gain from trade creation (P_1TP_2) and the partner gain from trade expansion (RP'_1P_2) outweigh the domestic and foreign losses from trade diversion ($F_2LF'_1N$ and $LF'_2F'_1$ respectively).

The sum of the gains from the change is given by the area $P_1TRP'_1P_2$, and the sum of the losses by $F_2F'_2F'_1N$. By adding P_1RT to the sum of the gains, and F_1F_2N ($=P_1RT$) to the sum of the losses, world gain or loss is seen to depend on whether $P_1P'_1P_2$ exceeds or falls short of $F_1F_2F'_2F'_1$. But the former area $P_1P'_1P_2=\frac{1}{2}RP_2.AC$ and the latter area $F_1F_2F'_2F'_1=F_2N.AC$, so that the world gains or loses according to whether RP_2 is greater or less than twice F_2N. Subtracting $F_2N=RT$ from both sides, it is readily seen that the world gains or loses according to whether TP_2 is greater or less than F_2N, that is, according to whether the amount of trade creation exceeds the amount of trade diversion or not. To put the point another way, the world gains or loses according to whether less than or more than half the expansion of the partner's trade is accounted for by trade diversion. The amount of the gain (loss) is one-half the product of the excess (deficiency) of trade creation over trade diversion and the amount of the tariff.[4] These results can, of course, be derived more simply and directly from the measure of the gain for the home and partner country, by cancelling out the two terms corresponding to the gain on the foreign terms of trade, and the loss of foreign producers' surplus.

Whether the world as a whole gains or loses from discriminatory tariff removal depends (on the assumptions of the Marshallian model employed here) on the very simple criterion of whether trade creation is greater or less than trade diversion. Moreover, it is intuitively obvious, and can be rigorously established,[5] that trade creation will be greater or less than trade diversion according as the effect of a price reduction in increasing

increase or decrease with t. But since (M_c-M_d) increases in absolute value, and (M_f-M_d) decreases, as t increases, there must be a critical value of t beyond which the gain is less or the loss greater the larger is t.

[4] The world gain or loss is

$$\begin{aligned} H.1+H.2+P.2-H.4-F.2 &= \tfrac{1}{2}pM_c+\tfrac{1}{2}(t-p)(M_d+M_c) \\ &\quad -(t-p)M_d-\tfrac{1}{2}pM_d \\ &= \tfrac{1}{2}t(M_c-M_d). \end{aligned}$$

[5] Substituting for M_c and M_d in terms of the slopes of the relevant demand and supply curves, as given in footnote 1, the expression for the world gain or loss given in footnote 4 becomes

$$\tfrac{1}{2}tp(d+s_h-s_f).$$

Hence the world gains or loses according as $d+s_h$, the slope of the home country's demand curve for imports, is greater or less than s_f, the slope of the foreign supply curve of imports.

import demand via extension of demand and contraction of domestic supply is greater or less than its effect in reducing foreign supply. In other words, the world as a whole gains if import demand is more sensitive to price than foreign supply, and vice versa.

A corollary of this result—that the world as a whole is more likely to gain, the lower the sensitivity of foreign supply to price—is of considerable interest. In conjunction with the fact that the loss inflicted on the foreign country (F.1+F.2) is greater the lower is this sensitivity, it leads to the paradoxical conclusion that the world as a whole is more likely to gain, the greater is the damage inflicted on the non-participating country.

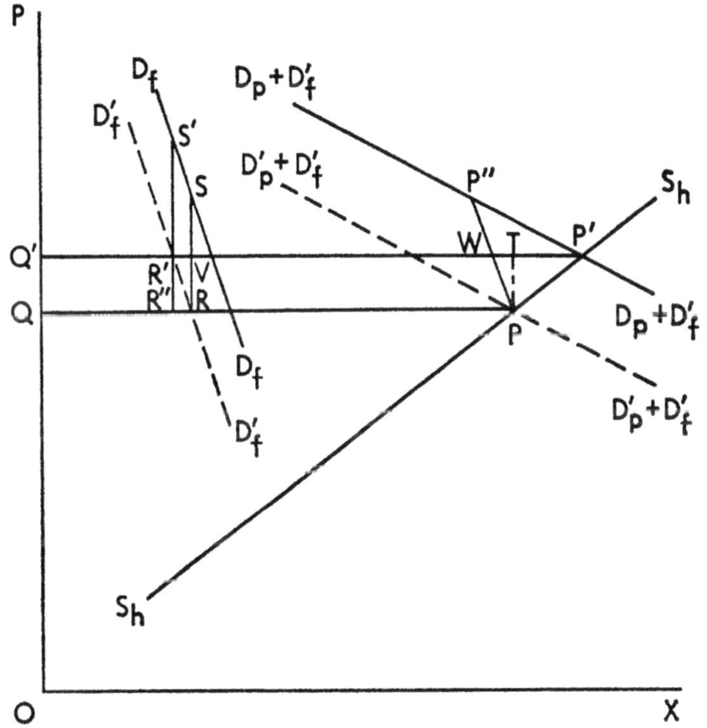

Fig. III.7

2. *Tariff Elimination: Exports to the Foreign Country*

In Fig. III.7, S_h is the home country's supply curve of exports; D_f is the demand curve of the foreign market, and D'_f that demand curve as reduced by the foreign country's tariff. $D'_p+D'_f$ is the combined foreign and partner demand curve for the home country's exports, when each imposes a tariff on imports. $D_p+D'_f$ is the combined foreign and partner demand curve for the country's exports, when the partner country's tariff is removed; since the combined demand curve is obtained by lateral addition of the foreign and partner demand curves, the point P″ on $D_p+D'_f$ corresponding to any point P on $D'_p+D'_f$ is found by drawing

PP″ parallel to D_f (the vertical distance between P and P″ is equal to the partner tariff).

With tariffs imposed by both importing countries, total exports are QP, of which QR goes to the foreign country and RP to the partner country. The producers' surplus earned by the home country is measured by the area below QP left of the supply curve S_h and right of the Y-axis. The foreign country enjoys tax revenue and consumers' surplus measured by the area bounded by the Y-axis, QR, RS, and D_f; the partner country enjoys tax revenue and consumers' surplus measured by the area bounded by D'_f, RP, PP″, and $D_p+D'_f$.

The effect of elimination of the partner country tariff is to increase exports to Q′P′, of which Q′R′ goes to the foreign country and R′P′ to the partner country: exports are diverted from the foreign to the partner market in the amount of R′V=WT, and new exports are created (to the partner market) in the amount TP′.

The home country's producers' surplus increases by QQ′P′P. The increase can be divided into the following parts:

H.1. The increased producers' surplus earned on surviving trade with the foreign country ('the gain on the foreign terms of trade'), QQ′R′R″.

H.2. The increased producers' surplus earned on trade diverted from the foreign to the partner country ('the gain from trade diversion'), R″R′VR.

H.3. The increased producers' surplus earned on the initial trade with the partner country ('the gain on the partner terms of trade'), RR′WP=RVTP.

H.4. The producers' surplus earned on the increase in the volume of exports ('the gain from trade creation'), PTP′.

The effect on the partner country consists of the net result of two conflicting effects:

P.1. The loss of consumers' surplus and tariff proceeds due to the increased cost of the former volume of imports ('the loss on the partner terms of trade', equal to the home country's gain on the partner terms of trade, H.3), RR′WP=RVTP.

P.2. The increase in consumers' surplus[6] due to the expansion of imports (through trade creation and trade diversion) as a result of tariff elimination, WP″P′.

The foreign country suffers a loss of tariff revenue and consumers' surplus which can be divided into the following parts:

F.1. The loss from the increased cost of the surviving volume of imports, QQ′R′R″.

F.2. The loss of tariff revenue on former imports diverted to the partner market, R′S′SR.

[6] Where the country produces some importable goods domestically, the gain consists of two parts: the gain in consumers' surplus from greater consumption, and the gain from replacement of higher-cost domestic production by lower-cost imports.

F.3. The loss of consumers' surplus[7] on former imports diverted to the partner market, R″R′R.[8]

The net gain to the home and partner countries combined is H.1+H.2+H.3+H.4−P.1+P.2=H.1+H.2+H.4+P.2. The various elements of gain can be grouped into two classes: the increase in producers' surplus from more favourable terms of trade with the foreign country (H.1), and the increase in producers' and consumers' surplus due to the expansion of exports to the partner country by trade creation and trade diversion (H.2+H.4+P.2).

The net gain or loss to the world as a whole is the difference between the gain to the home and partner countries and the loss to the foreign country, that is, H.1+H.2+H.4+P.2−F.1−F.2−F.3=H.2+H.4+P.2−F.2−F.3. Since H.2=R″R′VR=R″R′R+R′VR=F.3+WTP, the net world gain or loss is equal to PP″P′−R′S′SR, that is, to $\frac{1}{2}t_p(X_c+X_d)-t_fX_d$, where t_p and t_f are the partner and foreign tariffs, X_c is the amount of trade created, and X_d is the amount of trade diverted.

It follows easily that, if the tariffs are initially the same in the partner and foreign countries, the world gains or loses according as trade creation exceeds or falls short of trade diversion. This is the same criterion as was established for the case of discriminatory tariff elimination. The result is not surprising, since equal tariffs on exports to different countries are 'non-discriminatory' as between buyers in the same sense as equal tariffs on imports from different countries are non-discriminatory as between sellers, and removal of the tariff imposed on one buyer is discriminatory in the same sense as removal of the tariff imposed on one seller.

It follows also that the world is more likely to gain, the lower is the

[7] Where some importable goods are produced domestically, this loss consists of two parts: the loss of consumers' surplus due to reduced consumption and the loss due to substitution of additional higher-cost home production for imports.

[8] In symbols, let t_p and t_f be the partner and foreign tariffs, and p the increase in the net and foreign market price of exports when the partner tariff is removed; then (t_p-p) is the decrease in the partner market price. Let X_f and X_p be the initial volumes of exports to the foreign and partner countries, X_c and X_d the amounts of trade created and diverted by the change. Then the various gains and losses are

$$H.1=F.1=p(X_f-X_d)$$
$$H.2=p\,X_d$$
$$H.3=P.1=p\,X_p$$
$$H.4=\tfrac{1}{2}\,p\,X_c$$
$$P.2=\tfrac{1}{2}\,(t_p-p)\,(X_c+X_d)$$
$$F.2=t_f\,X_d$$
$$F.3=\tfrac{1}{2}\,p\,X_d.$$

It can easily be shown that $p=\dfrac{d_p\,t_p}{d_p+d_f+s_h}$

$$X_d=p\,d_f$$
$$X_c=p\,s_h,$$

where d_f, d_p, and s_h are the slopes of the foreign and partner demand curves and the home supply curve, referred to the Y-axis.

foreign tariff relative to the partner tariff; and it must gain if the foreign country imposes no tariff on imports.

Finally, since the amount of trade diversion will be less, and the loss to the foreign country from the increased cost of its imports greater, the less responsive is the foreign demand to price, the same paradoxical result emerges in this case as in the first: the world as a whole is more likely to gain from tariff elimination under a customs union, the more damage is inflicted on the non-participating country.

IV

ECONOMIC DEVELOPMENT AND INTERNATIONAL TRADE*

Economic growth gives rise to many problems of international economic adjustment. This lecture is concerned with the formal analysis of one group of such problems, the effects of economic growth of various kinds on the growing country's demand for im-

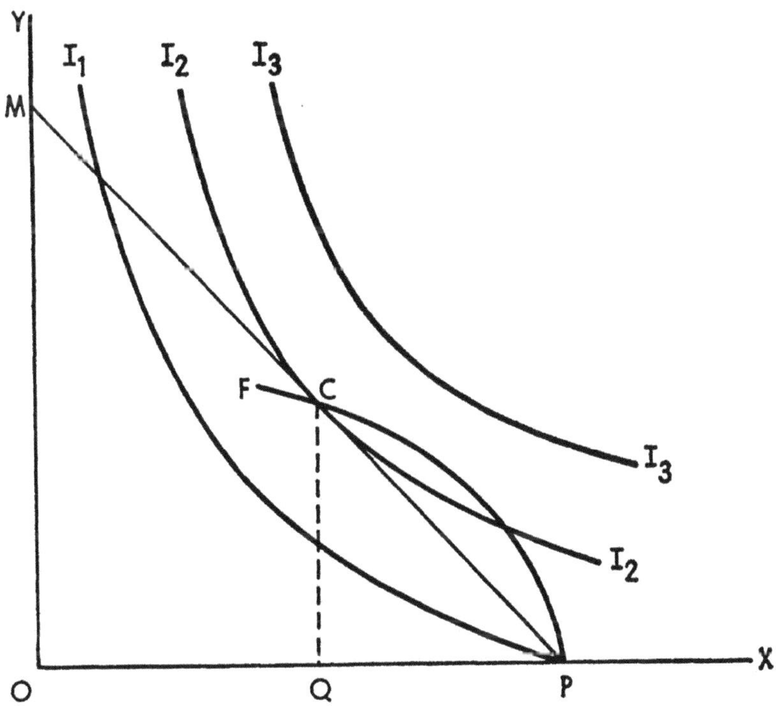

Fig. IV.1a

* Nationaløkonomisk Tidsskrift, 97 Bund 5–6 Hefte 1959, 253–72.

ports and dependence on international trade. The analysis may be treated in either of two ways: as an analysis of the nature of the equilibrium adjustment which growth requires of the international economy; and as a preliminary to analysis of the monetary problems which arise if the mechanism of international adjustment prevents or inhibits the attainment of the required new international equilibrium. The argument employs the standard two-country two-factor model, assuming constant returns to scale in production and perfectly competitive conditions. When we come to analyse the effects of specific types of economic growth, the model will be 'concretized' by making assumptions about the nature of the countries and the demand and supply conditions of the goods they produce.

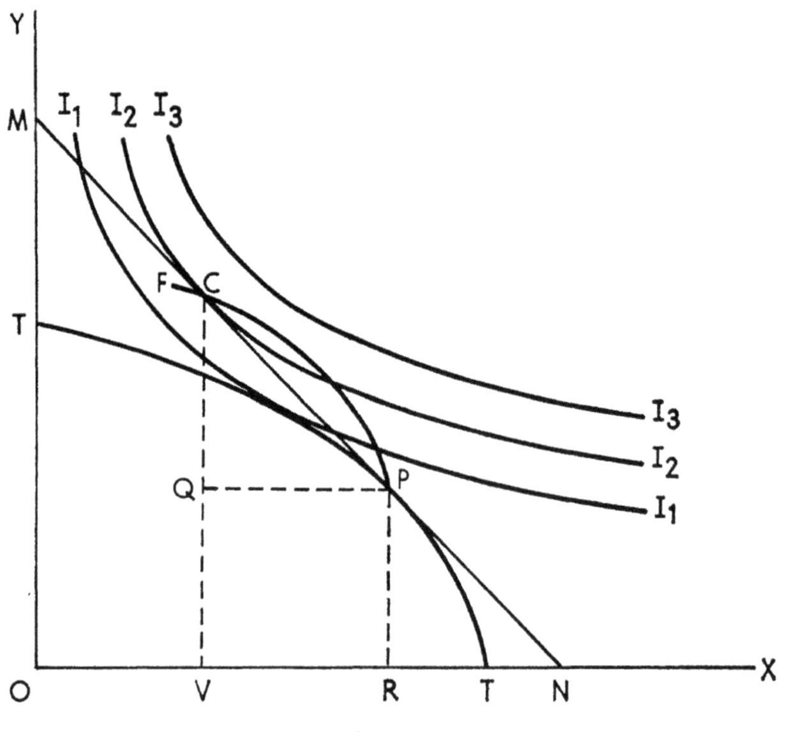

Fig. IV.1b

To begin with, let us recapitulate the general nature of the equilibrium established in international trade. Two cases may be distinguished, corresponding to complete and incomplete specialization of the country in production: these are represented in Figs. IV.1a and IV.1b. In both Figs. quantities of commodities X and Y are measured along the axes, and I_1, I_2, I_3 represent community indifference curves. The domestic production possibilities are represented by the fixed quantity OP in the complete specialization case, and by the transformation curve TT in the incomplete specialization case: the terms of trade open to the country on the world market are represented by the slope of the line PC. In equilibrium, the terms-of-trade line is tangent to a community indifference curve at C; and also, in the incomplete specialization case, to the transformation curve at P; the country produces the quantities represented by P (OP of X in case *a*, OR of X and PR of Y in case *b*) and consumes the quantities represented by C (OQ of X and CQ of Y in case *a*, OV of X and CV of Y in case *b*), exporting PQ of X to pay for imports of QC of Y. The value of the country's national product (national income), measured in terms of import goods, is represented by OM in each case; and the level of satisfaction enjoyed is I_2, as compared with the level I_1 that would be enjoyed if there were no international trade.

The foregoing account assumes that the country faces given terms of trade. In general, the terms of trade will not be given but will be variable and determined by the interaction in the market of the country's own willingness to trade, as determined by its preference system and production capacity (case *a*) or transformation curve (case *b*), and the willingness of the foreign country to trade, as determined by the same factors abroad. The foreign country's willingness to trade can be represented by an offer curve (PF in Figs. IV.1a and IV.1b) showing the quantities of Y the foreign country would export in return for imports of various quantities of X, the price at which each exchange would occur being shown by the ratio of the quantities of X and Y exchanged. In case *a*, the foreign offer curve has a fixed origin at the point corresponding to the domestic country's productive capacity, and international trade equilibrium is determined by the condition that the point at which an indifference curve is tangent to the (variable) terms of trade line must lie on the foreign offer curve: in case *b*, the origin of the foreign offer curve shifts along the transformation curve, as domestic production alters; and international trade equilibrium requires, in addition to the condition just stated, that the terms-of-trade line be tangent to the transformation curve at the point from which the offer curve originates. With the insertion of the foreign offer curve PF, the 'trade triangle' CPQ in Figs. IV.1a and IV.1b represents the equilibrium of international trade when the terms of trade are variable.

The effect of economic growth is to shift the production point P outwards along OX in case *a*, and the transformation curve TT outwards in case *b*. The analysis of the effects of growth can be pursued in two alternative ways: by assuming a given foreign offer curve and analysing the new international trade equilibrium that will result from growth, or by considering the effect of growth on the domestic country's demand for imports at the initial terms of trade. The latter is the approach adopted here, both because it enables the isolation of the effects of the growth of the economy and the development of concepts for the analysis of these effects, concepts which are directly applicable to economies whose terms of trade are fixed by the world market, and because, if the foreign offer curve is unchanged, the

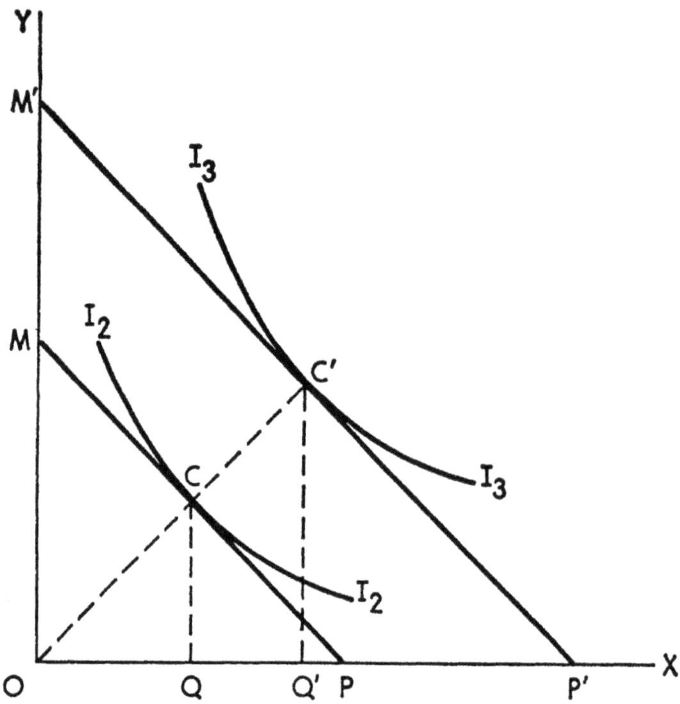

Fig. IV.2a

direction of change of the terms and volume of trade can be predicted from the effect of growth on the country's demand for imports at constant prices.

The general nature of the effect that economic growth would have on the growing country's demand for imports if growth occurred with unchanged terms of trade is illustrated in Figs. IV.2a and IV.2b. In each case, the production point shifts from P to P′, national income (product) measured in terms of imports from OM to OM′, the consumption point from C to C′, and the level of satisfaction enjoyed from I_2 to I_3. Imports demanded increase from CQ to C′Q′, and exports supplied from QP to Q′P′.

The question of economic interest is whether growth will increase the demand for imports more than proportionally to the increase in the value of the national product, in the same proportion as, or less than proportionally to the increase in the value of the national product. From the growing country's point of view, the question is whether growth makes the country relatively less self-sufficient, no more or less dependent on trade, or relatively more self-sufficient. From the point of view of the foreign country, the question is

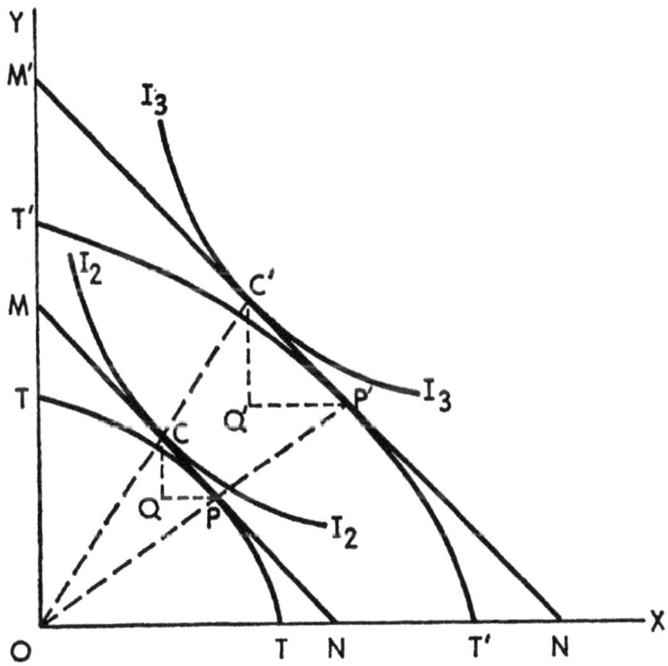

Fig. IV.2b

whether the market for its exports expands more than proportionally to, at the same rate as, or less than proportionally to the growth of this country. The three possibilities can be conceptualized in terms of three types of growth: pro-trade-biased growth, which increases the country's demand for imports and supply of exports more than proportionally to output; 'neutral' or unbiased growth, which increases the country's demand for imports and supply of exports in proportion to output; and anti-trade-biased growth, which increases the country's demand for imports and supply of exports less than proportionally to output. Figs. IV.2a and IV.2b represent a particular type of unbiased growth, in which production and consumption of each of the two goods, and therefore exports and imports, expand proportionally with income—as shown by the fact that M′M, C′C, and P′P all meet in the origin. In addition to the three general types of growth, two extreme cases can be distinguished: ultra-pro-trade-biased growth, in which more than the whole increase in national income is devoted to the purchase of imports so that the demand for

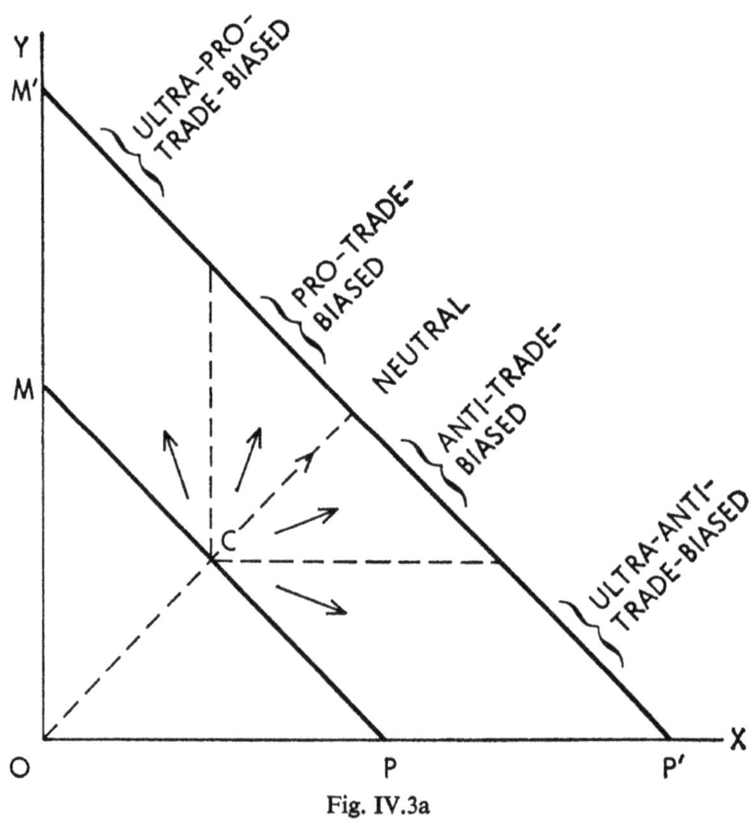

Fig. IV.3a

home-produced goods actually falls and the country becomes absolutely less self-sufficient; and ultra-anti-trade-biased growth, in which more than the whole increase in national income is devoted to the purchase of home-produced goods, so that the demand for imports actually falls and the country becomes absolutely more self-sufficient.

In the case of complete specialization, the type of growth is determined by the behaviour of the consumption of importables as the national product rises. Formally, it can be related to the 'output-elasticity of demand for importables'—the proportional change in quantity of importables demanded, divided by the proportional change in national output which causes the change in import demand: growth is pro-trade-biased, neutral, or anti-trade-biased according as this elasticity exceeds, equals, or falls short of one, ultra-anti-trade-biased if the elasticity is negative and ultra-pro-trade-biased if the elasticity exceeds the original ratio of national income to imports (an alternative way of expressing a negative output-elasticity of demand

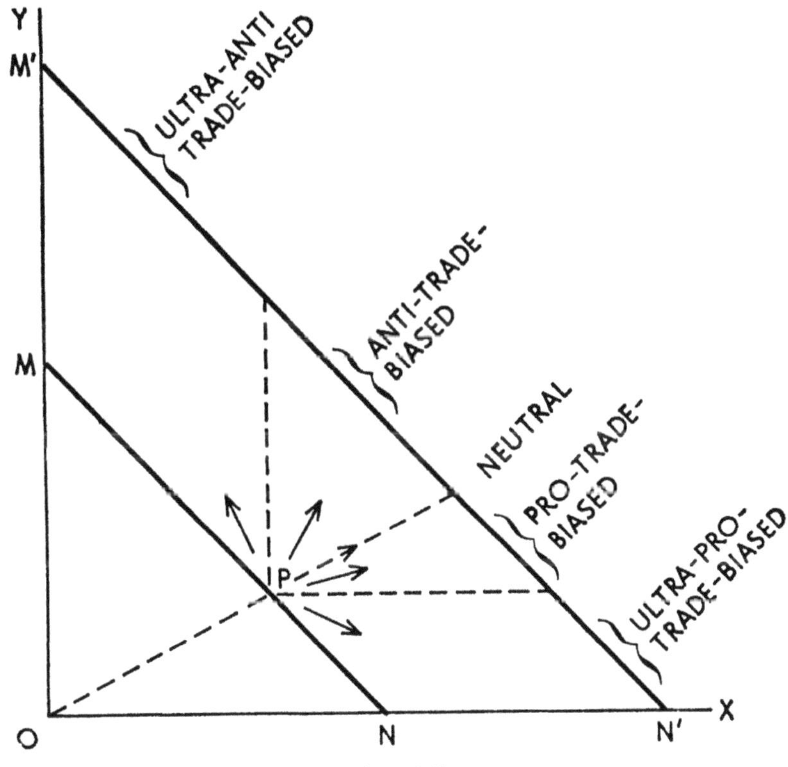

Fig. IV.3b

for exportables). The ranges of shift of the consumption point corresponding to the five possible types of growth are illustrated in Fig. IV.3a.

If growth is due to some other cause than population change, income per head will rise, and the type of growth will depend on the average income-elasticity of demand for imports: if imports are luxury goods, growth will be pro-trade-biased, if they are necessary goods growth will be anti-trade-biased; if imports are inferior goods growth will be ultra-anti-trade-biased and if exports are inferior goods growth will be ultra-pro-trade-biased. If, on the other hand, growth is due to population increase alone, it may be presumed that income per head will fall, so that in aggregate demand luxury goods will behave like necessities and conversely; the net effect of growth on demand will depend on the relations between population size and income per head, and between income per head and consumption per head of the good consumed, and a luxury good may even appear inferior in aggregate consumption. To simplify the following argument, and also because it seems reasonable to do so, cases of ultra-bias in the consumption shift will henceforth be ignored.

In the case of incomplete specialization, the effect of growth on the demand for imports depends on the combined behaviour of consumption and production. For analytical purposes it is convenient to consider separately the effects on the country's self-sufficiency of the consumption and production shifts associated with growth, before considering their combined effect. The consumption shift has already been analysed (the term 'demand for importables' rather than 'demand for imports' has been used deliberately to permit the argument to be extended to the case in which some importable goods are produced at home). The production shift can similarly be classified into five types, which can be formally described in terms of an 'output-elasticity of supply of importables'. If this elasticity exceeds one, so that domestic production of importables increases more than proportionally to national income and the country's production pattern becomes more self-sufficient, growth is anti-trade-biased; if the elasticity is negative, so that domestic production of importables falls, growth is ultra-pro-trade-biased; and so on. The ranges of shift of the production point corresponding to these types are shown in Fig. IV.3b. The determinants of the production shift will be discussed later; it would be possible, but is not worth while, to develop an analysis of output-elasticity of supply in terms of luxury, necessary and inferior production paralleling the analysis of output-elasticity of demand in terms of luxury, necessary and inferior consumption already presented.

The effect of growth on the demand for imports is the combined result of its effects on consumption demand and domestic supply; and the addition of the effects of the consumption and production shifts is complicated. If both shifts are biased in the same direction, or one is neutral, the combined effect is clearly pro-trade-biased or anti-trade-biased. If, however, the two shifts are biased in opposite directions, the net effect cannot be simply assessed. Because consumption of imports initially exceeds domestic production of them, biases of the same degree (as measured by the deviation from unit output-elasticity) but in opposite directions will not cancel out; instead, the bias on the consumption side will dominate unless the production shift is sufficiently more biased than the consumption shift. In other words, the degrees of bias must be compared. But where there is ultra-bias in the production shift and the possibility of contrary ultra-bias in the consumption shift is ruled out, some simplification is possible: ultra-anti-trade-bias in the production shift is sufficient to make the effect of growth ultra-anti-trade-biased, and ultra-pro-trade-bias in the production shift is sufficient to prevent growth being ultra-anti-trade-biased on balance.

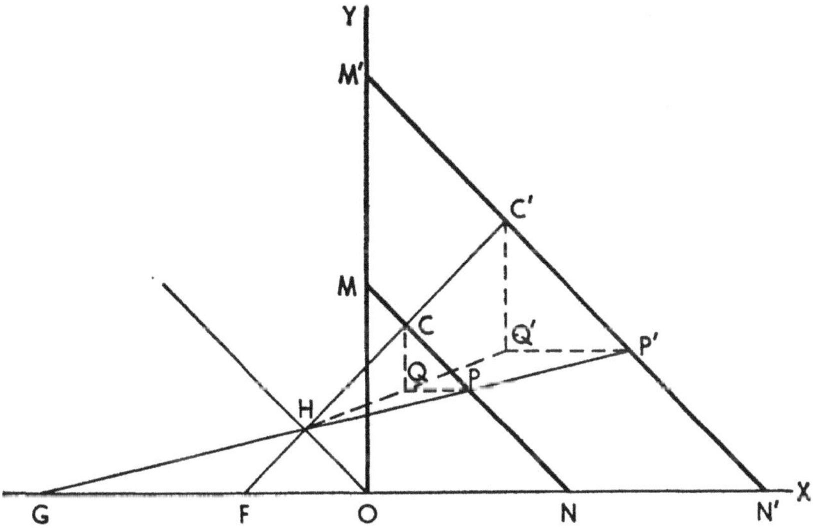

Fig. IV.4

The relation between the output-elasticities of consumption and production of importables, the production and consumption biases, and the overall bias of growth can be shown geometrically in terms of Fig. IV.4, which reproduces Fig. IV.2b but for clarity omits the transformation and indifference curves. The proportional changes in aggregate output, consumption of importables and production of importables are respectively:

$$\frac{MM'}{OM}=\frac{NN'}{ON},\ \frac{CC'}{FC}=\frac{NN'}{FN},\ \text{and}\ \frac{PP'}{GP}=\frac{NN'}{GN}.$$

Hence the output-elasticity of consumption of importables is $\frac{CC'}{FC}\div\frac{MM'}{OM}=\frac{ON}{FN}$, and the output-elasticity of production of importables is $\frac{PP'}{GP}\div\frac{MM'}{OM}=\frac{ON}{GN}$. The proportional change in demand for imports is $\frac{CC'}{HC}=\frac{PP'}{HP}=\frac{QQ'}{HQ}$, and the output-elasticity of demand for imports is $\frac{CC'}{HC}\div\frac{NN'}{ON}$. The magnitude of the latter, and hence the overall bias of growth, can be determined simply by comparing the slopes of OH and MN. If OH and MN are parallel, as in Fig. IV.4, $\frac{C'C}{HC}=\frac{NN'}{ON}$, the output-elasticity of demand for imports is unity and growth is neutral; if OH lies to the right of a line through O parallel to MN, $\frac{C'C}{HC}>\frac{NN'}{ON}$, the elasticity exceeds unity, and growth is pro-trade-biased; conversely, if OH lies to the left of the line through O parallel to MN, the elasticity is less than unity and growth is anti-trade-biased. By extension, if C'C and P'P meet in H at an obtuse angle growth is ultra-pro-trade-biased, while if H lies to the right of MN growth is ultra-anti-trade-biased. The bias of the consumption shift can be measured by the excess of the output-elasticity of consumption of importables over unity, and of the production shift by the excess of unity over the output-elasticity of production of importables (so that pro-trade-bias is positive and anti-trade-bias negative in each case). On these definitions the consumption bias is represented in Fig. IV.4 by $\frac{FO}{FN}$ and the production bias by $\frac{GO}{GN}$; $\frac{GO}{GN}$ is larger than $\frac{FO}{FN}$, thus demonstrating the point previously stated that where the biases are opposed the production bias must be larger than the consumption bias if the latter is not to predominate.

Ultra-pro-trade-biased growth and ultra-anti-trade-biased growth have been described as extreme cases, in terms of their effects on the growing country's self-sufficiency or dependence on trade. Before proceeding to discuss the likely effects on trade of growth due to particular causes, it seems appropriate to notice an alternative conception of extreme types of growth, a conception in terms of economic welfare which really belongs at a later stage of the argument but which it is convenient to introduce at this stage.

Let us assume that only the one country is growing, and consider the nature of the new international trade equilibrium that will result from its increased production, and the economic welfare that will be derived from it. Normally, at least so far as the argument up to this stage has taken us, we might expect that growth would increase the country's demand for imports, thereby worsening its equilibrium terms of trade and so imposing a loss of economic welfare as a partial offset to the gain in welfare associated with a higher level of production. This suggests two possible extreme cases. The first is the case in which the growing country's demand for imports falls instead of rises, so that its terms of trade improve and the benefit from increased production is augmented by a gain on the terms of trade; this case will occur when growth is ultra-anti-trade-biased, possible causes

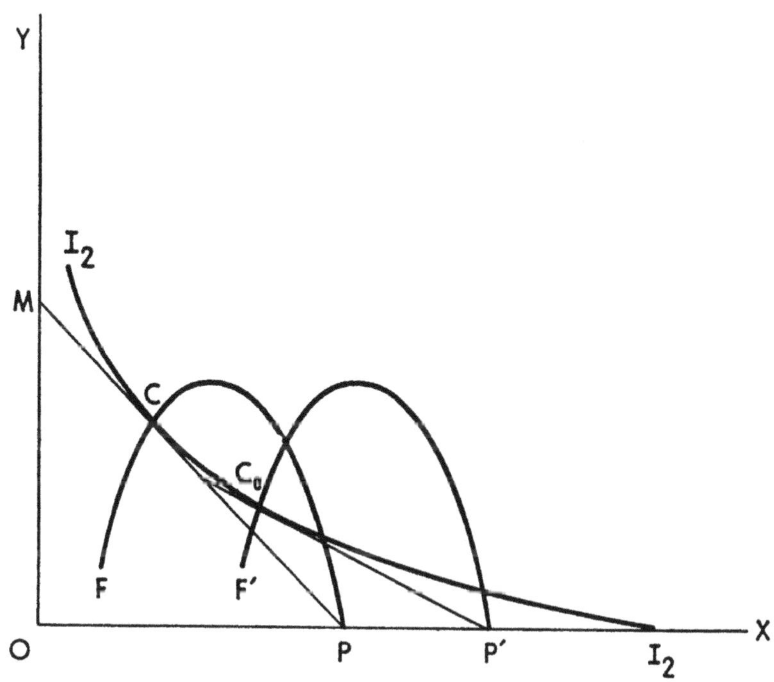

Fig. IV.5a

of which will appear in subsequent analysis. The other extreme is the case in which the terms of trade turn unfavourable to such an extent that the welfare loss from this cause more than offsets the gain from increased production, so that the country's growth leaves it worse off on balance. This is the case which Jagdish Bhagwati has described as 'immiserizing growth';[1] it is probably a *curiosum*, but worth analysing.

The simplest way of doing so is to illustrate the possibility of growth which leads to no welfare gain; this possibility is depicted in Figs.

[1] Jagdish Bhagwati, 'Immiserizing Growth: A Geometrical Note', *The Review of Economic Studies*, XXV(3), no. 68, June 1958, 201–5.

IV.5a and IV.5b, for the two cases of complete and incomplete specialization. In both Figs., C_e on the pre-growth indifference curve I_2 is the consumption point when growth has occurred and the terms of trade moved against the country sufficiently to preserve international trade equilibrium; in Fig. IV.5b, P_e is the new equilibrium production point on the new transformation curve.

In the complete specialization case, zero-gain growth obviously requires that foreign demand for the country's exports be inelastic. With a higher price of imports and the same level of indifference,

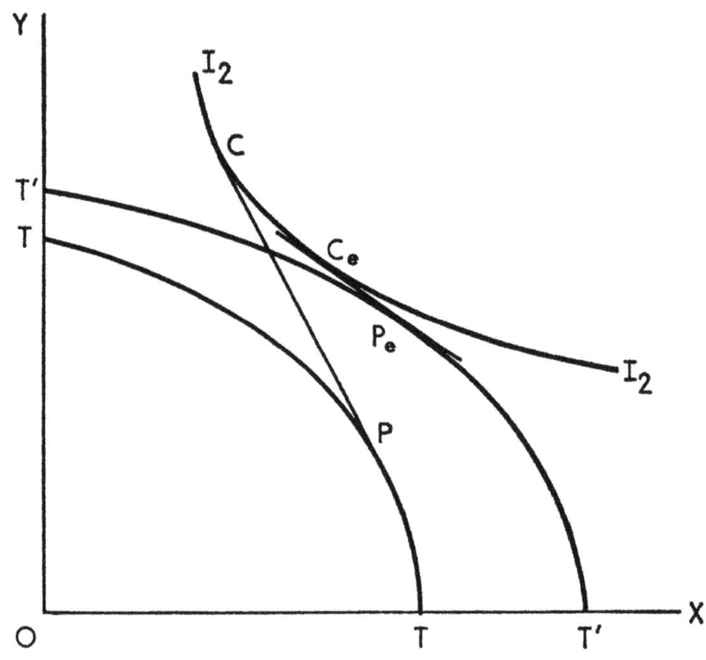

Fig. IV.5b

consumption of importables and therefore imports demanded must fall. For this to correspond to full international equilibrium, the foreigner must accordingly reduce the quantity of imports supplied when their price rises, or, what is the same thing, spend less of his goods on this country's exports when the price of the latter falls. This necessary condition for zero-gain growth in the complete specialization case is illustrated in Fig. IV.5a, where PF and P′F′ represent the (given) foreign offer curve drawn through the pre-growth and post-growth production points. In the incomplete specialization case, consumption of importables must also fall; but the demand for imports does not necessarily fall, since domestic production of importables may fall by more than consumption of them. Thus, zero-gain growth in this case requires *either* that the foreign demand for the country's exports be inelastic *or* that the country's growth be ultra-pro-trade-biased.

To return to the main line of the argument, the concepts of neutral, pro-trade-biased, anti-trade-biased, and ultra-pro- and ultra-anti-trade-biased growth, together with the distinction between the consumption, the production, and the overall effect of growth, must now be applied to analysing the effects of different types of growth. Following convention, we shall be concerned with three types of economic growth—technical progress, population increase, and capital accumulation—which are assumed to be analytically separable. And we shall consider their effects in two types of economy, one which exports manufactured goods in exchange for foodstuffs—a 'manufacturing country'—and one which exports foodstuffs in exchange for manufactured goods—an 'agricultural country'. Both countries are assumed to be only partially specialized—this is the more interesting case, and can readily be adapted to the case of complete specialization.

To make the analysis more concrete, it is assumed that food is labour-intensive in production and a necessary good in consumption, while manufactures are capital-intensive in production and a luxury good in consumption. Further, it is assumed that capital is better off than labour, so that the average and marginal propensities to consume manufactures are higher for capital than for labour, and the average and marginal propensities to consume food are higher for labour than for capital.

In considering the effects of growth, it is convenient to distinguish between technical progress, which alters the production functions of the economy, and population increase and capital accumulation, which increase the quantity of a productive factor without altering the production function. The effects of factor accumulation are the simplest to deal with, and will therefore be discussed first. For reasons which will become clear in the course of the argument, it is necessary to consider the production effects before the consumption effects.

The production effect of factor accumulation, for the simple model we are using, is given by a rather simple proposition sometimes described as 'the Rybczynski theorem';[2] if the terms of trade are constant, and one factor accumulates, there will be an absolute

[2] T. M. Rybczynski, 'Factor Endowment and Relative Commodity Prices', *Economica*, New series, XXII, no. 88, November 1955, 336–41. I first encountered the argument in a paper read by W. M. Corden in November 1954.

reduction in the production of the good which uses that factor less intensively, and the production of the good using that factor more intensively will increase by more than the value of the total increase in output. The proof of this proposition starts from the fact that, to keep the relative prices of the goods constant, it is necessary to keep factor prices constant, because an increase in the relative price of a factor will increase the relative cost of the good which uses that factor more intensively. To keep factor prices constant, it is necessary

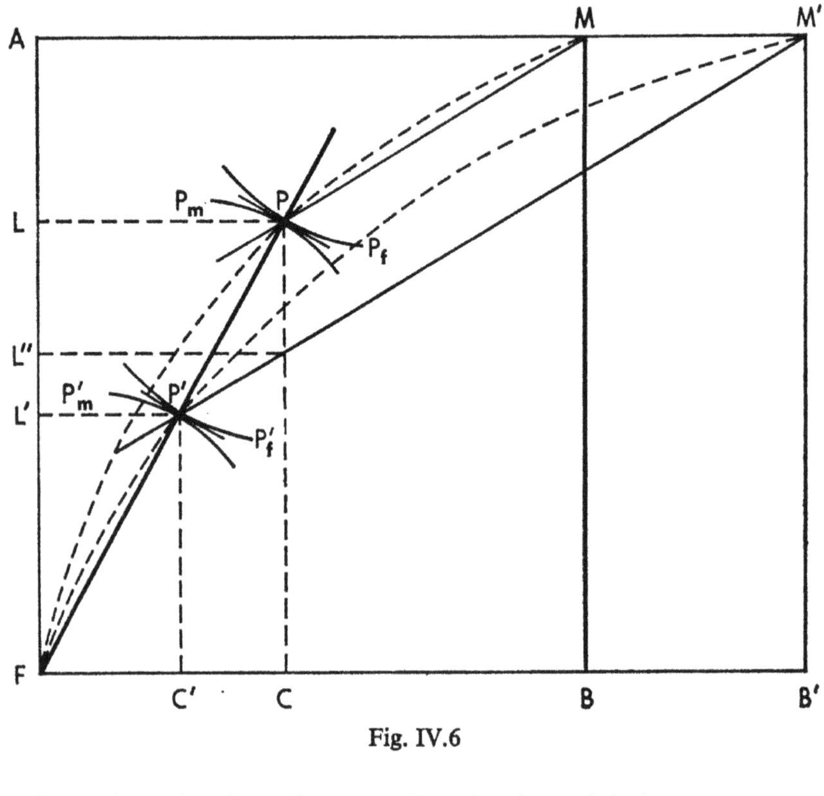

Fig. IV.6

to keep the ratio of one factor to the other in each industry constant, since it is this ratio which determines the relative marginal productivities and therefore the relative prices of the factors.

How is this to be done when the amount of one factor increases? Suppose there is an increase in the quantity of capital: then if labour and capital together are shifted out of the labour-intensive into the capital-intensive industry, labour will be released from the labour-intensive industry in greater quantities than are required to operate the released capital in the capital-intensive industry; and the surplus will be available to operate the additional capital.

This point can be illustrated by means of the production box-diagram, as in Fig. IV.6. In the diagram AF represents the initial endowment of labour, and AM the initial endowment of capital; production indifference curves for food are drawn in the box with F as origin, and for manufactures with M as origin; the points of tangency of indifference curves from the two origins, which constitute efficient allocations of resources between the two industries, form the contract curve FPM. Suppose that P is the pre-growth production point, the economy producing P_f food by using FL of labour and FC of capital in agriculture, and P_m of manufactures by using LA of labour and BC of capital in manufacturing; the labour: capital ratios in food and manufactures respectively are shown by the slopes of FP and MP, and the exchange ratio between labour and capital is given by the slope of the common tangent to P_f and P_m at P.

Now suppose that capital increases to AM′, shifting the origin of the manufactures production indifference curves to M′ and altering the contract curve to FP′M′. At P′, the point on the new contract curve with the same labour: capital ratio in each industry and therefore the same exchange ratio between factors as at P, production of food P'_f is lower than at P. The reduction of food production from P_f to P'_f releases LL′ of labour and CC′ of capital from agriculture; only L′L″ of the labour released is required to co-operate with CC′ capital in manufactures, leaving LL″ free to operate the additional capital MM′.

It follows from the foregoing argument that capital accumulation will reduce agricultural production and increase manufacturing production at constant terms of trade. Capital accumulation in the manufacturing country will therefore have an ultra-pro-trade-biased production effect; whereas capital accumulation in the agricultural country will have an ultra-anti-trade-biased production effect. Conversely, population growth will reduce manufacturing output and increase agricultural output; thus the production effect of population growth will be ultra-anti-trade-biased in the manufacturing country and ultra-pro-trade-biased in the agricultural country.

It also follows from the previous argument that, at constant terms of trade (and so long as the country remains incompletely specialized), all of the increase in output goes as income to the factor which is accumulating. On our assumption of differing marginal and average propensities to consume the goods, capital accumulation will increase the average proportion of income spent on manufactures, and population growth will increase the average proportion of income spent on food. Hence the consumption effect of capital accumulation will be anti-trade-biased in the manufacturing country and pro-trade-biased in the agricultural country, while the consumption effect of population growth will be the reverse in the two countries. As explained earlier, an ultra-anti-trade-biased production effect will dominate the consumption effect while an ultra-pro-trade-biased production effect will rule out an ultra-anti-trade-biased total effect. Hence capital accumulation in the agricultural country and population growth in the manufacturing country will be ultra-anti-trade-biased, while the opposite type of factor accumulation in each country may be anything from ultra-pro-trade-biased to anti-trade-biased, but will not be ultra-anti-trade-biased.

Let us now turn to the effects of technical progress. This is a complex problem, because such progress may not only go on at different rates as between industries, but may also affect factors of production differentially in the industry in which it occurs, as well as in the economy as a whole. A technique for dealing with biased technical progress, which permits the whole problem to be dealt with in a relatively simple fashion, has only recently been published by two young American economists.[3] The following argument employs a somewhat modified version of their technique. As before, we begin with the production effect.

Let us begin with the simplest case of technical progress, 'neutral' technical progress, defined as progress which reduces the quantities of the two factors required to produce a given quantity of output in the same proportion. Neutral technical progress has the initial effect of increasing the output of the industry in which it occurs, and lowering its cost of production at the initial factor prices. We are interested in the effect on production at constant relative prices and costs of the goods. In order to restore the initial relative prices, factors must shift from the other industry into this one: as they do so, the price of the factor used relatively intensively in this industry rises, and the price of the factor used relatively intensively in the other industry falls, so altering the relative costs of the goods and restoring the initial price ratio. Thus neutral technical progress in an industry leads to expansion of the output of that industry at the expense of the other, at given terms of trade; in other words, neutral progress is ultra-biased. It follows that neutral progress in manufacturing has an ultra-pro-trade-biased production effect in the manufacturing country, and an ultra-anti-trade-biased production effect in the agricultural country; while the effects of neutral progress in agriculture are exactly the reverse.

[3] R. Findlay and H. Grubert, 'Factor Intensity, Technological Progress, and the Terms of Trade,' *Oxford Economic Papers*, New Series, II, no. 1, February 1959.

Now consider technical progress which is biased, in the sense that it alters the optimum ratio of one factor to the other employed at the initial factor prices in the industry in which progress occurs. Such progress may be described as saving the factor whose optimum ratio to the other is reduced.[4] Biased progress has a dual initial effect: it lowers the cost of production in the industry, and it releases a quantity of the factor it saves. Its effects are therefore the same as those of a neutral technical change,[5] combined with an increase in the supply of the factor which is saved by the biased progress.

Again we are interested in the effect on production at constant commodity prices. As in the case of neutral technical progress, the reduction in cost requires a shift of factors into the industry where the progress has occurred. As in the case of factor accumulation, the factor released by progress must be absorbed by an expansion of production of the good which uses the factor relatively intensively, at the expense of production of the other good.

It follows that if technical progress saves the factor which is used relatively intensively in the industry where the progress occurs, both factors operate in the same direction, and the production effect will be even more ultra-biased than if progress were neutral. But if progress saves the factor used relatively intensively in the other industry, the two effects—cost-reducing and factor-saving—work in opposite directions, and the production effect may vary from one to the other extreme of ultra-bias, depending on the balance of cost-reducing and factor-saving effects.

The argument can be illustrated by reference to Fig. IV.7, which is reproduced (with emendations) from Findlay and Grubert. Capital is measured on the vertical axis, labour on the horizontal. The country's factor-endowment ratio is OR. The line through P_m and P_f represents the pre-progress factor price ratio, tangent to a manufacturing production indifference curve at P_m and an agricultural production indifference curve at P_f, these curves representing quantities of equal cost and value at the initial price ratio. OP_m and OP_f are the optimum factor-ratios in the two industries; and the allocation of production between the industries must be such that the two ratios, each weighted by the proportion of the labour force in the

[4] The bias is defined in terms of the effect of progress on the optimum factor ratio, rather than in terms of the relative reductions in quantities of factors required per unit of output, because progress may increase the quantity of one factor required per unit of output.

[5] Neutral technical progress (increased output in the industry) if the cost-saving effect outweighs the bias effect so that less of both factors is required per unit of output than before, neutral technical regress (reduced output in the industry) if more of the other factor is required per unit of output than before.

industry where the ratio is used, average out to the endowment ratio OR.

This diagram, incidentally, can be used to establish the Rybczynski theorem. Suppose that capital is accumulated, increasing the endowment ratio to OR′; for OP_m and OP_f to average out to the higher level OR′, the weight of OP_m must increase and that of OP_f decrease. That is, a larger proportion of the unchanged labour force must be

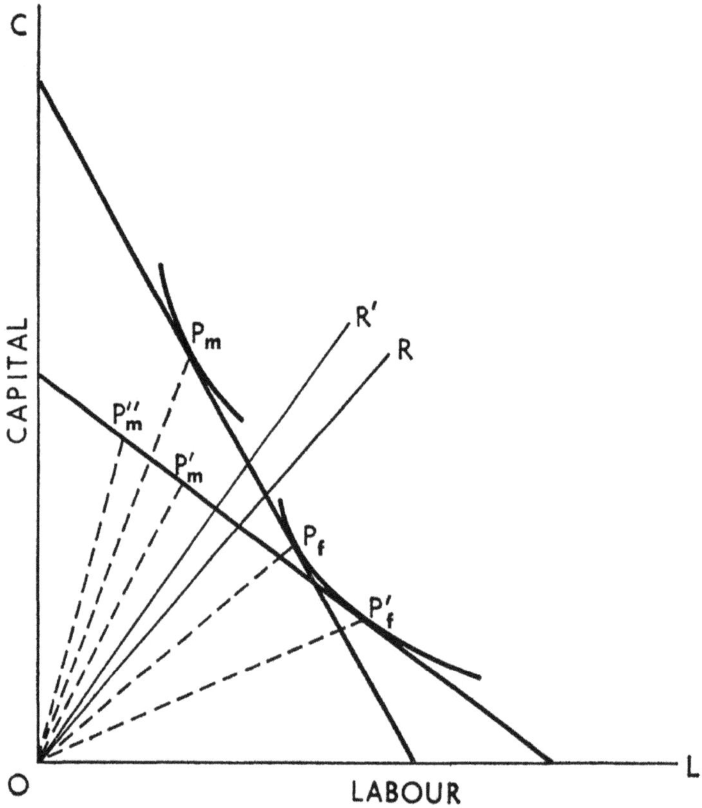

Fig. IV.7

employed in the capital-intensive manufacturing industry, and a smaller amount of labour in the labour-intensive food industry. Since capital : labour ratios are constant, production must vary with the amount of labour employed, falling in the labour-intensive industry.

To return to the effects of technical progress, suppose that there is technical progress in manufacturing, which shifts the production indifference curve for manufactures towards the origin O. At the initial factor prices, the cost of the quantity of manufactures represented by this indifference curve would now be less than the cost of the quantity of foodstuffs represented by the (unchanged) production indifference curve for agriculture. To keep the costs of the quantities of the goods equal, and so maintain the initial price ratio, factor prices must alter in favour of capital and against labour, to the factor-price ratio given by the new common tangent to the two production indifference curves, P'_m P'_f. As factor prices alter, labour will be substituted for capital in both industries.

The new capital : labour ratio in foodstuffs OP'_f is necessarily lower than the original one, owing to the substitution of cheaper labour for more expensive capital. If progress in manufacturing is capital-saving, neutral, or only slightly labour-saving, the capital: labour ratio in manufactures will also be lower than originally, as illustrated by P'_m. With a lower equilibrium capital : labour ratio in both industries, resources must have shifted out of the labour-intensive industry (foodstuffs) into the capital-intensive industry (manufactures) to maintain the overall average endowment ratio OR. Thus progress of these three types in manufacturing will be ultra-biased towards production of manufactures.

But if progress is sufficiently strongly labour-saving to offset the substitution effect of cheaper labour, the new capital : labour ratio in manufactures will be higher than the original. And with a higher capital : labour ratio in the one industry and a lower ratio in the other, the overall endowment ratio might have been maintained by a shift of resources in either direction (and to any extent) between the industries. Thus in this case the effect of technical progress in manufacturing may lie anywhere between the extremes of ultra-bias towards production of manufactures, and ultra-bias towards production of foodstuffs.

What about the consumption effect of technical progress? The restoration of the initial relative cost ratio involves lowering the relative price of the factor used less intensively in the industry where progress has occurred, and raising the price of the other. Thus more than the whole of the increase in national income due to progress goes to that factor which is used intensively in the industry in which the progress has occurred. In consequence, the proportion of expenditure out of national income on the good for which this factor's average and marginal propensity to consume is relatively high rises. It is even possible that total expenditure on the good preferred by the factor from which income is redistributed will fall; it will do so if the reduction in consumption due to straight income redistribution exceeds the increase in consumption due to the net increase in national income which accrues to the favoured factor. But it seems permissible to exclude this possibility of ultra-biased consumption effects through income-redistribution as an exceptional one. On this basis, it follows that progress in manufacturing, which reduces the income of labour and the proportional demand for food, will have an anti-trade-biased consumption effect in the manufacturing country and a pro-trade-biased consumption effect in the agricultural country; while the consumption effects of progress in agriculture will be the reverse.

Remembering that cases of ultra-anti-trade-biased and ultra-pro-trade-biased consumption effects have been excluded by assumption, the conclusions about the total effects of technical progress to which the foregoing analysis leads can be summarized as follows:

(*a*) The following types of progress will be ultra-anti-trade-biased:

(i) Neutral technical progress in agriculture in the manufacturing country;

(ii) neutral technical progress in manufacturing in the agricultural country;

(iii) capital-saving technical progress in manufacturing in the agricultural country;

(iv) labour-saving technical progress in agriculture in the manufacturing country.

(*b*) The following types of progress will be ultra-pro-trade-biased to anti-trade-biased, but not ultra-anti-trade-biased:

(i) Neutral technical progress in manufacturing in the manufacturing country;

(ii) neutral technical progress in agriculture in the agricultural country;

(iii) capital-saving technical progress in manufacturing in the manufacturing country;

(iv) labour-saving technical progress in agriculture in the agricultural country.

(*c*) The following types of progress can be biased in any way whatever from ultra-pro-trade-biased to ultra-anti-trade-biased:

(i) Capital-saving technical progress in agriculture in either country;

(ii) labour-saving technical progress in manufacturing in either country.

In brief, progress which is neutral or saves the factor used relatively intensively in the industry in which it occurs will be ultra-anti-trade-biased if it occurs in a country's import-competing industry, and ultra-pro-trade-biased to anti-trade-biased but *not* ultra-anti-trade-biased if it occurs in a country's export industry; progress which saves the factor used relatively intensively in the other industry than that in which the progress occurs may have any effect whatsoever.

TABLE

THE EFFECTS OF ECONOMIC GROWTH

Type of Growth	*Manufacturing Country* Production Effect	Consumption Effect	Total Effect	*Agricultural Country* Production Effect	Consumption Effect	Total Effect
Capital accumulation	UP	A	UP to A	UA	P	UA
Population Growth	UA	P	UA	UP	A	UP to A
Neutral technical progress						
(*a*) manufacturing	UP	A	UP to A	UA	P	UA
(*b*) agriculture	UA	P	UA	UP	A	UP to A
Capital-saving technical progress						
(*a*) manufacturing	UP	A	UP to A	UA	P	UA
(*b*) agriculture	UA to UP	P	UA to UP	UP to UA	A	UP to UA
Labour-saving technical progress						
(*a*) manufacturing	UP to UA	A	UP to UA	UA to UP	P	UA to UP
(*b*) agriculture	UA	P	UA	UP	A	UP to A

A: anti-trade-biased
P: pro-trade-biased
UA: ultra-anti-trade-biased
UP: ultra-pro-trade-biased

The production, consumption, and total effects of growth of the various types analysed in the argument so far on the growing country's demand for imports and supply of exports are summarized in the accompanying Table. The results in many cases are rather indefinite. It should perhaps be remarked that the chief reason why this is so lies in our original assumption that each factor prefers to consume the product in which it is employed intensively so that progress in that product, by redistributing income towards that factor, increases the relative demand for the product. If each factor preferred the product in which it was used less intensively, the consumption and production effects of progress would work in the same direction in many cases, giving unambiguous results. This may be confirmed by scrutiny of the summary Table: if factors' preferences for goods were the opposite of those assumed, the effects of growth of the types discussed would be *either* ultra-anti-trade-biased, *or* pro-trade-biased to ultra-pro-trade-biased, except in cases of capital-saving progress in agriculture and labour-saving progress in manufactures.

There are two further possible results of technical progress, suggested by Fig. IV.7, which should be mentioned, though it does not seem worth while to develop them in full. The first is that technical progress in one industry may reduce costs there so much that the country specializes completely on that product. In Fig. IV.7, the production indifference curve shifts so far towards the origin that either no common tangent exists, or the common tangent implies factor ratios inconsistent with the endowment ratio and non-negative production. This case is simply the extreme example of an ultra-biased production effect.

The second possibility arises when progress is so saving of the factor used intensively in the industry in which it occurs as to make the optimum ratio of that factor to the other at the initial factor prices lower than the endowment ratio in both industries. In this case, the saved factor cannot be absorbed (at the initial factor price ratio) by a shift of factors between industries; its relative price must fall, so that the consumption effect of progress is biased against the industry in which it occurs. The production effect of this kind of progress will entail complete specialization on the good in which progress occurs, at the initial commodity prices, provided that it can be assumed that with the original technology, the relative factor-intensities of the two industries would be the same at any factor price ratio. This assumption ensures that, as the price of the saved factor falls, the relative cost of producing the product in which progress has occurred, using the pre-progress technique, will fall. Thus it will never pay to produce the other product.[6] But since the reduction in the price of the saved factor will reduce the cost of producing this product with the old technique more than it will reduce the cost of producing it with the new technique, it is possible that, before the optimum factor-intensity with the new technique is raised to the endowment ratio, the old and new techniques become cost-indifferent. In this case, specialization will be accompanied by the use of that mixture of old and new techniques which demands factors in the average proportion of the country's endowment ratio.

[6] If factor-intensities with the old technique can reverse as the price of the saved factor falls, it is possible for there to exist a common tangent to the new production indifference curve for the industry where progress has occurred and the production indifference curve for the other industry such that (*a*) the optimum factor ratios lie on opposite sides of the endowment ratio, (*b*) the cost of production with the new technique is lower than with the old, in the industry where progress has occurred. In this case the country remains incompletely specialized at the initial commodity prices, this being made possible by a reversal of relative factor intensities in the two industries; the production effect here may be anywhere between the extremes of bias. The writer is indebted to Messrs. Findlay and Grubert for pointing out in correspondence the importance of condition (*b*), and so permitting the correction of an error in the original formulation of the argument.

The next step is to analyse the effects of growth in the two countries together, that is, of the growth of the world economy. If growth of the same type is going on in the two countries, conclusions about the movement of the terms of trade between them (i.e. between manufactures and food) can be drawn directly from the Table in many cases. For example, capital accumulation and neutral or capital-saving technical progress in manufactures turn the terms of trade in favour of the agricultural country, population growth and neutral or labour-saving technical progress in food turns the terms of trade in favour of the manufacturing country. But capital-saving progress in agriculture and labour-saving progress in manufactures may turn the terms of trade either way.

In the general case, with population increasing, capital accumulating, and technical progress being applied in both countries, the movement of the terms of trade will depend on the bias and the rate of growth in each country. This dependence can be expressed in the following formula:

$$R_{pm}=\frac{\varepsilon_a R_a-\varepsilon_m R_m}{\eta_a+\eta_m-1},$$

where R_{pm} is the rate of increase (decrease if negative) of the relative price of manufactures, R_a is the rate of growth of output in the agricultural country and ε_a its output-elasticity of demand for imports, R_m and ε_m are the rate of growth and output-elasticity of demand for imports of the manufacturing country, η_a and η_m are the two countries' price-elasticities of demand for imports, and $\eta_a+\eta_m-1$ is the 'elasticity factor' which determines the proportion of the initial value of trade by which a country's trade balance would improve if the price of its export good fell. The sense of the formula is that $\varepsilon_a R_a$ and $\varepsilon_m R_m$ are the rates of increase in the countries' demands for each other's goods; if these are unequal, equilibrium must be maintained by a relative price change whose magnitude will vary inversely with the elasticity factor.

Consideration of the effects of growth on the terms of trade suggests a concept of 'balanced growth'—growth of the two countries at rates which keep the terms of trade between them constant. Balance in this sense requires $\varepsilon_a R_a=\varepsilon_m R_m$; obviously, it is impossible if the output-elasticities of demand have opposite signs, the growth of one country being ultra-anti-trade-biased. In any case, the concept is of very limited usefulness, since 'balance' does not imply equal rates of growth of total output, let alone output per head. All that is implied by growth not being 'balanced' in this sense is that one of the countries is benefiting not only by the growth of its own output but by an improvement in its terms of trade, while the benefit the other derives from the growth of its output is reduced by a worsening of its terms of trade; it is even possible, as has been shown earlier, for a country to be worse off as the result of growth. If complete specialization is assumed, so that bias depends on consumption only, 'balanced growth' implies slower growth in the agricultural country unless growth is due to population increase.

In conclusion, some remarks on the extension of the analysis beyond the confines of the two-country two-good two-factor model seem called for. In the first place, recognition of a third factor, land, used predominantly in agriculture, introduces the classical problem of diminishing returns. If returns diminish strongly enough, the conclusions concerning the effects of population growth may be reversed—if there is no outlet on the land, the growing population may be forced into manufacturing. Second, allowance for a multiplicity of products introduces a variety of complications: rising income may lead to demands for foreign products formerly considered not worth their cost as compared with domestic substitutes; technical progress may be random, leading to sudden reversals of comparative advantage—for example, giving a capital-rich country a comparative advantage in producing a formerly labour-intensive product; and capital accumulation or population increase may alter a country's comparative advantage in particular goods—so that, for example, it may shift from labour-intensive to capital-intensive products in both manufacturing and agriculture. Thirdly, recognition of intermediate products which may be traded, and of the network of intersectoral transactions, greatly complicates the simple connection assumed in the foregoing between domestic demand for and supply of final goods, and the volume of international trade. Fourthly, allowing for the presence of many countries means that the movement of the terms of trade between manufactures and agricultural products depends on the nature and rate of growth in all countries together. One consequence of this is as follows: in the two-country model, 'general' growth of one country will tend to increase its demand for imports, so that if the other country does not grow or grows only slowly it will benefit from a favourable movement of its terms of trade; but if there are two groups of countries, the effect of world growth on a particular country depends not only on the relative rates of growth of the two groups, but also on its individual rate of growth as compared with the growth rates of others in its group. A country may lose by a low rate of growth because the rapid growth of others in its group turns the terms of trade against it.

APPENDIX

BIBLIOGRAPHY OF RECENT WORK ON TRADE AND GROWTH

Åkerman, Johan, 'The Problem of International Balance in Progressive Economies', *Economica Internazionale*, IV, no. 2, March 1951.

Asimakopulos, A., 'A Note on Productivity Changes and the Terms of Trade', *Oxford Economic Papers*, N.S., IX, no. 2, June 1957.

Aubrey, H. G., 'The Long-Term Future of United States Imports and Its Implications for Primary Producing Countries', *American Economic Review*, XLV, no. 2, May 1955.

Baldwin, R. E., 'Patterns of Development in Newly Settled Regions', *Manchester School of Economic and Social Studies*, XXIV, no. 2, May 1956.

Balogh, T., 'Static Models and Current Problems in International Economics', *Oxford Economic Papers*, N.S., I, no. 2, June 1949.

——*The Dollar Crisis: Causes and Cure* (Oxford: Blackwell, 1949).

——'The Dollar Crisis Revisited', *Oxford Economic Papers*, VI, no. 3, September 1954.

——'Progrès Technique et Bien-Être Internationale', *Économie Appliquée*, VII, no. 4, October December 1954.

——'Factor Intensities of American Foreign Trade and Technical Progress', *Review of Economics and Statistics*, XXXVII, no. 4, November 1955.

Bensusan-Butt, D. M., 'A Model of Trade and Accumulation', *The American Economic Review*, XLIV, no. 4, September 1954.

Bernstein, E. M., 'American Productivity and the Dollar Payments Problem', *Review of Economics and Statistics*, XXXVII, no. 2, May 1955.

Bhagwati, J., 'Immiserizing Growth: A Geometric Note', *Review of Economic Studies*, XXV(3), no. 68, June 1958.

——'International Trade and Economic Expansion', *The American Economic Review*, XLVIII, no. 5, December 1958.

——'Growth, Terms of Trade and Comparative Advantage', *Economia Internazionale*, XII, no. 3, August 1959.

Black, J., 'Economic Expansion and International Trade: A Marshallian Approach', *Review of Economic Studies*, XXIII(3), no. 62, June 1956.

Black, J. and Streeten, P., 'The Balance and Terms of Trade and Economic Growth', *Économie Appliquée*, X, no. 2, April 1957.

——'Appendix: A Mathematical Note on the Growth of a Two-Sector Economy', *Oxford Economic Papers*, N.S., IX, no. 3, October 1957.

Brems, H., 'The Foreign Trade Accelerator and the International Transmission of Growth, *Econometrica*, 24, no. 3, July 1956.

Bruton, H. J., 'Productivity, the Trade Balance and the Terms of Trade', *Economia Internazionale*, VIII, no. 3, August 1955.

Caves, Richard, *Trade and Economic Structure* (Cambridge, Massachusetts: Harvard University Press, 1960), especially chapters V, VI, IX.

Meade, J. E., *The Theory of International Economic Policy, Volume I: The Balance of Payments. Mathematical Supplement* (London: Oxford University Press, 1951), especially chapter VIII.

——*The Theory of International Economic Policy, Volume II: Trade and Welfare* (London: Oxford University Press, 1955), especially Part III, Appendix 8.

——*The Theory of International Economic Policy, Volume I: Trade and Welfare. Mathematical Supplement* (London: Oxford University Press, 1955), especially chapter XIX.

Mehta, F. A., 'Changes in the Terms of Trade as an Income Factor in World Trade, 1929–1938', *Indian Economic Review*, III, no. 3, February 1957.

——'The Effects of Adverse Income Terms of Trade on the Secular Growth of Underdeveloped Countries', *Indian Economic Journal*, IV, no. 3, July 1956.

Meier, G. M., 'A Note on the Theory of Comparative Costs and Long Period Developments', *Economia Internazionale*, V, no. 3, August 1952.

Mishan, E. J., 'The Long-Run Dollar Problem: A Comment', *Oxford Economic Papers*, N.S., VII, no. 2, June 1955.

Myint, Hla, 'The Gains from Trade and the Backward Countries', *Review of Economic Studies*, XXII(3), no. 59, June 1955.

——'The "Classical Theory" of International Trade and Underdeveloped Countries', *Economic Journal*, LXVIII, no. 270, June 1958.

North, D. C., 'Location Theory and Regional Economic Growth', *Journal of Political Economy*, LXIII, no. 3, June 1955.

Nurkse, R., 'A New Look at the Dollar Problem and the United States Balance of Payments', *Economia Internazionale*, VII, no. 1, February 1954.

——'Internal Growth and External Solvency', *Bulletin of the Oxford University Institute of Statistics*, XVII, no. 1, February 1955.

——'Relation Between Home Investment and External Balance in the Light of British Experience 1945–55', *Review of Economics and Statistics*, XXXVIII, no. 2, May 1956.

——*Patterns of Trade and Development* (Stockholm: University of Stockholm Press, 1959).

Pigou, A. C., 'Long-Run Adjustments in the Balance of Trade', *Economica*, XX, no. 79, August 1953.

Prébisch, R., 'Commercial Policy in the Underdeveloped Countries', *American Economic Review*, XLIX, no. 2, May 1959.

Ramaswami, V. K., 'The Effects of Accumulation on the Terms of Trade', *Economic Journal*, LXX, no. 279, September 1960.

Rostow, W. W., 'The Terms of Trade in Theory and Practice', *Economic History Review*, Second Series, III, no. 1, 1950.

Rybczynski, T. M., 'Factor Endowment and Relative Commodity Prices', *Economica*, XXII, no. 88, November 1955.

Sargent, J. R., 'Productivity and the Balance of Payments: A Three-Country View', *Bulletin of the Oxford University Institute of Statistics*, XVII, no. 1, February 1955.

Savosnick, K. M., 'The Box Diagram and the Production Possibility Curve', *Ekonomisk Tidsskrift*, LX, no. 3, September 1958.

Seton, F., 'Productivity, Trade Balance and International Structure', *Economic Journal*, LXVI, no. 264, December 1956.

Singer, Hans W., 'The Distribution of Gains Between Investing and Borrowing Countries', *American Economic Review, Papers and Proceedings*, XL, no. 2, May 1950.

Streeten, P., 'Productivity Growth and the Balance of Trade', *Bulletin of the Oxford University Institute of Statistics*, XVII, no. 1, February 1955.

Tatemoto, M., 'Productivity Growth and Trade Balance', *Osaka Economic Papers*, VI, no. 1, September 1957.

Tinbergen, J., 'The Influence of Productivity on Economic Welfare', *Economic Journal*, LXII, no. 245, March 1952.

Triantis, S. G., 'Economic Progress, Occupational Redistribution and International Terms of Trade', *Economic Journal*, LXIII, no. 251, September 1953.

United Nations (Raul Prebisch), *The Economic Development of Latin America and its Principal Problems* (Lake Success: United Nations, 1950).

Verdoorn, P. J., 'Complementarity and Long-Range Projections', *Econometrica*, XXIV, no. 4, October 1956.

Viner, J., *International Trade and Economic Development* (Oxford: Clarendon Press, 1953).

——'Stability and Progress: The Poorer Countries' Problem', in D. Hague, ed., *Stability and Progress in the World Economy* (London: Macmillan, 1958).

Williams, J. H., *Economic Stability in the Modern World*, The Stamp Memorial Lecture (University of London, 1952).

PART TWO: MONEY

V

MONETARY THEORY AND KEYNESIAN ECONOMICS*

What is the subject-matter of monetary theory? What is monetary theory about? This question brings us directly to the heart of the Keynesian revolution. Monetary theory before the Keynesian revolution was concerned primarily with the theory of the price level, the determination of the general level of prices. Associated with the price level was the question of economic fluctuations, which were connected with movements in the price level through the effects of rising prices in redistributing income from rentiers to entrepreneurs, increasing profit expectations and stimulating investments. Falling prices, on the other hand, redistributed income from entrepreneurs to rentiers, reduced profit expectations and depressed investment.

It is to be observed that classical monetary theory was not directly concerned with the level of employment, which entered only incidentally in connection with economic fluctuations. The classical theorists assumed a tendency to full employment of the economic system as a consequence of flexibility in wages and prices, and attributed unemployment to rigidity of wages and prices. We might note that, contrary to what some Keynesians have alleged, the classical economists did not assume automatic full employment. In their system full employment was a deduction from wage-price flexibility. On the other hand, they did not—as the Keynesians have shown—adequately investigate the effects of wage-price flexibility on employment and wrongly applied the analysis of a single commodity or factor to the economy as a whole.

Nor did classical theory investigate directly the theory of the rate of interest, which was held to be determined by real forces and not by monetary forces. The classical theorists did, however, introduce

* *Pakistan Economic Journal*, VIII, no. 2, June 1958, 56–70.

monetary forces to explain price trends and fluctuations, for example in the well-known form of the analysis of the effects of a divergence between the real and the market rate of interest.

To summarize, the classical theory was mainly concerned with the determination of the price level and with economic fluctuations, and was not directly concerned with the level of employment and the theory of interest. The essence of the Keynesian revolution was to shift the subject-matter of monetary theory, placing the emphasis on the level of employment as the central subject of monetary theory and posing the determination of the rate of interest as a specifically monetary problem. In the Keynesian theory, monetary forces influence the equilibrium rate of interest and do not merely, as in classical theory, exercise a transitional influence on market rates during periods of disequilibrium. On the other hand, in Keynesian theory the theory of the price level is reduced to a relatively minor role. Keynes took the level of money wages as given (through measuring all his variables in wage units) and assumed a closed economy. On this assumption there could be only three causes of a change in the price level: a change in the level of employment, a change in the wage unit and a change in technique of production, that is, a change in productivity. Of these three, Keynes was not concerned with changes in productivity, and the use of the wage unit left only variation in the level of employment as a cause of changes in the price level.

In addition to reducing the theory of the price-level to a minor role, Keynes practically removed economic fluctuations from the picture. Although Keynesian concepts have since provided the means of clarifying considerably the mechanism of economic fluctuations and cycles, the theory, as Keynes presented it, was not concerned with cycles: it was a static theory.

In summary, Keynes shifted the determination of the level of employment and the rate of interest from real theory into monetary theory, and reduced the former subject-matter of monetary theory—the price level and the economic fluctuations—to a minor position. In what follows I shall be concerned with various arguments centring on the question whether Keynes was right or not in doing this; with subsequent developments of Keynesian concepts as a result of theoretical discussion and practical experience; and with an evaluation of the present position of Keynesian theory in the light of experience over the past twelve years.

First, let me summarize briefly Keynes's theory. Its essence was an attack on the classical assumption of a tendency towards full employment and substitution for it of the possibility of under-employment equilibrium. The argument centred on the independence of decisions to save from decisions to invest. In a modern economy decisions to save are taken by a large number of individual households and firms but decisions to invest are taken by a specialized group of entrepreneurs. There is, therefore, no guarantee that the desire to save will find expression in investment, or that an increased desire to save will be matched by increased investment. Instead, the increased desire to save may run to waste through unemployment, the increased savings of some being offset by reduction in the savings of others brought about by increased unemployment, total saving being made to correspond with the amount of investment that entrepreneurs want to do by a reduction of aggregate income.

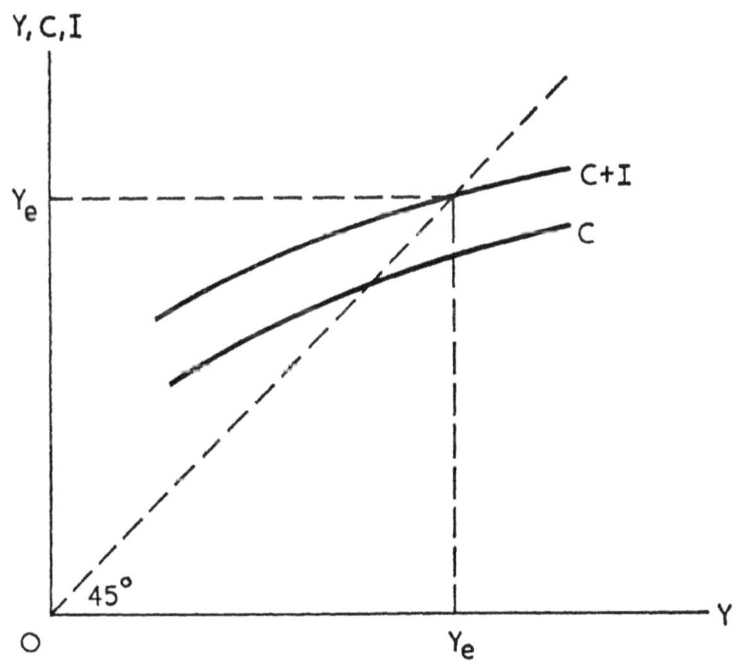

Fig. V.1

Now according to classical theory, this could not happen: it would be prevented by a change in the rate of interest which would reduce saving and increase investment so as to make them balance at full employment. But, Keynes argued, the classical theory of interest involved indeterminacy, because it neglected the dependence of saving on income. Through variations in the level of income, savings and investment could be equated at any level of the rate of interest, and would not necessarily be equated at the full-employment level of income. (I shall return to this question of indeterminacy later on.)

So much for Keynes's attack on the classical theory; let us now turn to his own theory. I shall begin with a simple version of that theory which may be put as follows: output and employment are determined by the demand for output, which comes from two sources —consumption demand and investment demand. Investment decisions, which depend on entrepreneurial profit expectations and other factors, are taken for granted at this stage. Consumption demand depends largely on the level of income (other influences, including the rate of interest, are recognized but dismissed from the argument) and when income rises, consumption is certain to rise but not as much as income—in other words, as income rises, saving rises.

On this assumption the level of income is determined by the level of investment. Investment is taken as given by factors lying outside the theory; income must be such that saving equals investment and income is the sum of the consumption from this level of income and investment.

This theory of income determination may be represented by two diagrams which are commonly employed in the literature: in the first (Fig. V.1) we measure income and output (Y) along both axes and draw a 45° line; at any point on this line the quantities measured on the two axes are equal. We then draw a curve to represent the relation between consumption (C) and income. The vertical distance between this line and the 45° line represents saving (the unconsumed part of income). The diagram assumes that below some level of income the community will consume more than its income, that is, it will dissave; and that as income rises, consumption will increase but less than income. We now add the fixed amount of investment to the consumption that would take place at various levels of income, thus obtaining the curve C+I which represents the demand for output at different levels of income. The intersection of this line with the 45° line determines the equilibrium level of income (Y_e). At a lower level of income and output demand for output will exceed output, and output and income will rise: conversely, at a higher level of income, demand for output will fall short of output, so output will fall. Another version of the same diagram is presented in Fig. V.2, which plots saving (S) as a function of income; the equilibrium level of income is that for which saving is equal to the given level of investment (I). The second diagram is more commonly used and has been described by Schumpeter as the 'Keynesian cross' (by analogy with the Marshallian cross of the demand and supply curves).

This diagram shows the determination of the level of output and employment. For some purposes we are concerned with the relation between an initial change in demand for output and the total change in income to which it gives rise. This is the theory of the multiplier. Since an increase in investment will raise income and the increase in income will raise consumption, thereby raising the demand for output still further, the total increase in income will be some multiple of the initial increase in investment. In the simple theory just presented, the multiplier will be the reciprocal of the marginal propensity to save. In the early years after the publication of the *General Theory*, a great deal of the literature was devoted to elaboration of the theory of the multiplier. This literature, however, is not relevant to my main theme, so I shall not attempt to deal with it.

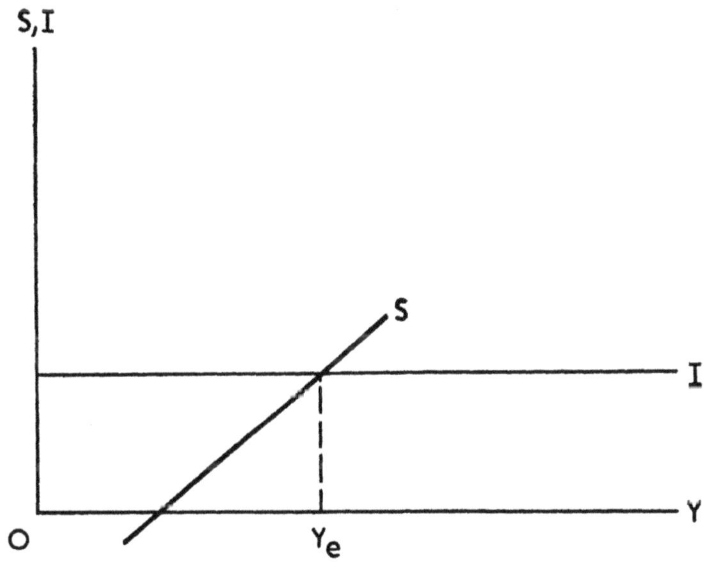

Fig. V.2

What I have just presented is a very simple version of the Keynesian theory. It is incomplete and unsatisfactory because it leaves both the rate of investment and the rate of interest undetermined. In the full version of the Keynesian theory, the rate of investment is determined by the balancing of the rate of return on investment, which Keynes termed 'the marginal efficiency of capital', against the rate of interest, the rate of investment being determined by the condition that, at the margin, the rate of interest and the marginal efficiency of capital should be equal. The rate of interest, in turn, is determined by the quantity of money and the demand for it, which Keynes analysed under the description of 'liquidity preference'.

The quantity of money is assumed to be determined by the monetary authorities. The demand for money is divided into two parts—the transactions demand (including the demand for precautionary balances) which depends on the level of money income, and the speculative demand. The speculative demand arises from the fact that, if the rate of interest is expected to rise, an owner of cash may do better not to invest it in securities immediately, but to wait until he can buy those securities at a lower price (higher yield). The lower the actual rate of interest relative to some 'normal' level, the less the sacrifice of interest in not investing immediately, and the more likely a rise in the rate in the near future; consequently the greater the relative attraction of holding cash, and the greater the demand for money to hold as speculative balances. (Keynes, and even more so his followers, tended to write of the speculative demand for money as depending only on the actual rate of interest, and varying with it; this has given rise to confusion and misunderstanding, since it leaves implicit the role of expectations of future rates.) Keynes also held that at some low rate of interest, the demand for idle balances might become completely interest elastic, thus putting a bottom stop to the rate of interest.

Notice that this theory seems to imply a one-way chain of causation: the rate of interest is determined by the demand for and supply of money: the level of investment is determined by the rate of interest and the marginal efficiency of capital; and the level of income and consumption is determined by the level of investment and the propensity to save. There is, apparently, no reverse influence of saving and investment on the rate of interest; and this feature has led to much discussion and criticism of Keynes's theory. But the appearance is misleading: in fact, the Keynesian system is an interdependent system, in which all the variables influence each other, for the reason that the transactions part of the demand for money depends on the level of income, which in turn depends on the desires to save and invest. Appreciation of this interdependence dispels much of the startling novelty of Keynes's theory of interest as he presented it.

The full Keynesian theory, in which the interest rate, income, saving and investment, demand for money and supply of money are all mutually interdependent, can be represented very conveniently by a diagram developed by Professor J. R. Hicks,[1] which has proved so useful that it has become a standard tool of monetary theory.

[1] J. R. Hicks, 'Mr Keynes and the "Classics"; A Suggested Interpretation', *Econometrica*, 5, no. 2, April 1937, 147–69, reprinted as Chap. 4, 461–76, in American Economic Association, *Readings in the Theory of Income Distribution* (London: Allen and Unwin, Philadelphia: The Blakiston Press, 1946).

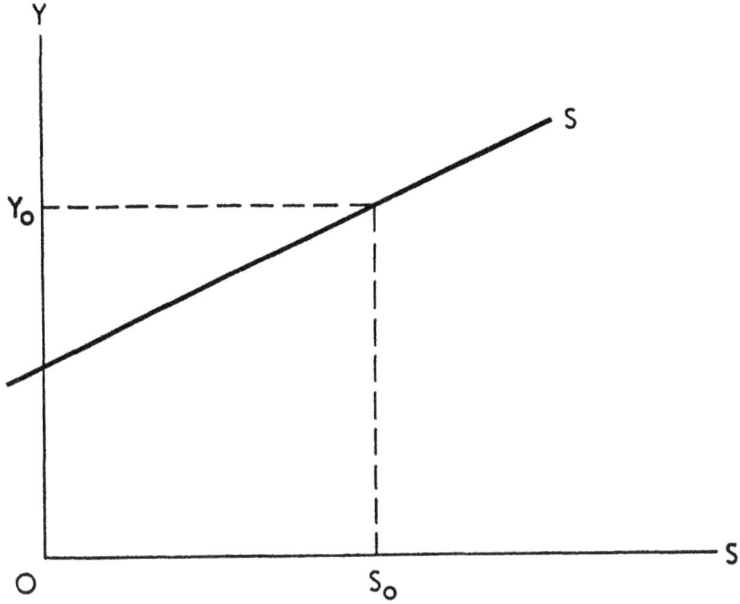

Fig. V.3a

Fig. V.3a represents the relation between saving and income, and Fig. V.3b the relation between investment and the rate of interest.

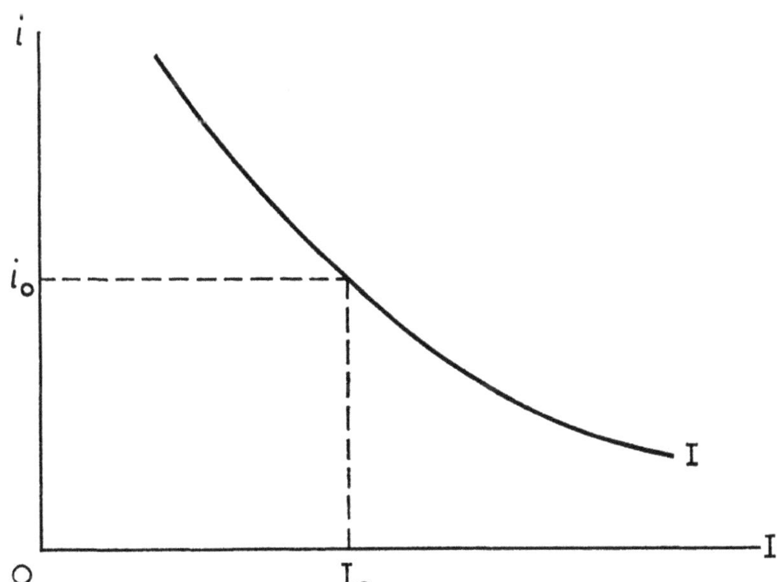

Fig. V.3b

From these two relations may be deduced the relation between the rate of interest and the level of income which will ensure equality between saving and investment, that is, will maintain equilibrium between the demand for and supply of output. This relation, known as the IS curve, is shown in Fig. V.3c; it represents the requirements of equilibrium in the 'real' sector of the economy. The IS curve will be downward-sloping, since at a lower rate of interest investment will be greater, saving must be greater, and consequently income must be greater.

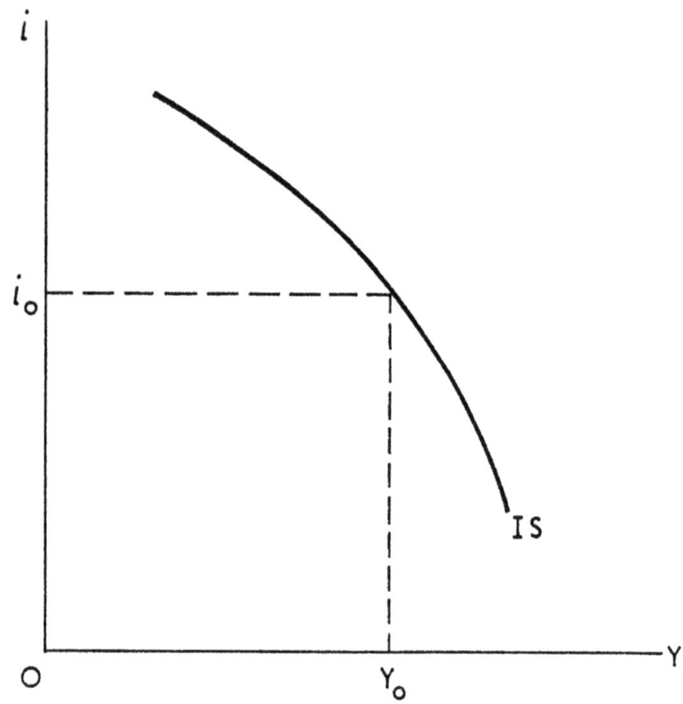

Fig. V.3c

Fig. V.4a represents the relation between the demand for and the supply of money. The upper right-hand quadrant represents the speculative demand for money, or the demand for speculative balances (M_2) as a function of the rate of interest. The lower left-hand quadrant represents the transactions demand for money (M_1), on the assumption that the transactions requirement is a fraction k of national income. The actual amount of money in existence $M(=M_1+M_2)$ is represented by a bar, which can be shifted along the M_1M_2 axis to derive the relation between the rate of interest and

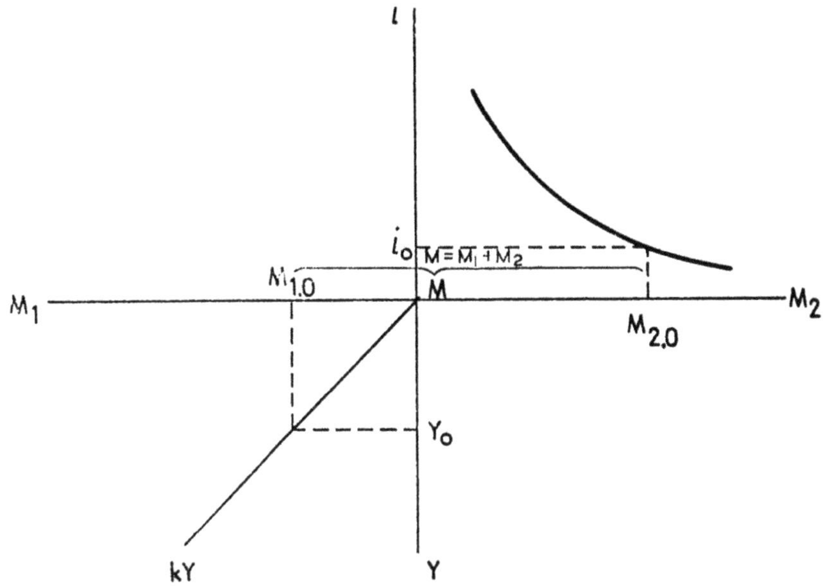

Fig. V.4a

the level of income at which the demand for money will just equal the amount of it available, that is, which will maintain equilibrium between the demand for and supply of money. This relation, known as the LM curve, is shown in Fig. V.4b; it represents the requirements

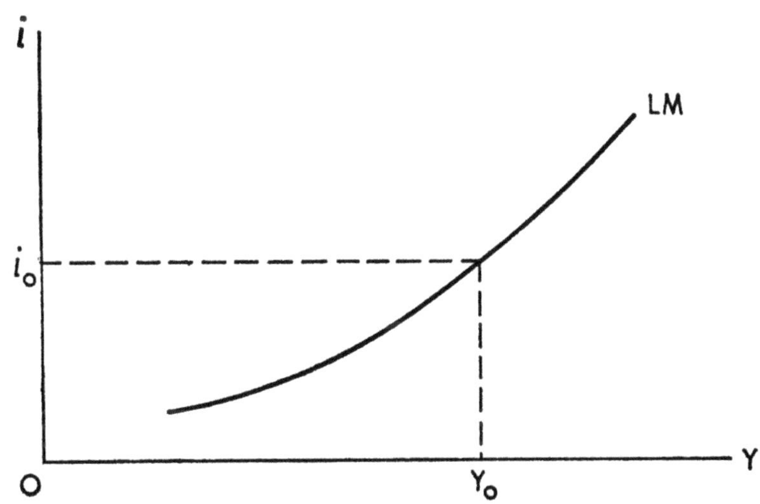

Fig. V.4b

of equilibrium in the 'monetary' sector of the economy. The LM curve will be upward-sloping, since at higher levels of national income more money will be required for transactions, leaving less available for idle balances, and to induce speculators to hold less idle money, the rate of interest must rise.

The IS and LM curves are combined in Fig. V.5, which shows the determination of the rate of interest and the level of income at the levels which ensure simultaneous equilibrium in the monetary and real sectors. This diagram may be described as 'the Hicksian cross' after its inventor; it can be adapted to take account of more general assumptions than Keynes made—for example, that saving depends

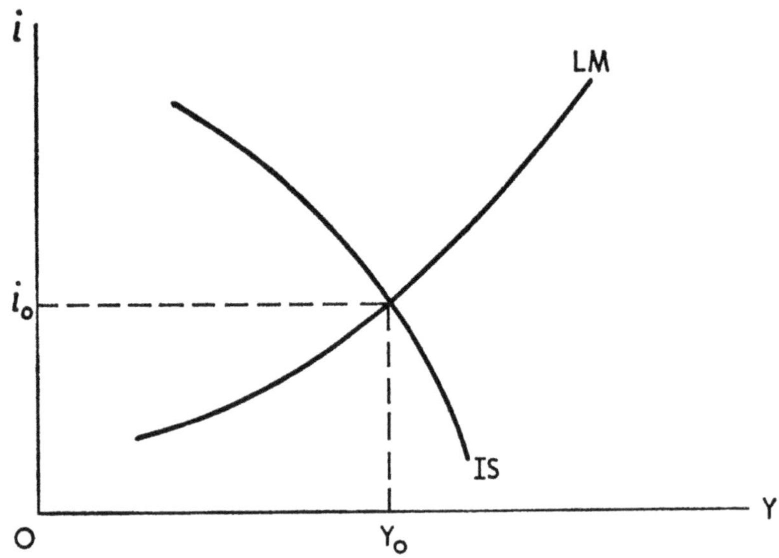

Fig. V.5

partly on interest rates and investment partly on income, and that both demands for money depend on both income and the interest rate; and it can be used to expound a number of important propositions and solve a number of problems in monetary theory.

For completeness, I shall fill out this diagrammatic picture of Keynesian theory with two further diagrams which illustrate significant aspects of his analysis, namely the determination of the price level and the concept of 'involuntary unemployment'. Fig. V.6 depicts the supply curve of output (X_s), on Keynes's assumptions that labour is the only variable factor, diminishing returns prevail, and competition ensures that supply is determined by the equality of price and marginal cost. The different combinations of real output and price level consistent with a given value of output may be represented by a rectangular hyperbola; the equilibrium price level and output are given by the intersection with the aggregate supply curve of the hyperbola representing the level of income determined from Fig. V.5. (I neglect certain complications arising from the fact that movement along the X_s-curve will probably alter the distribution of income, and the income-saving relation.) Fig. V.7 represents the relation between the real wage earned by labour (the marginal productivity of labour) and the quantity of labour employed (the MP_L curve); and the relation between the real wage earned and the quan-

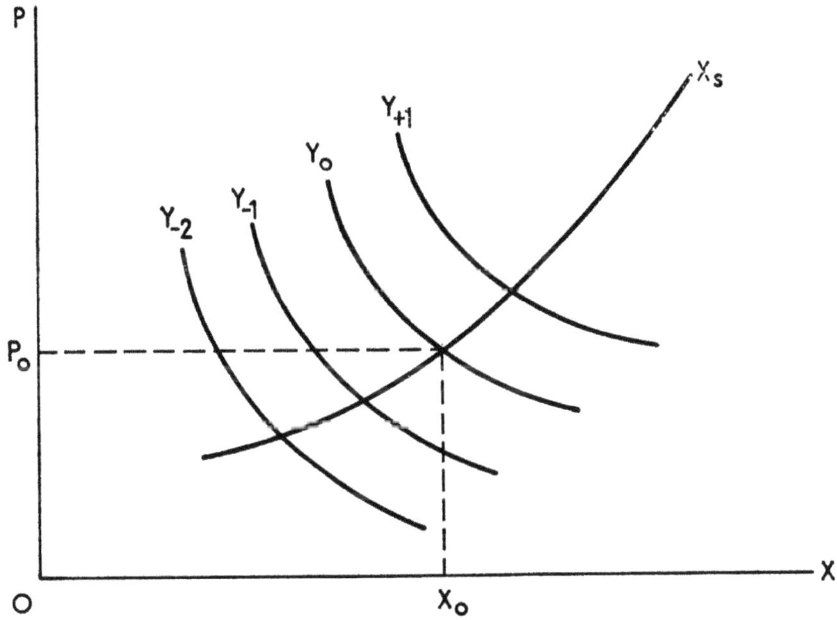

Fig. V.6

tity of labour supplied (the L_s curve). In classical theory, the intersection of these two curves determines the levels of employment and income; in Keynesian theory, however, the levels of employment and the real wage are determined by aggregate demand, the level of employment (L_0) being derived from the level of output (Fig. V.6) by means of the technological relation between them. The difference between actual employment at the real wage so determined (L_0) and the labour that would be offered at that real wage (L_E) measures the amount of 'involuntary unemployment' (L_E-L_0). (The diagrams, though not the economics, could be simplified by measuring unemployment in terms of the additional output it could produce, recognizing that the price level varies inversely with the real wage, and inserting a supply curve of labour in Fig. V.6.)

Let me now turn from exposition of the Keynesian theory to discuss some of the arguments and controversies to which it has given rise, and some of the recent developments of Keynesian concepts. In discussing the former, I shall ignore most of the minor controversies which have figures in the literature, and confine myself to what I consider the important issues.

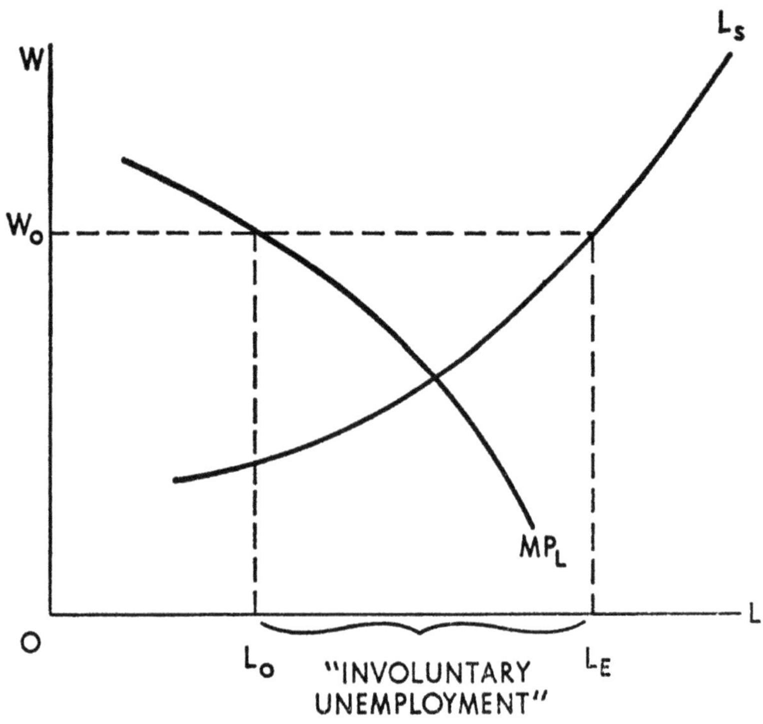

Fig. V.7

The chief argument pertaining to Keynes's theory of employment relates to the question whether Keynesian under-employment equilibrium depends on the assumption of rigid wages, which Keynes introduced into the theory by measuring all magnitudes in wage units. The answer to this question hinges on the effect on employment of a larger volume of money, since the effect of a wage cut in the system is the same as the effect of an increase in money supply (with a fall in wages and prices, less money is required for transactions, more is available for speculative balances). With a larger quantity of money, the rate of interest will tend to be lower and the level of investment higher; the question is whether a sufficient increase in the money supply (wage cut) will lead to full employment; if so, under-employment equilibrium is dependent on rigidity of wages.

Within the Keynesian framework, two cases in which increased money supply will not lead to full employment can be distinguished. First, liquidity preference may set a bottom limit to the rate of interest at a level above that required for a full-employment level of investment. Second, the IS curve may be so interest-inelastic that, at positive interest rates, investment does not increase, or savings fall, to a level consistent with full employment. (Since a negative interest rate is impossible when people have the alternative of holding money, we need not consider this possibility, which would require a policy of subsidizing investment or taxing savings.) The two cases mentioned can be combined in one statement: full employment will not be achieved by monetary expansion (wage cuts) if saving from a full-employment income would exceed investment at the lowest rate of interest the money market will allow.

The foregoing argument, however, assumes Keynes's own view of the factors which determine consumption. Against it may be brought an argument originated by Pigou,[2] which incorporates the assumption that consumption depends on wealth (assets) as well as income. The argument is that, as money wages and prices fall, the real value of cash balances rises, and the increasing real wealth of cash-holders will lead them eventually to increase their consumption. This is the so-called 'Pigou effect'; I should point out that it assumes token money or money backed by gold, since in the case of money backed by private debt the debtor becomes poorer in real terms as the cash-holder becomes richer, and the net effect on consumption is unpredictable. However, if we are prepared to assume that the Government is indifferent to changes in the real value of its debts, the Pigou effect can be extended to the public's holdings of Government debt, or of cash backed by Government debt.

In my opinion, though not, I should add, in the opinion of all Keynesians, the Pigou effect finally disposes of the Keynesian contention that under-employment equilibrium does not depend on the assumption of wage-rigidity. It does. How serious a criticism of Keynesian theory is this? Not, I think, a very important one. The

[2] A. C. Pigou, 'The Classical Stationary State', *Economic Journal*, LIII, no. 212, December 1943, 343–51; see also Don Patinkin, 'Price Flexibility and Full Employment', Chap. 13 in American Economic Association, *Readings in Monetary Theory* (London: Allen and Unwin, Philadelphia: The Blakiston Press, 1951).

heat engendered by the argument over it can largely be attributed to the desire of Keynes and his followers to reject the idea that cuts in wage-rates are the appropriate way to cure depressions. That argument is a policy argument, involving political and dynamic considerations not relevant to the consideration of Keynesian theory as a purely static theory.

The criticism does have significance in a broader context, though this is a consequence of the challenging way in which Keynes presented his theory—as a general theory of which the classical theory was a special case. It turns out that Keynes's theory is a special case of the classical—or rather of the neo-classical theory, since a satisfactory 'classical' theory was not worked out until after the Keynesian revolution. But this sort of argument about a theory is not particularly interesting; what is more important is that Keynes's theory started from an empirically relevant special assumption, derived some important meaningful results from it, and provided an approach which has since proved its usefulness for a wide range of problems.

Let me now turn from the Keynesian theory as a theory of employment to the Keynesian theory as a theory of interest. Here there have been several interesting controversies. The most fundamental has been the debate, initiated by Keynes, over whether the rate of interest is a real or a monetary phenomenon (the latter, of course, being Keynes's own view). This debate has two versions, of which the less important is the Cambridge battle over whether real or monetary (speculative) factors dominate actual credit markets.[3] That is really an empirical question; I shall confine myself to two remarks on it. The first is that, since Keynes's speculative demand for money is based on the relation between actual and expected rates of interest, there is nothing to prevent 'real' forces, in the shape of the profitability of investment, from entering into liquidity preference. On the other hand, it is not valid in my opinion to dismiss the Keynesian liquidity preference theory on the grounds that it is a 'bootstrap' theory of interest[4]—since interest is a relation between the present and the future, expectations must inevitably influence the rate as determined in the market.

[3] See D. H. Robertson, 'Mr Keynes and the Rate of Interest', *Essays in Monetary Theory* (London: Staples Press, 1940), Chap. 1; Joan Robinson, 'The Rate of Interest', *Econometrica*, 19, no. 2, April 1951, 92–111, reprinted as Chap. 1 of *The Rate of Interest and Other Essays* (London: Macmillan, 1952); R. F. Kahn, 'Some Notes on Liquidity Preference', *The Manchester School of Economic and Social Studies*, XXII, no. 3, September 1954, 229–57.

[4] J. R. Hicks, *Value and Capital*, 2nd edition (Oxford: Clarendon Press, 1946), 164. Contrast R. F. Kahn, *op. cit.*

The theoretically more important version of the debate has centred around the proposition that the so-called 'classical dichotomy' is invalid.[5] In classical theory (the argument runs) relative prices and the rate of interest are determined independently of the quantity of money, whereas the quantity of money influences the general price level (money prices) but not relative prices. This independence of relative price determination from absolute price determination has been shown to be invalid. The argument has been complex and mathematical, but its essence can be simply put: if people are to hold money, their demands for goods must depend in part on the value of their money-holdings, which must therefore influence relative prices as well as the absolute price level.

If it is assumed that utility depends on the quantities of goods consumed and on the *real* value of cash balances, it is possible to retain the classical result that an increase in the (nominal) quantity of money will raise the price level but leave relative prices and the rate of interest unchanged. But this conclusion is not very relevant or interesting for a modern economy, where money is created by the banking system against debt and its quantity is altered by open-market operations.[6] In general, the quantity of money must be regarded as influencing all decisions; and the rate of interest is inevitably 'a monetary phenomenon'.

Let me now deal briefly with two other controversies about Keynesian interest theory. The first is the 'loanable funds *versus* liquidity preference' debate—the argument as to whether the rate of interest is determined by the demand and supply of money, as Keynes maintained, or by the demand and supply of securities, as Robertson and others maintain.[7] We can approach this question by dividing the

[5] D. Patinkin, 'The Indeterminacy of Absolute Prices in Classical Economic Theory', *Econometrica*, 17, no. 1, January 1949, 1–27; W. B. Hickman, 'The Determinacy of Absolute Prices in Classical Economic Theory', W. Leontief, 'The Consistency of the Classical Theory of Money and Prices', C. G. Phipps, 'A Note on Patinkin's "Relative Prices" ', *Econometrica*, 18, no. 1, January 1950, 9–20, 21–4, 25–6; D. Patinkin, 'The Invalidity of Classical Monetary Theory', and K. Brunner, 'Inconsistency and Determinacy in Classical Economics', *Econometrica*, 19, no. 1, January 1951, 134–51 and 152–73; D. Patinkin, *Money, Interest and Prices* (Evanston, Illinois: Row, Peterson and Co., 1956).

[6] L. A. Metzler, 'Wealth, Saving, and the Rate of Interest', *Journal of Political Economy*, LIX, no. 2, April 1951, 93–116; D. Patinkin, 'Keynesian Economics and the Quantity Theory', in K. K. Kurihara, ed., *Post-Keynesian Economics* (London: Allen and Unwin, 1955), 123–52.

[7] D. H. Robertson, *op. cit.*; J. R. Hicks, *Value and Capital* (Oxford: Clarendon Press, 1938), Chap. XII, 153–62; W. Fellner and H. M. Somers, 'Alternative Monetary Approaches to Interest Theory', *Review of Economic Statistics*, XXIII, no. 1, February 1941, 43–8; *idem*, 'Note on "Stocks" and "Flows" in Monetary Interest Theory', *Review of Economics and Statistics*, XXXI, no. 2, May 1949,

economy into three markets—the markets for output, cash, and securities. According to a principle known as Walras's law, the sum of the excess demands in these three markets must be identically equal to zero; in symbols,

$$X_g + X_m + X_s = O.$$

It is clear that if the market for goods is in equilibrium ($X_g = O$), equilibrium in either of the other markets implies equilibrium in the remaining one, so that on this assumption it makes no difference whether we say that the equilibrium rate of interest is that which equates the demand for and supply of cash, or that which equates the demand for and supply of securities—the two theories amount to the same thing. To put the same point another way, in full-equilibrium positions the rate of interest equates both the demand and supply of money and the demand and supply of securities. But if the market for output is not in equilibrium, we can no longer say that the rate of interest is determined in either one of the other two markets, unless we assume that the remaining market behaves in such a way that we can lump it together with the commodity market—'liquidity preference' assuming that excess demand for output (investment greater than saving) is financed by bond sales, and 'loanable funds' assuming it is financed by running down cash balances.

A similar controversy relates to the allegation recently made by Professor Hansen, that the Keynesian theory as well as the classical theory is indeterminate.[8] Whereas Keynes charged the classics with neglecting the dependence of saving on income, Hansen charges Keynes with neglecting the dependence of the transactions demand for money on income. In my opinion, Professor Hansen's argument is invalid: as I have already pointed out, the Keynesian theory appears to be one of one-way causation but is in fact a theory of interdependence and mutual determination; it is determinate.

Let me now turn from the controversies stirred up by Keynesian revolution to post-Keynesian developments of Keynesian concepts.

145–6; L. R. Klein, *The Keynesian Revolution* (New York: Macmillan, 1947), 117–23; L. R. Klein, 'Stock and Flow Analysis in Economics', W. Fellner and H. M. Somers, 'Stock and Flow Analysis: Comment', L. R. Klein, 'Stock and Flow Analysis: Further Comment', K. Brunner, 'Stock and Flow Analysis: Discussion', W. Fellner and H. M. Somers, 'Stock and Flow Analysis: Note on the Discussion', *Econometrica*, 18, no. 1, January 1950, 236–41, 241–5, 246, 247–51, 252.

[8] Alvin H. Hansen, 'Classical Loanable Funds and Keynesian Interest Rate Theories', *Quarterly Journal of Economics*, LXV, no. 3, August 1951, 429–32 and *A Guide to Keynes* (New York: McGraw-Hill, 1953), Chap. 7, 140–53; also Edward T. Nevin, 'Professor Hansen and the Keynesian Interest Theory', and Alvin H. Hansen, 'Comment', *Quarterly Journal of Economics*, LXIX, no. 4, November 1955, 637–41 and 641–3.

The most interesting developments have been those relating to the consumption function, which were stimulated by the failure of the prediction of a major post-war slump, and the apparent contradiction between Kuznets's finding that in the long run the proportion of income saved is constant, and the evidence of time-series and budget studies that saving is a rising proportion of income in the short run.[9] The effort to reconcile the short-run and the long-run propensities to save has stimulated several reformulations of the theory of the consumption function: Tobin has introduced the influence of assets (as well as income) on consumption, Duesenberry has employed the hypothesis that individual consumption behaviour depends on relative rather than absolute income, Friedman that consumption is governed by 'normal' rather than actual income, Modigliani and Brumberg that consumption is governed by maximization of utility over the consumer's whole life.[10] These and other contributions all have in common the reintroduction of utility-maximization into the theory of the consumption function.

On the side of the inducement to invest, the most important development has been the introduction of the relation between capital-stock and output (in the form either of the accelerator or of the capital-output ratio) as a determinant of investment decisions. This has permitted the conversion of the static equilibrium Keynesian system into cycle and growth models. Useful work has also been done on inventory cycles—Keynes himself tended to think in terms of fixed capital investment as the dominant determinant of income.[11]

[9] On the failure of the forecasts, see L. R. Klein, 'A Post Mortem on Transition Predictions of National Product', *Journal of Political Economy*, LIV, no. 1, February 1946, 289–308; for Kuznets's data, see Simon Kuznets, 'Capital Formation, 1879–1938', 53–78 in Wesley C. Mitchell and others, *Studies in Economics and Industrial Relations* (Philadelphia: University of Pennsylvania Press, 1941).

[10] James Tobin, 'Relative Income, Absolute Income, and Savings', 135–56 in *Money, Trade and Economic Growth, in honor of John Henry Williams* (New York: Macmillan, 1951); James S. Duesenberry, *Income, Saving, and the Theory of Consumer Behavior* (Cambridge: Harvard University Press, 1949); Milton Friedman, *A Theory of the Consumption Function* (Princeton: Princeton University Press, 1957); Franco Modigliani and Richard Brumberg, 'Utility Analysis and the Consumption Function: An Interpretation of Cross-Section Data', 383–436 in Kenneth K. Kurihara (ed.), *Post-Keynesian Economics* (London: Allen and Unwin, 1955, New Brunswick: Rutgers University Press, 1954).

[11] M. Kalecki, *Essays in the Theory of Economic Fluctuations* (London: Allen and Unwin Ltd., 1939), 116–49; N. Kaldor, 'A Model of the Trade Cycle', *Economic Journal*, L, no. 1, March 1940, 78–92; R. M. Goodwin, 'Econometrics in Business-Cycle Analysis', in A. H. Hansen, *Business Cycles and National Income* (London: Allen and Unwin, New York: Norton, 1951), 417–68; P. A. Samuelson, 'Interaction Between the Multiplier Analysis and the Principle of Acceleration', *Review of Economic Statistics*, XXI, no. 2, May 1939, 75–8; J.

The theory of liquidity preference has been improved in a variety of ways by closer analysis of the motives for holding money. The most important development, however, has been the extension of the liquidity-preference concept to take account of more alternatives than the simple bonds—cash choice assumed by Keynes. Generally speaking, the tendency has been to move towards a generalized theory of asset-holding, suitable for application to the analysis of monetary and fiscal policy. In this connection the Keynesian assumption of a fixed quantity of money has been modified to permit the banking system to exercise a liquidity preference of its own.

Before concluding I should like to say something about how well Keynesian theory has stood up to the experience of war-time economic problems and the war and post-war inflation. It is agreed, I think, that Keynesian theory provided a far better basis for understanding the nature of the war-time economic problem and the causes of inflation than did previous theory. It made it clear that the war-time economic problem is not the financing of the war effort but the adjustment of aggregate demand to the capacity of the economy to produce; and that the source of inflation is an excess demand for output. (Both of these propositions are applicable to the problems of development planning.)

On the other hand, Keynesian theory has shown definite weaknesses as a theory of prices. In Keynesian theory, the level of money-wages is taken as given, and alterations in it are not explained by the theory. Inflation models have been built by assuming relations between aggregate demand and the rates of wage or price change or between wage and price changes; but while they describe the inflationary process they do not explain it very well. The problem of explaining the differing price histories of different countries during and since the war has led to a certain tendency to return to the Quantity Theory of Money as an explanation of inflation, and to explain post-war inflation as a result of the war-time expansion of the money supply.[12] It is clear that the accumulation of money during the war has had an important effect; but I would myself prefer to employ a neo-Keynesian explanation, based on the accumulation of assets relative to income (these assets including both money and Government debt) rather than one which stressed the quantity of money *per se*.

R. Hicks, *A Contribution to the Theory of the Trade Cycle* (Oxford: Clarendon Press, 1950); R. F. Harrod, *Towards a Dynamic Economics* (London: Macmillan, 1948); L. A. Metzler, 'The Nature and Stability of Inventory Cycles', *Review of Economic Statistics*, XXIII, no. 2, August 1941, 113–29.

[12] See, for example, A. J. Brown, *The Great Inflation: 1939–1951* (London: Oxford University Press, 1955).

I conclude with a general evaluation of the Keynesian revolution. As a theory for dealing with problems of employment, inflation, and economic planning, it constitutes, in my opinion, a great and pervasive advance, the essence of which is to look at the relations between aggregate demand for and availability of resources, rather than at the quantity of money. In monetary theory, its main contribution has been to emphasize the function of money as an asset, alternative to other assets, and to break the quantity-theory assumption that there is a direct connection between money quantity and aggregate demand. On the other hand, the theory as Keynes presented it is misleading in many ways, and needs much adaptation to fit non-depression conditions; and the Keynesian approach does tend to play down the influence of monetary conditions, which may at times be very important.

VI

THE *GENERAL THEORY* AFTER TWENTY-FIVE YEARS*

What should one say in an address commemorating the twenty-fifth anniversary of a book?[1] Normally, one thinks of the publication of a book as a birth of new ideas; and the appropriate occasion for a speech is either the day the youth attains his majority, when he is congratulated on the achievement of adult status and a brilliant future is predicted for him, or the day the old man retires, when he is congratulated on a life-time of productive labour and wished a peaceful old age. A twenty-fifth anniversary suggests a marriage—a union of ideas with literary expression, so to speak—and the appropriate speech is one which compliments the couple on their success in solving the problem of marital adjustment, and congratulates them on the number and promise of their progeny, while tactfully refraining from mentioning that in its early years the marriage was judged by many to be a mistake and doomed to failure. It is in this spirit that I wish to commemorate the Silver Anniversary of the *General Theory* in this lecture. We have had the coming-of-age party in the Revolutionary days of the late 1930s, and the pension presentation ceremony in the obituary assessments of the late 1940s.[2] We are now

* *American Economic Review*, LI, no. 2, May 1961, 1–17.

[1] John Maynard Keynes, *The General Theory of Employment, Interest and Money* (London: Macmillan, 1936). Subsequent page references are to this edition.

[2] S. E. Harris (ed.) *The New Economics: Keynes's Influence on Theory and Public Policy* (New York: A. A. Knopf, 1947); R. F. Harrod, *The Life of John Maynard Keynes* (London: Macmillan, 1951); also E. A. G. Robinson, 'John Maynard Keynes, 1883–1946', *Economic Journal*, LVII, no. 225, March 1947, 1–68; J. A. Schumpeter, 'John Maynard Keynes—1883–1946', *American Economic Review*, XXVI, no. 4, September 1946, 495–518; P. A. Samuelson, 'Lord Keynes and the General Theory', *Econometrica*, 14, no. 3, July 1946, 187–200.

well into the post-Keynesian era;[3] and it seems more appropriate at this point to take stock of the intellectual capital embodied in the *General Theory* than to debate whether the investment should be considered the foundation of our fortune or written off as a dead loss.

To keep the subject within bounds, I propose to concentrate on the *General Theory* and to use it as a basis for discussion. I shall first discuss the book as economic literature. My excuse for so doing is that the book long ago attained the status of a classic—meaning a book that everyone has heard of and no-one has read—and the translation of its untidy construction into neat models suitable for geometric and mathematical manipulation, effective as it proved in converting economists to the Keynesian school, has obscured some characteristics of Keynes's methods of analysis which are relevant to the evaluation of his theory. From the book I shall proceed to the theory presented in it, considering it first as monetary theory and then as a theory of income and employment. I shall then comment, more briefly, on the policy implications of the theory. In each case I shall be concerned to assess Keynes's ideas in the context of subsequent developments; and I shall conclude with a summary assessment of the contributions of the *General Theory* to modern economics.

I. THE 'GENERAL THEORY' AS ECONOMIC LITERATURE

Not even the most ardent admirer of Keynes's powers as an expositor of economic ideas and a literary stylist would wish to have his reputation in these respects judged solely by the *General Theory*. Arresting phrases and brilliant passages there are, as everyone who has read it remembers, but the book as a whole is not easy to read and master, and it has not become easier with the passage of time. In support of this judgment one need only refer to the fact that no less than three successful books aimed at guiding the reader through the *General Theory* have appeared at intervals in the past twenty-five years—those of Joan Robinson, Dudley Dillard, and Alvin Hansen[4]—not to speak

[3] Kenneth K. Kurihara (ed.), *Post-Keynesian Economics* (New Brunswick: Rutgers University Press, 1954, and London: Allen and Unwin, 1955).

[4] Joan Robinson, *Introduction to the Theory of Employment* (London: Macmillan, 1937); Dudley D. Dillard, *The Economics of John Maynard Keynes; the Theory of a Monetary Economy* (New York: Prentice-Hall, 1948); Alvin H. Hansen, *A Guide to Keynes* (New York: McGraw-Hill, 1953). At a more advanced level, reference should be made to Mabel F. Timlin, *Keynesian Economics* (Toronto: University of Toronto Press, 1942); Oscar R. Lange, *Price Flexibility and Employment* (Bloomington, Indiana: Principia Press, 1944); Lawrence R. Klein, *The Keynesian Revolution* (New York: Macmillan, 1947).

of less well-known monographs and the countless interpretative articles which still continue to appear.

For the difficulty of the *General Theory* there are a variety of reasons. At the literary and expository level, there is the evident strain of the 'long struggle of escape . . . from habitual modes of thought and expression' mentioned by Keynes in his Preface. There is also the non-rigorous Cambridge style of theorizing, the didactic Marshallian style,[5] in which awkward complications are hidden in plain view and common sense is allowed to run away with the argument, a style which Keynes defended in his critical remarks on mathematical economics. Keynes was a less successful practitioner of this style than Marshall, presumably because he spent less effort on it; it never became fashionable to dismiss new work with the crushing remark 'It's all in Keynes', though of course much of it was, and one of the pleasures of re-reading the *General Theory* is to spot the passages which anticipate such later developments as Lange's 'Optimum Propensity to Consume' or Harrod's *Dynamic Economics.*[6] There is the intrusiveness of Keynes the philosopher, interrupting the argument to muse on the social virtues and vices of the organized speculative markets on which he had made his own and his College's fortune, or to dilate rather pretentiously on the essential properties of interest and money. And above all there is the pervading influence of Keynes the born propagandist, with his instinct for dramatizing his ideas, and his Cassandra complex, fortified as polemicists often are by a certain obtuseness in understanding the arguments of his adversaries. It is startling, even at this date, to read on from the mild statement of the Preface that 'A monetary economy, we shall find, is essentially one in which changing views about the future are capable of influencing the quantity of employment and not merely its direction'[7]—a statement which even then must have appeared platitudinous in the extreme to business cycle theorists—to the scathing attack on the (neo)classical theory of value and production which followed.

In directing his attack at the neoclassical concept of an economic system equilibrating at full employment, and presenting a general theory of underemployment equilibrium of which the neoclassical theory was a special case, Keynes's polemical instinct was surely

[5] Cf. Laurence E. Fouraker, 'The Cambridge Didactic Style', *Journal of Political Economy*, LXVI, no. 1, February 1958, 65–73.

[6] Oscar Lange, 'The Rate of Interest and the Optimum Propensity to Consume', *Economica*, New Series, V, no. 17, February 1938, 12–32, reprinted as Chap. 8, 169–192, in American Economic Association, *Readings in Business Cycle Theory* (Philadelphia: Blakiston Press, 1944); R. F. Harrod, *Towards a Dynamic Economics* (London: Macmillan, 1948).

[7] *General Theory*, vii.

right, both because neoclassical ways of thinking were then a major obstacle to sensible anti-depression policy and because, for professional economists, the concept of equilibrium has always had far more intellectual sex-appeal as an analytical companion than its opposite, disequilibrium. But his concentration on equilibrium was in the longer run inimical to his purpose, since his central theoretical contribution—that in a monetary economy the stability of employment in the face of changes in aggregate demand for output depends on the uncertain monetary effects of changes in money wage levels, which changes may themselves be slow—could be and was easily converted into a demonstration that his underemployment equilibrium depended on wage rigidity or on special empirical assumptions about the monetary consequences of wage changes. I shall return to this point later; for the present, let me merely remark that the polemical spirit impedes the argument.

These are idiosyncracies of method of presentation; more fundamental difficulties for the reader are inherent in the analytical content of the book. In the first place, it is difficult for a modern reader to appreciate, after twenty-five years of rapid theoretical development, the extreme limitations of the concepts then available for dealing with economic aggregates and economic dynamics. Keynes tells us that 'The three perplexities which most impeded my progress in writing this book, so that I could not express myself conveniently until I had found some solution for them, are: firstly, the choice of units of quantity appropriate to the problems of the economic system as a whole; secondly, the part played by expectations in economic analysis; and thirdly, the definition of income.'[8] These perplexities reflect the absence, in the Marshallian partial-equilibrium tradition, of a clear notion of real income; the lack of a technique of dynamic analysis in the Hicksian sense, explicitly incorporating expectations; and the fact that national income accounting was in its infancy. In resolving these perplexities, Keynes was thrown strongly back on the very classical tradition he was seeking to attack. His choice of the wage unit depended on the extremely questionable classical view that labour is a uniquely homogeneous aggregate. His treatment of expectations in terms of *states* of expectation, and especially his distinction between short-term and long-term expectations, incorporated the pseudo-dynamics of the Marshallian distinction between short-period and long-period analysis. And his laborious discussion of the definition of income was essentially an elaboration of the Marshallian short-period theory of the firm. More fundamentally, the theory of the book is constructed on the model of Marshallian

[8] *General Theory*, 37.

I have dwelt on the difficulty of the *General Theory* as a book, not with the intention of leading up to the remark that in the 1930s the effort required to open the oyster led those who were successful to overvalue the intellectual pearl within—which is true but trite—but to emphasize the necessity of distinguishing between the *General Theory* as one of the great books in our literature and the general theory as a system of analysis, and to enable me to place the book conveniently in its historical setting. In so doing, I have stressed the extremely Marshallian character of Keynes's theory, which I regard not as a qualification of his achievement but as a measure of the limitations which his powers of original thinking enabled him to transcend. The *General Theory* is built on Marshallian concepts. In the light of subsequent developments, it is also possible to detect Marshallian influences at a more subtle level, in Keynes's concentration on the propensity to consume. His emphasis on personal saving behaviour to the neglect of corporate saving behaviour reflects Marshall's inability to integrate the modern corporation into his system of economic analysis. More fundamentally, his stress on current income receipts as the prime determinant of current consumption expenditure, and particularly his deduction of the form of the income-consumption relationship from an *a priori* 'fundamental psychological law', reflects the general weakness of the Cambridge School in dealing with capital in its relation to economic behaviour. Indeed, if one seeks for a single peg on which to hang a discussion of both the criticism and the elaboration of this and other aspects of Keynes's theory, one can find it in the inadequate attention paid in the *General Theory* to problems of capital theory.

II. THE 'GENERAL THEORY' AS ECONOMIC THEORY

Let me now turn from the *General Theory* as economic literature to the general theory as economic analysis. In considering the analysis of the *General Theory*, I find it convenient to distinguish between the economic theory contained in the book, and the set of ideas about economic policy associated with that theory. The policy implications of the *General Theory* helped to foster the rapid propagation of Keynesian theory in the 1930s and '40s, and constitute the essence of the Keynesian Revolution at what may be called the popular level of economic thought. But these policy implications spring from certain central themes of the *General Theory*—that the economic system does not tend automatically to maintain full employment, and that what determines employment is aggregate expenditure—rather than from the details of the theory of income, employment, interest and money presented in the book; and Keynesian ideas on economic policy have evolved in response to contemporary experience along a path sufficiently independent of the evolution of Keynesian theory to warrant separate treatment. I therefore propose to discuss the theory first, and then to turn to the policy ideas.

The theory presented in the book can be considered from two points of view. As Keynes presented it, it is a theory of the determination of income and employment, in which the emphasis is thrown on the determinants of effective demand and monetary factors play a subsidiary role. But it can also be considered as a monetary theory, in which the emphasis is thrown on the demand for money as an asset alternative to other assets. The distinguishing feature of the first theory is the concept of the propensity to consume; the distinguishing feature of the second is the speculative demand for money—'liquidity preference proper'. Both theories are developed on the assumption—to which Keynes did not always consistently adhere—of a given level of money wages, an assumption incorporated in his device of measuring all aggregates in wage units. It is this assumption which makes Keynes's monetary theory a theory of interest rather than of prices, and which raises the central theoretical questions about both his monetary theory and his theory of under-employment equilibrium.

Before I discuss these theories in detail, let me note briefly that Keynes's way of presenting them as static equilibrium theories led in each case to a violent and prolonged controversy which has turned out in retrospect to be sterile. I refer to the controversy over the savings-investment identity, and the loanable funds *versus* liquidity preference, stocks *versus* flows, debate. The savings-investment controversy turns on the question of how savings and investment can be identical and yet their equality be a condition of income equilibrium; the answer is simply that the term 'savings' (or 'investment') is being used in two senses—variously distinguished as *ex post* and *ex ante*, realized and intended, actual and desired—of which the latter is the theoretically relevant one.[13] Most theorists have long since ceased to worry about the necessary identity of savings and investment, since insistence on it clutters up dynamic analysis; but it survives as a bewildering element in various Keynesian theories of income dis-

[13] D. H. Robertson, 'Mr Keynes and the Rate of Interest', *Essays in Monetary Theory* (London: Staples Press, 1940), Chap. 1; Alvin H. Hansen, *Monetary Theory and Fiscal Policy* (New York: McGraw-Hill, 1949), Appendix B, 219–25 and *A Guide to Keynes* (New York: McGraw-Hill, 1953), Chap. 2, Section 4, 58–64.

tribution,[14] and, in the form of the proposition that investment creates its own savings, continues to inhibit clear thinking on problems of promoting economic development.

The liquidity preference-loanable funds debate turns on the question of whether the rate of interest is better regarded as equilibrating the flow of funds on to and off the market for securities, or as equilibrating the demand for and supply of the stock of cash. The answer, which is now so deeply embedded in mathematical argument that no one can be sure he has got it right,[15] seems to be that the stock-flow distinction is irrelevant, since either theory can be expressed in stock or flow terms; and that it makes no difference whether one works with money or securities, provided, first, that one is concerned only with the determination of the equilibrium level of the rate of interest, and second, that one realizes that this is a general equilibrium problem which can be reduced only by artifice to a problem of equilibrium in one market. In more formal terms, if one assumes to begin with that the markets for goods and factors are in equilibrium, equality between the demand for and supply of money implies equality between the (stock and flow) demand for and supply of loans, and *vice versa*. The two theories become different, however, when applied to dynamic analysis of disequilibrium situations, since liquidity preference theory implies that the rate of interest rises only in response to an excess of the demand for over the supply of money, whereas loanable funds theory implies that it rises only in response to an excess of supply of over demand for securities, and when the goods and factors markets are out of equilibrium an excess demand for money does not necessarily imply an excess supply of securities. In a dynamic context, the loanable funds theory definitely makes more economic sense; and the sustained resistance of Keynesians to admitting it, evident most notably in the prolonged defence in the English literature of the proposition that an increase in the propensity to save lowers the interest rate only by reducing the level of income,[16] is a credit to their ingenuity rather than their scientific spirit.

[14] For example, Nicholas Kaldor, 'Alternative Theories of Distribution', *Review of Economic Studies*, XXIII(2), no. 61, 1955–56, 83–100; Joan Robinson, *The Accumulation of Capital* (London: Macmillan, 1956).

[15] The argument that follows is based on Don Patinkin, 'Liquidity Preference and Loanable Funds: Stock and Flow Analysis', *Economica*, New Series, XXV, no. 4, November 1958, 300–18; but my understanding of the controversy is largely derived from an unpublished manuscript, 'A Survey of Monetary Theory', by F. H. Hahn.

[16] Joan Robinson, 'The Rate of Interest', *Econometrica*, 19, no. 2, April 1951, 92–111, reprinted as Chap. 1 of *The Rate of Interest and Other Essays* (London: Macmillan, 1952); R. F. Kahn, 'Some Notes on Liquidity Preference', *The Manchester School of Economic and Social Studies*, XXII, no. 3, September 1954, 229–57.

1. *The* General Theory *as Monetary Theory*

With these preliminaries out of the way, I turn first to Keynes's general theory considered as a monetary theory. As I have stated, the distinguishing feature of this theory is the emphasis placed on the demand for money as an asset alternative to other yield-bearing assets, rather than as a medium of exchange, together with the crucial role assigned to uncertainty of expectations about future interest rates in determining the shape of the demand curve for money as a function of the rate of interest. Thus Keynes made the analysis of the demand for money explicitly a branch of capital theory, whereas the role of money as a form of wealth-holding has been left implicit in the neoclassical analysis. His theory of the demand for money is, however, misleadingly presented, very confused, and, as a theory of demand for money in capital theory terms, seriously incomplete; so that much work has been required of interpreters and critics by way of clarifying and extending his central ideas.

As to misleading presentation, I have already made the point that Keynes's method of presenting a single general equilibrium system in two separate parts—an income theory in which the rate of interest enters exogenously, and a monetary theory in which income enters exogenously—creates the false impression, of which Keynes himself was the chief victim, that holding securities is the only relevant alternative to holding money, and that the classical alternatives of spending money on consumption or investment play no part in determining the demand for money and the rate of interest. This is incorrect, since the latter alternatives enter the transactions demand for money via their role in determining the levels of income associated with different levels of the rate of interest—as is immediately clear from Hicks's reformulation of the *General Theory* in his classic IS—LM diagram.[17]

As to confusion, I need only mention the transmogrification of the precautionary and speculative motives for holding money between the two chapters in which they are discussed.[18] The precautionary motive starts as the senior partner, entrusted with the important business of avoiding uncertainty about future rates of interest, while the speculative motive is the junior partner who looks after the possibility of profiting from a fall in security prices on an organized market. But when next we meet them, the speculative motive has taken over

[17] J. R. Hicks, 'Mr Keynes and the "Classics"; A Suggested Interpretation', *Econometrica*, 5, no. 2, April 1937, 147–59, reprinted as Chap. 24, 461–76, in American Economic Association, *Readings in the Theory of Income Distribution* (Philadelphia: Blakiston Press, 1946).

[18] *General Theory*, Chapters 13 and 15.

the whole business of asset management, and the precautionary motive has been reduced to a poor relation eking out his existence in the household of transactions demand. That the speculative motive in Keynes's final formulation of it includes the precautionary is not generally recognized in the post-Keynesian literature, even though the precautionary motive provides the ultimate rationale of the 'liquidity trap'.[19] James Tobin's important article on 'Liquidity Preference as Behaviour Towards Risk'[20] does distinguish clearly between the two elements in Keynes's analysis of the demand for money as an asset; but it does not identify them with the two motives that Keynes described.

As to incompleteness, there is first the fact that Keynes dealt only cursorily with transactions demand, which he explained on classical lines of personal convenience and economic structure and took to be a simple proportion of income. Thus demand for money in his theory depends partly on income, in a way not rigorously analysed, and partly on the influence of current and expected interest rates on the preferred disposition of wealth. Subsequently Baumol and Tobin have shown[21] how transactions demand can be treated as a problem in capital (specifically, inventory) theory, and that the demand so derived varies inversely with the rate of interest and is subject to economies of scale.

Far more serious, however, are the limitations resulting from Keynes's procedure of conducting his analysis on the assumption of a given wage/price level and lumping all securities together in an aggregate yielding a single rate of interest. Aggregation undoubtedly tends to exaggerate the importance of the speculative, as distinct

[19] When Keynes comes to explain why the speculative motive will normally lead to increasing demand for money as the rate of interest falls, he offers two different explanations, both of which stress the avoidance of possible loss. (*General Theory*, 202.) One is the increased risk of illiquidity as the current rate falls below the 'safe' rate, the other the reduction in the insurance provided by the current yield against possible capital loss if the rate rises. Only the first, which depends on a definite view of what the rate should be, is properly speaking speculative; the second, which depends only on the possibility that the rate may rise from its current level, is more appropriately described as precautionary. Since the assumption on which the first explanation rests will obviously be belied by experience, Keynesian writers have usually preferred to rest 'the liquidity trap' on the second. See the article by Tobin referred to below.

[20] James Tobin, 'Liquidity Preference as Behavior Towards Risk', *Review of Economic Studies*, XXV(2), no. 67, February 1958, 65–86.

[21] W. J. Baumol, 'The Transactions Demand for Cash: An Inventory Theoretic Approach', *Quarterly Journal of Economics*, LXVI, no. 4, November 1952, 545–56; James Tobin, 'The Interest-Elasticity of Transactions Demand for Cash', *Review of Economics and Statistics*, XXXVIII, no. 3, August 1956, 241–7.

from the precautionary, demand for money, since it overlooks the likelihood that, with a wide variety of equities and fixed-interest securities of varying maturity available, speculation will take the form of movements between securities of different types rather than between securities and cash. It is Keynes's emphasis on the speculative as against the precautionary motive that more orthodox monetary theorists have tended to find objectionable. The assumption of a given wage/price level excludes the influence of price expectations on the assets demand for money, and the associated necessity of distinguishing between real and nominal interest and between fixed-interest-bearing securities and equities; Keynes's attempt to circumnavigate these complications by confining the influence of price-level expectations to the marginal efficiency of capital is not convincing.[22]

The theory of liquidity preference has since been extended by Keynesian writers—Joan Robinson, Richard Kahn, and others[23]—to comprise choices between money, bills, bonds, and equities, and more generally between a multiplicity of assets; but the influence of price-level expectations on asset choices has generally been neglected by Keynesian writers, important though that influence has become on investor behaviour since the war. For explicit analysis of it one must turn to the modern quantity theory literature, where Milton Friedman's restatement of the quantity theory of money[24] goes far towards providing a synthesis of Keynesian and classical approaches to the demand for money in capital theory terms.

As a theory of the demand for money as an asset, Keynes's liquidity preference theory is incomplete in another significant respect. His concern with the short run in which the stock of physical capital is given, together with his assumption of a given wage level, enabled him to develop the demand for money as a function of current and expected interest rates without explicitly introducing the value of assets. This omission led him into analytical errors of far-reaching significance. In the first place, he did not distinguish between increases in the quantity of money resulting from gold discoveries or budget deficits, and those resulting from open market operations,

[22] *General Theory*, 142.

[23] Joan Robinson, 'The Rate of Interest', *Econometrica*, 19, no. 2, April 1951, 92–111, reprinted as Chap. 1 of *The Rate of Interest and Other Essays* (London: Macmillan, 1952); R. F. Kahn, 'Some Notes on Liquidity Preference', *The Manchester School of Economic and Social Studies*, XXII, no. 3, September 1954, 229–57; Ralph Turvey, *Interest Rates and Asset Prices* (London: Allen and Unwin, 1961).

[24] Milton Friedman, 'The Quantity Theory of Money—A Restatement', Chap. I, 3–21, in Milton Friedman (ed.), *Studies in the Quantity Theory of Money* (Chicago: University of Chicago Press, 1956).

though the former involve a net increase in the quantity of assets held by the public and the latter do not.[25] Secondly, in treating the effect of a reduction in money wages as a reduction in the transactions demand for money—a procedure which incidentally commits the heinous crime of building money illusion into the assets demand for money[26]—he overlooked the effect of the wage reduction in increasing the public's real wealth—the Pigou-Haberler-Patinkin wealth effect.[27] In each case, the significance of the oversight lies less in its implications for the demand for money than in the neglect of the effects of the increase in real wealth on aggregate demand. Keynes's neglect of the wealth-effect of deficit finance undoubtedly contributed to misunderstanding of the postwar consequences of the methods adopted for financing the war; and the wealth-effect of wage reduction has become the foundation of the proof that his underemployment equilibrium depends on rigid wages. The value of wealth, and its dependence on the price level, have since been integrated with other determinants of behaviour in Keynesian theory.

So far I have been discussing Keynes's theory of the demand for money and subsequent developments of it. I have taken his central contribution to be his conception of money as an asset whose usefulness springs from uncertainty about future asset prices, and the chief limitation of his analysis to be his concentration on expectations of future changes in interest rates as the determinant of the assets-demand for money. I now turn to the deeper issues raised by Keynes's treatment of the demand for and supply of money as determining the rate of interest rather than the level of prices. As Modigliani showed in his classic *Econometrica* article,[28] this treatment depends on Keynes's assumption of rigid wages: with perfect wage and price flexibility, liquidity preference and the nominal quantity of money would determine the level of prices and not the rate of interest in Keynes's model, unless a liquidity trap intervenes. But an economy

[25] *General Theory*, 200.

[26] *General Theory*, 263. The implicit assumption that the assets demand for money is independent of the price level involves money illusion.

[27] A. C. Pigou, 'The Classical Stationary State', *Economic Journal*, LIII, no. 212, December 1943, 343–51, and 'Economic Progress in a Stable Environment', *Economica*, New Series, XIV, no. 55, August 1947, 180–90; Gottfried Haberler, *Prosperity and Depression* (Geneva: League of Nations, 1941), 3rd ed., 242, 389, 403, 491–503; Don Patinkin, 'Price Flexibility and Full Employment', Chap. 13 in American Economic Association, *Readings in Monetary Theory* (Philadelphia: Blakiston Press, 1951).

[28] Franco Modigliani, 'Liquidity Preference and the Theory of Interest and Money', *Econometrica*, 12, no. 1, January 1944, 45–88, reprinted as Chap. 11 in American Economic Association, *Readings in Monetary Theory* (Philadelphia: Blakiston Press, 1951).

with perfect price flexibility is not the economy with which Keynes was concerned, and it is not an interesting economy to posit for theorizing about the problems with which he wanted to deal. In this judgment I derive support from the fact that the quantity theory has ceased to be a theory of prices, and has become the theory that there is a stable demand function for money[29]—a formulation which leaves open the question whether the demand and supply of money determine interest or prices or both.

To leave the matter there, however, is to confine the issue to short-run analysis, whereas it goes much deeper. The fundamental contention of Keynesian monetary theory is that a monetary economy is essentially different from a barter economy—that money is not merely a veil but exercises an influence of its own in the working of the economy.[30] To examine the validity of this contention it is necessary to investigate the role of money in an economy with wage and price flexibility, allowing for the wealth effect of price-level changes. Such investigation is the object of the two major works in monetary theory published since the *General Theory*—Patinkin's *Money, Interest and Prices* and Gurley and Shaw's *Money in a Theory of Finance*.[31] These show (the one largely by inference, the other directly) that in an economy in which a variety of assets exists and money is created by purchase of such assets by a banking system, changes in the supply of and demand for money have a long-run and not merely a short-run influence on the real equilibrium of the economy. The present position can be summarized in the statement that Keynes was right to attack Say's Law, but he attacked it for the wrong reason. Properly understood, the significance of Say's Law is not that it makes the decision to save identical with the decision to invest, but that it excludes money altogether from any influence on economic behaviour.[32]

2. *The General Theory of Income and Employment*

I have been discussing the *General Theory* as a monetary theory; but its main purpose and contribution is the theory of income and employment. Keynes's great achievement was to cut through the conceptual complexity and literary looseness of contemporary monetary theory to an aggregative general equilibrium model of the economy

[29] Milton Friedman (ed.), *Studies in the Quantity Theory of Money* (Chicago: University of Chicago Press, 1956), 4.

[30] *General Theory*, Chap. 2.

[31] Don Patinkin, *Money, Interest and Prices* (Evanston, Illinois: Row, Peterson, 1956); John G. Gurley and Edward S. Shaw, *Money in a Theory of Finance* (Washington: Brookings Institution, 1960).

[32] Don Patinkin, *Money, Interest and Prices* (Evanston, Illinois: Row, Peterson, 1956), Chap. VIII, Section 7, 119–21.

which, once grasped, was simple, readily manipulable, and above all relevant to contemporary problems. The elements in this model, aside from liquidity preference and the quantity of money, are the propensity to consume, the investment demand schedule, and the aggregate supply schedule relating employment to output. Keynes's analysis of the last two of these was thoroughly classical in general outline—extraordinarily so in view of the contemporary eruption of monopolistic and imperfect competition theory. The novel and intriguing element in the theory was the propensity to consume, together with its *alter ego*, that inexhaustibly versatile mechanical toy, the multiplier.

The propensity to consume made the theory of income determination a simple theory in which income was determined by the amount of fixed capital investment, the multiplier playing a role analogous to that of velocity in the quantity theory. The concept of income as the main determinant of expenditure, which Keynes confined to personal consumption behaviour, lent itself readily to extension by others to the spending behaviour of Government, of corporations, of nations in their external transactions, and of an economy disaggregated into output-producing or income-receiving sectors. The statistical estimation of the consumption function offered itself as an important exercise for the emerging discipline of econometrics; and early analysis of time-series and cross-section data seemed abundantly to confirm the hypothesis that consumption is a stable function of income.

Alas for the consumption function, it dismally failed the test of forecasting postwar unemployment. This failure, together with the paradox disclosed by Kuznets's data on the long-run constancy of the savings ratio,[33] prompted a rapid independent development of the theory of the consumption function, and led to substantive modifications of Keynesian income theory. Both developments have been concerned with the same shortcoming of the theory as Keynes presented it, the neglect of the influence of wealth on consumption, a neglect inherent in Keynes's short-period approach and concealed by his deduction of the shape of the propensity to consume from an unexplored 'psychological law'. The various hypotheses used to reconcile the short-run variability with the long-run constancy of the savings ratio, ranging from 'secular upward drift'[34] through the

[33] Simon Kuznets, 'Capital Formation, 1879–1938', 53–78 in Wesley C. Mitchell and others, *Studies in Economics and Industrial Relations* (Philadelphia: University of Pennsylvania Press, 1941).

[34] Alvin Hansen, *Fiscal Policy and Business Cycles* (London: Allen and Unwin, New York: W. W. Norton, 1941), 233.

influence of highest previous income[35] or value of assets[36] to the more intellectually exciting life-plan[37] and permanent income theories,[38] are all concerned at one or another level of sophistication with the influence of wealth on consumption.[39] Correspondingly, it has become customary to include the value of wealth in some form among the variables on which the Keynesian behaviour propensities depend, both to give explicit recognition to the influence of wealth on consumption in the long run and to incorporate the neglected wealth-effect of wage and price level changes.

Meanwhile, the propensity to consume and the multiplier have dwindled to relative insignificance both in the purer sort of monetary theory and in popular Keynesian economics. For pure theory, the essential Keynesian concept is the functional dependence of aggregate expenditure on itself in its income-generating capacity. The division of expenditure into consumption and investment is a superfluous complication once one drops the restrictive assumption that consumption depends only on income and investment only on the rate of interest, and permits both to change autonomously; similarly, the multiplier is a tiresome way of comparing general equilibrium positions. At the popular level, the essential Keynesian idea is the dependence of income, employment, and (more recently) the rate of inflation on the level of aggregate spending, together with the understanding that economic policy can attack spending at a variety of points; the notion of consumption as a passive respondent to investment is appropriate, if at all, to a *laissez faire* society, not to one with conscious economic policies. But the propensity to consume survives as an integral part of modern business cycle and growth theory; it

[35] James S. Duesenberry, *Income, Saving, and the Theory of Consumer Behavior* (Cambridge: Harvard University Press, 1949); Franco Modigliani, 'Fluctuations in the Saving-Income Ratio; a Problem in Economic Forecasting', *Studies in Income and Wealth*, XI (New York: National Bureau of Economic Research, 1949), 371–441.

[36] James Tobin, 'Relative Income, Absolute Income, and Savings', 135–56 in *Money, Trade and Economic Growth, in honor of John Henry Williams* (New York: Macmillan, 1951).

[37] Franco Modigliani and Richard Brumberg, 'Utility Analysis and the Consumption Function: An Interpretation of Cross-Section Data', 383–436 in Kenneth K. Kurihara (ed.), *Post-Keynesian Economics* (New Brunswick: Rutgers University Press, 1954).

[38] Milton Friedman, *A Theory of the Consumption Function* (Princeton: Princeton University Press, 1957).

[39] For an interesting approach on these lines, see W. Hamburger, 'The Determinants of Aggregate Consumption', *Review of Economic Studies*, XXII(1), no. 57, 1954–55, 23–34, and 'The Relation of Consumption to Wealth and the Wage Rate', *Econometrica*, 23, no. 1, January 1955, 1–17.

modern capitalism, what is left of the general theory of income and employment? The contribution of the *General Theory* to modern economics is certainly not Keynes's specific model of income determination, for not only is his consumption function too simple but his theory of investment is incomplete and has had to be extended to make it usable. Rather, the contribution lies in the general nature of Keynes's approach to the problem of income and employment. In the first place, he concentrated attention on the expenditure-income and income-expenditure relationships, which are much easier to understand and apply than the quantity theory relationships and which provide, in the multiplier analysis, a key to dynamic processes of change. In the second place, he provided a useful macro-economic general equilibrium model for the analysis of a monetary economy in which capital accumulation is a specialized activity financed by the issue of marketable securities. In pure monetary theory Keynes's crucial distinction between consumption and investment decisions has been dropped, and the model refined into the four-market system comprising goods, labour, money and 'bonds'[48]—two flows and two stocks—but the distinction remains essential to cycle and growth theory. Indirectly, also, Keynes stimulated the development of modern dynamic theory.[49] Finally, what is most important for scientific economics but can easily be used to denigrate Keynes's work, he set out his theory in a model in which the important variables and relationships are specified in a form suitable for statistical measurement and testing. The stimulation given by the *General Theory* to the construction and testing of aggregative models may well prove to be Keynes's chief contribution to economics in the longer perspective of historical judgment, since the application of capital rather than income concepts to monetary theory may well produce better and more reliable results, and the present predominance of the income-expenditure approach prove to be a transitional stage in the analysis of economic behaviour.

III. THE POLICY IMPLICATIONS OF THE 'GENERAL THEORY'

This brings me to the policy implications of the *General Theory*, which I have hitherto postponed discussing. At this date there is no need to labour the point that the *General Theory* deserves much of the credit for the fact that the maintenance of high and stable employment is now accepted as a Governmental responsibility, or that

[48] Don Patinkin, *Money, Interest and Prices* (Evanston, Illinois: Row, Peterson, 1956), Part Two.

[49] I am indebted for this point to Robert Clower.

Keynes's theory of effective demand is the origin of the modern theory of economic policy. What calls for comment, rather, is the bias that the majority of Keynesians have drawn from the *General Theory* against allowing money, and consequently monetary policy, an important role in determining the level of activity of the economy. This bias has meant that Keynesian theory has proved a poor guide to the dominant postwar policy problem of inflation, and that the Keynesian approach to this problem has tended to degenerate into a confused and often obstructive eclecticism. Now, a bias against money and monetary policy was not characteristic of Keynes's work as a monetary theorist—rather the opposite—and money and the demand for it play an essential role in the *General Theory* itself. It is true that the presentation of the theory plays down the role of money, and that despite its title the book contains almost nothing on the theory of inflation; but Keynes did state clearly that full employment conditions would require a different analysis, and he had after all dealt extensively with such conditions in the *Treatise*. (The *Treatise* is in fact much more relevant to postwar conditions than the *General Theory*—but that would require another lecture.)

It is an interesting question why a theory in which money is important should have turned into the theory that money is unimportant. Part of the explanation lies in certain features of the *General Theory* I have already mentioned, that diverted attention from the influence of money and of price expectations on spending. Part of it lies in the hardening of certain of Keynes's conclusions into rigid dogmas in the hands of his disciples—notably the hardening of his legitimate criticisms of the quantity theory into militant opposition to any form of quantity theory reasoning, and the hardening of his opinion that monetary policy might be ineffective in combating a collapse of the marginal efficiency of capital into the conflicting dogmas (*a*) that monetary restriction is dangerous because it might precipitate such a collapse, (*b*) that monetary restriction is useless because it will have a negligible effect on effective demand. Part of it is that for obvious reasons Keynesians have tended to be politically left of centre, a position associated with distrust of central bankers—particularly in England, due to the part the Bank of England played in the restoration of the gold standard and the downfall of the second Labour Government. Much of it is simply that the 'vulgar Keynesians' seized on the simplest and most striking version of the Keynesian system—autonomous investment and the multiplier—as the essence of it, ignoring the monetary analysis as an irrelevant complication.

Whatever the explanation, the result has been that in analysing inflation Keynesians have tended to fall back on one or other of two approaches based on components of the *General Theory*, rather than on the complete model. One approach is based on the crude effective demand model of income determination; combined with the expenditure-income-expenditure sequence, this leads into the demand-pull theory of inflation. The other approach is based on Keynes's habit of treating the wage unit as exogenous; combined with the income-expenditure-income sequence, this leads into the cost-push theory of inflation. The one approach leads towards the prescription of fiscal policy to remedy inflation, the other towards the prescription of some form of wage and price control. Neither prescription is very realistic for postwar capitalist economies: fiscal remedies are difficult to graft on to high-level budgets dominated by defence expenditure and structural social welfare programmes; wage and price controls are inconsistent with a free enterprise system, and especially with the principle of free collective bargaining. Both approaches, by ignoring or suppressing the monetary side of Keynesian theory, concentrate on the mechanism rather than the causation of inflation; and both virtually assume away the possibility of controlling inflation by monetary means.

Not all Keynesians have been sceptical about monetary policy, especially after experience of it since 1951. Keynesian theory has in fact had a formative influence on modern ideas on monetary policy. The theory of effective demand suggests the question of what precise effects monetary policy has on spending, a question which it is important to ask owing to the tendency of central banks to judge their policies by their effects on interest rates and credit conditions in the markets with which they are immediately concerned. This question has stimulated the search for the effects of monetary policy on particular sectors of the economy, and also furnished the rationale for a broader and more selective approach to the techniques of monetary control. On the other hand, the search for specific impacts of monetary policy tends to promote underestimation of its influence; so does the Keynesian concern with interest rates as determinants of effective demand—which also tends to play into the hands of central bankers—since it is only too easy to fall into the habit of identifying an increase or decrease in interest rates with a deflationary or inflationary policy. Similarly, the theory of liquidity preference, in a more indirect way, has played a part in the evolution of the modern theory of central banking, according to which the function of the central bank is the broad one of controlling the liquidity of the economy rather than the narrow one of controlling the quantity of currency and demand deposits.[50] Again, the recognition of the monetary role of financial intermediaries and other credit-granting institutions which this entails can easily lead back to scepticism about the potentialities of monetary policy. But these are matters far removed from the *General Theory*.

IV. CONCLUSION

Let me conclude by summarizing briefly the main points I have made in this lecture. The *General Theory* is an uncommonly untidy book, which bears the strong imprint of the Marshallian tradition from which it sprang. Nevertheless, it has shifted the emphasis of monetary theory to the role of money as an asset with special properties in an uncertain world, and forced recognition of the fact that a monetary economy is fundamentally different from a barter economy. It provided a simple and comprehensible aggregative model of the economy, which not only facilitated the analysis of aggregative problems but greatly stimulated the development of econometric work with such models. It explained why the competitive capitalist economy does not automatically maintain a satisfactory level of employment, and outlined the theory of remedial policy, thereby promoting a revolution in ideas on the responsibilities of Government in such a system. On the other hand, the book was weak at a crucial point, in its neglect of the influence of capital on behaviour; and its influence has been to distract attention from the role of money in the functioning of the economy. I have not, in this lecture, been able to survey the contributions of Keynes's ideas to the many specialized branches of theory —international economics, public finance, business cycles, economic growth, economic planning, to mention the major ones—where they have proved extremely fruitful. But no-one could hope, in a single lecture, to take a census of the progeny of the *General Theory*.

[50] *Report of the Committee on the Working of the Monetary System* (London: HM Stationery Office, 1959).

VII

PLANNING AND THE MARKET IN ECONOMIC DEVELOPMENT*

Economic development is a field of study in which economists have only recently begun to specialize, and in which consequently there is as yet no settled body of economic doctrine. I must therefore begin with the warning that what I am about to present is not the agreed view of a representative group of economists, but rather my own opinions. Though I have drawn on the literature of development and of economic theory in forming these opinions, I cannot say that the results constitute an authoritative statement of the present position of economics.

The fundamental causes of economic growth are not a subject with which economists have dealt much in the past, and they are not a subject with which economists can claim to be qualified by training and technique to deal now. My subject is not, however, the causes of economic development, but planning and the market in economic development; this involves the theory of markets, and on that subject economists by profession have a great deal to say. Indeed, from the time of Adam Smith, the theory of markets has been the core of economics as a social science.

It is true that the full ramifications of the market as an instrument of social and economic organization were not appreciated from the start by the classical economists. The English classical economists understood the functions of commodity markets; but they did not link the theory of distribution to the pricing process. The integration of the theory of factor prices with the theory of commodity markets was left to J. B. Say, and later Walras and Marshall, to work out. But the relation between the market and economic development lay at the centre of the foundations laid by Adam Smith. Smith was con-

* *Pakistan Economic Journal*, VIII, no. 2, June 1958, 44–55.

cerned with economic development, and at the heart of his work was the market, determining the extent of specialization and division of labour and the limits to increasing productivity.

In recent times, there has been a retreat both in economic theory and in economic policy from the nineteenth-century ideal of the unfettered market as a principle of economic organization. But the economic pros and cons of this retreat have been fully debated, and the economist consequently has a great deal to say about the relative merits of the market as contrasted with other methods of economic organization, and the circumstances appropriate to each.

The subject of planning and the market in economic development is, therefore, one which falls definitely within the field of the economist. Before I go on to discuss it, I must define more precisely what I mean by it. 'Planning and the market' may be interpreted in two different ways. First, it may refer to the contrast between direction of the economy by Government and the policy of *laissez-faire*. This is not my subject, though in a wider philosophical and historical context it offers much to discuss. For example, though *laissez-faire* and direction are often regarded as opposites, if one looks to the history of economic development one finds (as Professor Easterbrook has shown[1]) that economic development is almost invariably a process in which planning and direction on the one hand and freedom of enterprise on the other play their part, and are mixed. There is almost no case in which economic development has been entirely planned or entirely unplanned. The usual pattern is one of some framework of control by Government, within which the entrepreneur provides his services—a mixture of bureaucracy and enterprise, in which bureaucracy takes care of the major risks of development and enterprise faces and overcomes the minor ones. Another relevant point that Easterbrook makes is that an economy which succeeds in finding a formula for growth tends to repeat that pattern after it has become inappropriate. For example, Britain has gone on trying to work the internationally-orientated pattern of her nineteenth-century development; Russia has been very successful in developing heavy industry but has not yet solved the problem of agriculture.

The alternative interpretation takes planning, in the sense of a general direction of the economy, as an established principle, and considers the market as an alternative to other and more direct means

[1] Professor Easterbrook's analysis was presented in the Marshall Lectures at Cambridge University in the spring of 1956. Unfortunately these lectures have not been published, but some of the ideas are available in W. T. Easterbrook, 'Long Period Comparative Study: Some Historical Cases', *Journal of Economic History*, XVII, no. 4, December 1957, 571–95.

of detailed control. Given the general framework of economic planning, there is still a choice between two alternative methods of looking after the details. One is by direct detailed planning by a central authority, the other is by leaving the working out of details as far as possible to the operation of the market. (There is a third alternative, in which the Government is itself the entrepreneur and investor, which I shall consider later.)

This alternative interpretation is the one I shall be using: I shall discuss the question of the market mechanism as against detailed planning as an instrument of economic development. I should like to make it clear from the start that I am going to make a strong case for the market, as the preferable instrument of economic development, on two main grounds. The first is that the achievement of the desired results by control methods is likely to be especially difficult and inefficient in an underdeveloped economy; at this point I should like to remind you that a large part of Adam Smith's argument for *laissez-faire* was the inefficiency and corruption he saw in the Governments of his time. The second is that the remedies for the main fault which can be found with the use of the market mechanism, its undesirable social effects, are luxuries which underdeveloped countries cannot afford to indulge in if they are really serious about attaining a high rate of development. In particular, there is likely to be a conflict between rapid growth and an equitable distribution of income; and a poor country anxious to develop would probably be well advised not to worry too much about the distribution of income.

I am going to make a fairly strong case for the market, because the market figures relatively little in the literature of economic development, and the theoretical analysis which economics has developed in relation to markets is often overlooked or disregarded. Before getting down to business on the subject of markets, I should like to explore a little the question why, in the theory and policy of 'economic development', so little scope is usually allowed to the operation of market forces. There have been, I think, three main groups of factors at work.

In the first place, there seems to be in human societies a set of social and psychological factors favouring intervention in the market. In this connection it is important to remember that the free market as commonly understood is essentially a characteristic of the nineteenth century—before then, and since, the common feature of economic organization has been intervention in the market. What are these factors? One of them, I believe, is the impatience of idealists and would-be reformers with the working of the market, and their desire to take direct action to improve things, according to their criteria of improvement: this attitude reflects the intellectual arrogance typical of reformers. The attitude is reinforced by the fact that the defects of market organization seem obvious to anyone, or can be made to seem so, whereas the socio-economic functions of the market are obscure and difficult to appreciate. The discovery of these functions was indeed the great achievement of the classical economists, and constitutes the only claim that economics has to the status of a science. The obscurity of the market's functions makes it easy, also, to confuse opposition to unattractive features of the free enterprise system which express themselves through the market, such as inequality of income and wealth, with opposition to the market as a mechanism of organization.

Opposition to and dislike of the market for the reasons I have just discussed is frequently allied with a positive belief in the desirability of Government intervention in the market, and a faith in the disinterestedness and effectiveness of such intervention. Belief in the desirability of Government intervention in the western world is associated with the spread of socialist ideas, and in its modern form can be traced back to Benthamite utilitarianism; elsewhere, it can probably be associated with the nature of the State as the dispenser of justice in primitive economies. Belief in the efficiency and disinterestedness of Governmental intervention is associated with the growth of the modern career civil service, with its standards of incorruptibility, particularly in Britain and countries influenced by the British example. (This explains why the belief is less prevalent in the United States than in other English speaking countries.) It is, in my opinion, an important question for underdeveloped countries whether their civil services are of the calibre required to administer the kinds of social and economic programmes adopted in the advanced economies.

Opposition to the market as a means of economic organization is also inherent in the characteristics of an established and functioning civil service. One of these characteristics, a corollary of the standards of administrative efficiency and 'public service', is a natural propensity to regulate. A good civil service, or a bad one, is rarely prepared to decide that non-intervention is the best policy; and to the bureaucratic mind the functioning of the price system as a regulator appears mere disorder and chaos. Another characteristic is an antipathy towards enterpreneurship; the entrepreneur is an agent of change, and as such disturbs the orderliness of the economy and makes it more difficult to regulate. This is not, of course, a universally valid generalization: civil services have, at times, played important entrepreneurial roles themselves, though usually under the pressure of political events. One special feature of the generally anti-entrepreneurial attitude of civil servants, noted by P. T. Bauer in his studies of West African trade,[2] is specially relevant to underdeveloped economies. This is the antipathy of the British-trained type of civil servant, literate and 'responsible', to the semi-literate and socially unacceptable type of individual who possesses the knack of making money by trading—the small-scale entrepreneur on whose activities economic development from a low level may well depend.

These characteristics of civil services are important in considering the uses and limitations of control methods in economic development. The economist, or any other intelligent man, can easily think up ways in which market processes could be improved on by means of controls, assuming that he administers them himself and has infinite time in which to do so. But would the conclusion in favour of controls be the same if it were accepted that their administration had to be entrusted to a 'responsible' civil servant of the British type, let alone a civil service with a less ingrained tradition of honesty and disinterestedness?

A third factor antithetical to the market has been the character of modern economics itself, as applied to economic planning. Modern economics has been strongly influenced by the theoretical revolutions of the 1930s, which were inimical to competition and the market. On the one hand, both the theory of monopolistic competition and the new welfare economics have been excessively concerned with criticisms of the efficiency of the market mechanism, criticisms formulated from a static viewpoint not obviously relevant to growth problems. On the other hand, the Keynesian revolution fostered aggregative thinking to the neglect of older ideas of substitutability in production and consumption (which in turn have receded into the limbo of mathematical economics); and the habit of aggregative thinking has to some extent been reinforced by the modern emphasis on statistical verification which has necessarily postulated simplicity of economic relationships.

In addition to these theoretical developments, development economics has been strongly influenced by the nature of the major problems with which economics was concerned before it turned to 'development', namely mass unemployment and war finance, which inculcated the habit of thinking about economic structure as given, and of applying other criteria than consumers' choice. Two features of wartime economic planning are frequently overlooked in the attempt to

[2] P. T. Bauer, *West African Trade: A Study of Competition, Oligopoly and Monopoly in a Changing Economy* (Cambridge: Cambridge University Press, 1954), especially Chaps. 11–12, 145–71.

carry over its concepts and techniques to peacetime planning. In the first place, the battery of controls applied in war-time rested very heavily on a strong appeal to patriotism. The application of similar techniques might be possible in an underdeveloped country which could mobilize and concentrate all the instruments of communication and propaganda on the single aim of development; but the capacity of most countries to do this is doubtful, especially as development presents no single dramatic objective comparable to victory. Secondly, in spite of the propaganda and the patriotic appeal, war-time economic policy in most countries ran into serious difficulties with the resurgence of the market in the form of black markets of various kinds, shop shortages, incentive problems, and so on.

I have been discussing various reasons why thinking about economic development has been inimical to, or neglectful of, market considerations. I now want to recapitulate briefly the various economic functions of the market and the price system as a method of economic organization. I shall be brief, as the argument is a familiar one.

In the first place, the market rations supplies of consumer goods among consumers; this rationing is governed by the willingness of consumers to pay, and provided the distribution of income is acceptable it is a socially efficient process. Secondly, the market directs the allocation of production between commodities, according to the criterion of maximum profit, which, on the same assumption, corresponds to social usefulness. Thirdly, the market allocates the different factors of production among their various uses, according to the criterion of maximizing their incomes. Fourthly, it governs the relative quantities of specific types of labour and capital equipment made available. Fifthly, it distributes income between the factors of production and therefore between individuals. Thus it solves all the economic problems of allocation of scarce means between alternative ends.

These are static functions; but the market also serves in various ways to provide incentives to economic growth. Thus the availability of goods through the market stimulates the consumer to seek to increase his income; and access to the market provides an opportunity for inventors of new goods and technical improvements to profit from their exploitation. Moreover, the market serves particularly to provide an incentive to the accumulation of capital of all kinds: first to the accumulation of personal capital in the form of trained skill, since such skill earns a higher reward; and second to the accumulation of material capital, since such capital earns an income.

The argument, then, is that a properly functioning market system would tend to stimulate both economic efficiency and economic growth. And it is important to note that the market does this automatically, while it requires no big administrative apparatus, no central decision-making, and very little policing other than the provision of a legal system for the enforcement of contracts.

All this sounds very impressive; but it is clearly not the whole of the story. What, then, are the objections to the market, how serious are they, and what should be done about them in the context of economic development? I shall discuss these questions in some detail. But first I shall state briefly the central theme of my discussion. It is that in many cases the objections to the market can be overcome by reforming specific markets, so as to bring them closer to the ideal type of market; and that to overcome other objections to the market may be very expensive and may not prove to be worthwhile—in other words, the defects of the market mechanism may on balance be more tolerable than they look at first sight.

Now, what are the objections to the market? They can, I think, be classified into two main types. One type of objection is that the market does not perform its functions properly. The other type of objection is that the results produced by the functioning of the market are undesirable in themselves.

I begin with the first type of objection, that the market does not perform its function properly. Here it is useful to draw a distinction between two quite different sorts of cases—those in which the market operates imperfectly, and those in which a perfectly functioning market would not produce the best results.

Imperfect operation of the market in an underdeveloped country may be attributable to ignorance, in the sense of lack of familiarity with market mechanisms and of awareness of relevant information, or to the prevalence of other modes of behaviour than the rational maximization of returns from effort. In the first case, the appropriate Governmental policy would seem to me to be, not to assume from the market the responsibility for allocative decisions, but to disseminate the knowledge and information required to make the market work efficiently and provide the education required to use it. The second case implies a more fundamental obstacle, not only to the use of the market but also to economic development itself, and suggests that successful economic development requires a basic change in social psychology. To my mind, it raises a serious question of fact. Is it really true that people in underdeveloped countries are strangers to the idea of maximizing gains? The idea that they are is very common in the literature and policy-making of economic development; one of its manifestations is the implicit assumption that both supplies and demands are completely price-inelastic. I am very sceptical about this, partly because of Bauer's work and partly because at least some of the actions of Governments in underdeveloped areas presuppose that even the poorest producers are susceptible to price incentives. I personally do not think one is justified in assuming as a general proposition that ignorance and illiteracy necessarily imply that men are not interested in making money. If it is true, there will be serious difficulties in the way of economic development; but again, the appropriate Governmental policy would seem to be to educate the people in the practice of rational economic behaviour.

Even if the market functions perfectly, it will not produce the best possible results by its own criteria if there is a difference between social and private benefit or cost. This type of case may be particularly relevant to economic development; it includes the case of increasing returns to scale, and can be extended to include the possibility that technical progress or capital accumulation tend to proceed more rapidly in industry than in agriculture. But it raises an immediate question of fact—whether divergences between social and private benefit or cost are numerous and important or not. This is an important question, but one on which we do not know very much for certain. The theory of increasing returns is logically intriguing, but the influence of increasing returns still has to be disentangled from that of technical progress in historical growth. Again, it is a fact that few advanced countries are not industrial; but this by itself does not establish the wisdom of a policy of forced industrialization in an underdeveloped country. Aside from the question of fact, the existence of divergences between social and private returns does not necessarily indicate a need for the Government to replace the market mechanism; instead, the operation of the market can be perfected by the use of appropriate taxes and subsidies to offset any divergences between social and private returns.

I now turn to the second type of objection to the market, the point of which is not that the market does not work in the way it should, but that the results produced are undesirable in themselves. Here, I think, there are two major objections to the market. The first is that the income distribution produced by the market is unjust and socially undesirable. The distribution of income through the market depends on the wealth and talents of different individuals, and on their individual skill in seeing a profitable opportunity of employing their money or labour. If they make a wise or lucky choice, they may obtain a much higher income. The objection is that this method of determining the distribution of income is not just. But if you attempt to intervene in the distribution of income, you immediately encounter the problem that such intervention interferes with the efficiency of the market system. If people are not allowed to enjoy the income they could obtain by their decisions, their decisions in turn will be affected, and the efficiency of the system will be impaired. There is, therefore, a conflict between economic efficiency and social justice. The extent and importance of this conflict is likely to vary according to the state of economic development. The more advanced a country is, the more likely are its citizens to have consciences about the distribution of income, and to accept the high taxation necessary to correct it without disastrously altering their behaviour; and on the other hand, the higher the level of income reached, the less serious will be any slowing down of the rate of growth brought about by redistribution policies. An advanced country can afford to sacrifice some growth for the sake of social justice. But the cost of greater equality may be great to any economy at a low level of economic development that wishes to grow rapidly, particularly as it is evident that historically the great bursts of economic growth have been associated with the prospect and the result of big windfall gains; it would therefore seem unwise for a country anxious to enjoy rapid growth to insist too strongly on policies aimed at ensuring economic equality and a just income distribution. I should add that the problem may not be in fact as serious as I have made it out to be, since in the course of time rapid growth tends in various ways to promote a more equal distribution of wealth.

At this point I should like to digress on a special aspect of the conflict between the market principle and considerations of social justice, which appears in some underdeveloped countries, the conflict created by opposition on moral grounds to the payment and receipt of interest.[3] Now the view that interest is a bad thing is economically nonsensical (unless it is merely a terminological dispute) until the economy has reached a stage at which no more capital can usefully be employed. I am not here referring to the administrative difficulties of removing interest from the economy, but to the economic principle involved. The problem of underdeveloped countries centres around the scarcity of capital. If capital is scarce, there should be both an incentive to the accumulation of it by saving, and a device for rationing supplies of it among alternative uses. These are the functions of interest. If you 'abolish interest' in the sense of forcing interest to be called by some other name, as was the practice in the Middle Ages, the result will merely be inconvenience; but if you abolish interest in the economic sense, the result will be the loss of the economic services

[3] This digression was a response to the seminar discussions that accompanied the Pakistan Refresher Course; in the seminar it became clear that many students were bothered by the conflict between economic principles and the Muslim injunction against the taking of *riba*.

performed by interest. On the one hand, the amount of private saving will be reduced and its allocation to investment distorted by the restriction of investment to activities over which the saver has personal control. On the other hand, insofar as there is a pool of investment funds (created, say, by taxation or monetary expansion, or made available by foreign aid), some method will have to be found for rationing it out among competing claims if it is to be used efficiently. This problem has in fact arisen in Russia, where the engineers and planners who assess investment projects have had to work out concepts which amount to the rate of interest, to fill the gap created by the refusal of Marxian dogma to recognize that capital has a scarcity value and is productive.

The same sort of argument makes it seem undesirable for the Governments of underdeveloped countries to use their monetary policy to favour themselves with low rates of interest. Governments now often enjoy the privilege of paying a rate of interest of 2½ or 3 per cent; this encourages them to think, and to plan, as if capital were easily available. There seems no reason why Governments should enjoy low rates of interest when capital is scarce; on the contrary, it promotes wasteful investment and also, for reasons explained below, tends in the long run to promote inequality of income distribution.

I have been discussing the objection to the results of the market system on the grounds that it produces an undesirable distribution of income. A second objection of the same sort is that the free market will not produce as high a rate of growth as is desirable. I think there is a strong case for this objection, because people's actions in regard to saving and investment depend very much on their guesses about the future. Now people are likely to know their own current requirements better than the Government. But the requirements of the future have to be looked at not from the individual or family point of view or that of the nation as a collection of individuals, but from the point of view of the ongoing society. The needs of society in the future, many economists agree, tend to be underprovided for by the free market.

Even if the conclusion that state action is desirable to raise the rate of growth is accepted, this conclusion nevertheless does not carry with it a number of corollaries which are often attached to it. In particular, it does not necessarily imply that the state ought to undertake development saving and investment itself. Private enterprise may be more efficient than the Government in constructing and operating enterprises, so that the best policy may be to stimulate private enterprise by tax concessions, subsidies, and the provision of cheap credit. Similarly, it may be preferable to stimulate private saving by offering high interest rates, rather than by forcing savings into the hands of the state by taxation or inflation. One argument against a policy of low interest rates and forced saving is that it may in the long run contribute to the inequality of income distribution. The reason is that the poor or small savers are mainly confined to low-yielding fixed-interest investments, directly or indirectly in Government debt, because these are safe and easily available, whereas the larger savers can invest their money in higher-yielding stocks and shares or directly in profitable enterprises. There is, therefore, an opportunity here for Government both to stimulate saving for development and to improve the distribution of income.

There is another reason for being wary of the proposition that the state should undertake development investment itself—the danger that if the Government undertakes investment itself, especially if its adminstrators are not too clear on their objectives, the result will be the creation of vested industrial interests inimical to further development, and resistant to technical change.

To summarize the foregoing argument from the point of view of development policy, it seems to me that much of development planning could usefully be devoted to the improvement and strengthening of the market system. This does not imply the acceptance of all the results of *laissez-faire*, especially with respect to the rate of growth; but there are reasons for thinking that too much emphasis on a fair or ethical distribution of income can be an obstacle to rapid growth.

The argument I have presented has been concerned mainly with one side of the case for the market. The other side concerns the costs and difficulties of controls, in terms of the manpower costs of the administration they require, and their effects in creating profit opportunities which bring windfall gains to some members of the community and create incentives to evasion which in turn require policing of the controls. I have touched on that side of the argument sufficiently frequently to make it unnecessary to elaborate on it further.

Instead, I shall comment briefly on international markets in relation to economic development, since so far I have been implicitly concerned with internal markets. Economic development planning inevitably has a strong autarkic bias, by reason both of its motivation and of the limitation of the scope of control to the national economy. Nevertheless, international trade can play an important part in stimulating and facilitating the development process. Access to foreign markets for exports can permit an economy with a limited domestic market to exploit economies of scale, and the potentiality of such exports can serve as a powerful attraction for foreign capital and enterprise. Similarly, the capacity to import provided by exports can give a developing economy immediate access to the products of advanced technology, without obliging it to go through the long and perhaps costly process of developing domestic production facilities. Economic nationalism and excessive fear of the risks of international trade, by fostering aversion to exploiting the advantages of the international market, can therefore retard economic development unnecessarily.

One further comment on the international aspects of the market and economic development seems to me worth making. Discussion of the international side of development has been mostly concerned with commodity trade and commercial policy. But in fact one of the most important ways in which the world market system is imperfect is with respect to the international mobility of capital and labour. The problem of international capital movements has received a fair amount of attention, labour mobility and immobility much less. Now, the process of economic development in the past, especially in the nineteenth century, was characterized by vast movements, not only of capital, but also of labour, about the world. The mass movement of labour between countries has now been more or less shut off by the growth of nationalism. I believe it is important to recognize this restriction on international competition, and its implications for programmes of economic development. It means—looking at the world economy as a whole—that the solution to the problem of maximizing world output cannot be approached directly, by bringing labour, capital, technology, and natural resources together at the most efficient location; instead, the other productive factors have to be brought to the labour. To a large extent, 'the economic development of underdeveloped countries' is a second-best policy,[4] in which gifts of capital and technical training by advanced to underdeveloped countries are a compensation for the unwillingness of the former to consider the alternative way of improving the labour to resources ratio, movement of the labour to the resources. The fact that development is a second-best policy in this respect may impose severe limitations on its efficiency and rapidity.

To conclude, I have been concerned with the role of the market in economic development; and I have aimed at stressing the economic functions of the market, in automatically taking decisions about various kinds of allocations of economic resources, and the place in economic development programmes of improvements in market

[4] See J. E. Meade, *The Theory of International Economic Policy, Volume II: Trade and Welfare* (London: Oxford University Press, 1955), and R. G. Lipsey and Kelvin Lancaster, 'The General Theory of Second Best', *Review of Economic Studies*, XXIV(1), no. 63, 1956–57, 11–33.

organization and methods. I have been advocating, not a policy of *laissez-faire*, but recognition of the market as an administrative instrument that is relatively cheap to operate and may therefore be efficient in spite of objectionable features of its operations. The general assumption on which I have been arguing is that economic development is a process of co-operation between the state and private enterprise, and that the problem is to devise the best possible mixture.

VIII

THE POLITICAL ECONOMY OF OPULENCE*

'Economics is the science which studies human behaviour as a relationship between ends and scarce means which have alternative uses.'[1] Lionel Robbins' well-known definition of their subject is one which most economists would probably accept, at least as a description of their workaday activities. The definition allows—and it was specifically framed by its author to allow—for the pursuit of other ends than purely material ends; but in practice economists devote themselves predominantly to the study of the allocation of material means between ends conceived and defined in material terms. Inherent in the way economists set about their task is the implicit assumption that material means are scarce and material wants are pressing—in short that economic society is materially poor, and resources must not be wasted.

This assumption permeates the theoretical apparatus of the subject: it also directs what economists have to say about economic policy. In the debate which has been going on over the general problem of inflation, for example, economists have been divided between those who stress the loss of production and potential growth of output that results from anything less than full employment of labour, and those who stress the loss of production and potential growth of output that results from the misallocation of resources brought about by inflation. Again, in making comparisons between the Russian and Western economic systems, economists have generally tended to accept as their standard of performance the rate of growth of output per head, a standard which gives away most of

* *Canadian Journal of Economics and Political Science*, 26, no. 4, November 1960, 552–64.

[1] Lionel Robbins, *An Essay on the Nature and Significance of Economic Science*, Second Edition (London: Macmillan, 1935), 16.

the positive points on the Western side. In both cases, the adoption of the output standard implicitly assumes that the economic problem is of prime importance.

The assumption that the economic problem is of prime importance is obviously gratifying to the self-esteem of the economics profession; but that does not necessarily make it valid. It has in fact been powerfully challenged in Professor J. K. Galbraith's book of two years ago, *The Affluent Society*.[2] No doubt many of you have read this book; at the very least you must have heard it mentioned in the cocktail-party conversation of those people who can afford to read only one book a month. Nevertheless, I shall summarize it briefly, since it forms the starting point of this paper.

Galbraith argues that classical economics was formed in and shaped by an atmosphere of grinding poverty for the mass of the population. In that environment, the economic problem appeared as a tripartite one: the inadequacy of production, which expressed the prevalence of poverty and the grimness of the human lot; the inequality of distribution, which accentuated the insufficiency of production to provide more than a miserable standard of living for the masses; and the insecurity of income, which reinforced the misery of inadequacy. Accordingly, the problem of economic policy was to increase production and mitigate inequality and insecurity: and since scarcity of resources was the apparent cause of poverty, and the more efficient use of these resources the way to increase production, the need to increase production placed severe limits on the pursuit of policies aimed directly at overcoming inequality and insecurity.

Production, inequality, and insecurity were the economic problems of the nineteenth century. But, Galbraith argues, these problems are no longer with us. Technological progress on the one hand, and the modern corporation on the other, have solved the problem of production. At the same time, the rising trend of average income has both rendered inequality of income less blatantly obvious and removed its social and political sting; while the expansion of production, together with the development of the social conscience, has pretty well solved the problem of insecurity.

But the solution of the economic problems of the nineteenth century through expansion of production raises new problems, because this solution involves our economic society in a rat-race in which people have to be persuaded by high-powered advertising and hidden persuasion to buy the goods which the business men think up to produce. Real scarcity has been succeeded by contrived scarcity, and the successful functioning of the economy depends on reiterating

[2] J. K. Galbraith, *The Affluent Society* (London: Hamish Hamilton, 1958).

the contrivance. One consequence is the growth of consumption financed on the instalment plan, and the associated increase in potential instability of the economy. Another is the problem of chronic inflation, which is associated with the fact that the solution of all three nineteenth-century problems is tied to keeping individuals employed at high pay. Most important, the necessity of, and insistence on, sustained expansion of production carries with it a number of attitudes inimical to sensible economic policy. The old emphasis on efficiency leads to bitter opposition to efforts by entrepreneurs, farmers, and workers to increase their security of income by price agreements, government subsidies and restrictive practices of various kinds. Luxurious living, which drives the whole machine, becomes the necessary cost of production, so that the margin of resources available for social uses such as defence is unduly small in relation to national income. In particular, the assumption that it is private consumption that counts, together with the emphasis on the scarcity of resources and the need for efficiency, creates strong resistance to the provision of public services and collective consumption goods by tax-financed governmental activity.

Thus Galbraith's argument; and I must say that I find it extremely convincing, at least in its broad outline. It is, I believe, important to recognize that, judged by any reasonable historical or comparative standard, the citizens of the Western industrial countries are in fact very well off, that the economic problem is not all that pressing, and that the belief that it is leads economists (and the general public, in its views on economic matters) into inconsistencies and false positions on economic policy. In insisting on these points, Galbraith is performing an important service—regardless of what one thinks of his choice of audience to which to address himself, and the tone in which he writes. Nor can his argument be dismissed by pointing out what is true, that the force of his reasoning assumes the continuation of an unequal distribution of income, a relatively low level of social services and public investment in education, a limited defence effort, and a limited contribution to the assistance of underdeveloped economies. All of these are things which important sections of public opinion (including Galbraith himself)[3] would like to see changed, and the changing of which could make the growth of production of pressing importance; but as there seems little prospect that they will be changed at all radically, to make a point of them is to miss the point. The point is that we live in a rich society, which nevertheless in many respects insists on thinking and acting as if it were a poor society.

[3] *Ibid.*, Chaps. 18–25.

Not only do I believe that Galbraith is right in emphasizing the fact of affluence; I also think there is much justice in his claim that economics is not adjusted to this central fact of modern life. But—and this 'but' is not, I hope, entirely due to my inability to multiply my academic income by writing a best-selling denunciation of my profession—I think he goes much too far in asserting that marginal production is of no real use to people, so that economics is of no importance. Moreover, he lets himself off much too easily by contenting himself with satirizing demand theory; indeed, he makes a serious error in contending that the indifference curve technique precludes the notion of a hierarchy of more and less essential wants[4]—though it is, I suppose, barely conceivable that Harvard has not yet heard of the Engel curve. And he offers no suggestions on what economists might usefully occupy themselves with, in the affluent society.

This brings me to the subject of this paper. Suppose we start from the Galbraith view of the economy, as one which is well off and tending to grow progressively more so, more or less automatically, through the institutionalization of capital accumulation and technical progress in the modern corporation. (If the idea of starting from Galbraith is distasteful, one can start equally well from W. W. Rostow's recent book, *The Stages of Economic Growth*,[5] according to which the United States and other advanced countries have embarked on the historical phase of high mass consumption, in which compound-interest growth is built into the structure of the economy.) Then how should economic doctrine be formulated, to be as illuminating as possible a guide to the economic system of such an economy?

Economics so formulated I call 'the political economy of opulence'. The term 'opulence' goes back at least as far as Adam Smith, who uses it occasionally as a synonym for wealth; this brings the subject into the grand tradition of English classical economics. I use the term 'political economy', instead of the more recent 'economics' or the more technical 'economic theory', as an excuse for a broad, discursive political-philosophical approach, and a willingness to deal with difficult theoretical questions by sage circumlocution; this brings the subject still more into the grand tradition of English classical economics. I am not, however, prepared to follow that

[4] *Ibid.*, Chap. 10, sec. 4, 115–18.

[5] W. W. Rostow, *The Stages of Economic Growth* (Cambridge: Cambridge University Press, 1960). An abridged version, under the title 'Rostow on Economic Growth', may be found in *The Economist*, CXCII, no. 6051, August 1959, 409–16.

tradition all the way into the adumbration of a complete system of thought, suitable for entombment in an 871-page volume, the sapience of whose footnotes could only be fully appreciated after two generations of careful study.[6] Instead, I shall skim through the main branches of an elementary course in economic principles, suggesting ways of looking at various problems which seem to me more fruitful and enlightening than the ways in which these problems are generally treated. Much of what I shall say, however, is merely a restatement of approaches which can already be found in the literature.

The logical place to begin is with the theory of consumption and demand. This is also the most interesting place to begin, since it is on the consumption side that the phenomena and special problems of opulence appear most clearly, and economic theory seems most remote from reality.

The theory of demand is a johnny-come-lately in economic analysis. Its master-creator, Alfred Marshall (hallowed be his name), approached it from a broadly sociological, if somewhat stuffily Victorian, point of view. Since his time, however, the trend has been to reduce the theory of demand to the bare logic of choice. We assume an individual of given preferences, or at least of a given consistency, choosing between different given commodities, endowed with a given income and facing given prices. The main conclusion to which the theory leads is that the demand curve slopes downwards —except that it may not.

I submit that the juice has long since been squeezed from this particular *lemma,* and that there is a great deal to be gained in the way of understanding how the economy works by turning from sharpening our axioms to developing the implications of the generalization laid down by Marshall (in Book III, chapter II of the *Principles,* before the marginal utility and the tea-drinking set in): 'although it is man's wants in the earliest stages of his development that give rise to his activities, yet afterwards each new step upwards is to be regarded as the development of new activities giving rise to new wants, rather than of new wants giving rise to new activities.'[7] In other words, the purpose of economic organization is not merely to satisfy wants, but to create wants. Further, in assessing the nature of the system from the point of view of welfare, it is I think important to keep in mind a notion which has been stressed for many years by F. H. Knight, that one of the basic human social character-

[6] Compare for example Alfred Marshall, *Principles of Economics,* Eighth Edition (London: Macmillan, 1920, xxxiv+871).

[7] *Ibid.,* 89.

istics is a continuing desire to improve and educate one's tastes.[8]

Progress takes the form both of satisfying wants more fully, and of raising the standard of wants. In technical jargon, it is expressed both in improvements in the production function, and in improvements in the consumption function. A natural corollary is that, just as it pays the entrepreneur to invest in improving the technique of production in order to adjust the product more profitably to the want, so it pays him to invest in improving the technique of consumption in order to adjust the want more profitably to the product; in short, it pays to advertise. In both cases, 'improvement' from the standpoint of the producer's profit may consist in adulteration as udged by some objective standard of performance.

The fact that wants are created, and not original with the individual, raises a fundamental philosophical problem whether the satisfaction of wants created by those who satisfy them can be regarded as a social gain. This is a question which is ignored, and hence implicitly answered in the affirmative, by welfare economics of both the older 'superiority of the competitive system' and the newer 'subsidy, tax, and lump sum redistribution' varieties, both of which assume stable and independently-given consumer preferences. Yet it is a question which has persistently troubled observers of the influence of advertising; and it is a crucial question for the age of opulence, one of whose chief characteristics is the promotion of wants by advertising.

To begin with, it must I think be recognized that the creation of wants by advertising does not by itself justify dismissing these particular wants as inferior to others, or the resources required to gratify them as wasted. All economically relevant wants are learned, and, what is more important, all better taste has to be acquired by study and practice. Even the presumption that one knows better than other people what is good for them, which underlies a large part of the argument of Galbraith and other critics of advertising and is formalized in the distinction drawn by the Cambridge school between rational and irrational preferences,[9] is acquired by education—the best education, of course. Thus the problem of whether the creation and satisfaction of wants by advertised production constitutes a genuine increase in welfare cannot be settled simply by distinguishing base material from elevated spiritual types of wants, and asserting the priority of the latter over the former. Rather, the

[8] See F. H. Knight, *The Ethics of Competition* (London: George Allen and Unwin, 1935), especially 'Ethics and the Economic Interpretation', 19–40.

[9] R. F. Kahn, 'Some Notes on Ideal Output', *Economic Journal*, XLV, no. 177, March 1935, 1–35, especially 24ff.

answer depends in both cases on whether there exist generally accepted standards for distinguishing better from worse taste, standards which can themselves be learned, and a social process by which such standards are in fact learned and enforced. I am myself inclined to the view that the creation and satisfaction of wants by advertised production does result in social gain, on the grounds that there are generally accepted standards for distinguishing meretriciously from genuinely superior products, and, equally important, that there are social and governmental processes which set to work when the exploitation of helpless consumers becomes flagrant. If this be denied for commercial products, I do not see how it can be asserted for educational, cultural, and artistic activities.

The creation of wants raises serious problems for welfare economics and for any theory of economic policy. It also raises problems for positive economics, by making it difficult to predict the direction of evolution of demand.[10] This difficulty is aggravated by the tautological fact that increasing income implies the gratification of less and less essential wants. In particular, the margin of want-satisfaction tends to move from the physiological to the psychological and sociological: the physiological needs are satiated, the psychological and sociological become necessities, while the luxuries are psychiatric —hence the Hidden Persuaders and Motivational Research.[11] The sociological emphasis inherent in a high-consumption economy is further reinforced by the hierarchical nature of the bureaucratic production unit which makes opulence possible—to the Organization Man, goods are status symbols, to be bought and used as such.[12]

The consequence of these characteristics of opulence is that the most interesting (and commercially valuable) problems of demand analysis may well lie outside the present static and physiologically orientated concepts of consumer theory. Nevertheless, it seems to me that more can be done with the existing tools of economic analysis in analysing demand in the age of opulence than is usually done. Notably, a great deal more understanding can be derived by regarding consumption typically as the process of enjoying the services of consumer capital, rather than as the consumption of a flow of perishable goods. Not tea, but TV, is the exemplary commodity of the age of opulence.

[10] For a more extended discussion of the problems raised for both normative and positive economics by the creation of wants, with particular reference to advertising, see my 'The Consumer and Madison Avenue', *Current Economic Comment*, 22, no. 3, August 1960, 3–10.

[11] See Vance Packard, *The Hidden Persuaders* (New York: D. McKay, 1957).

[12] See W. H. Whyte, *The Organization Man* (New York: Simon and Schuster, 1956).

To conceive of the typical consumer good as an item of consumer capital equipment requires a number of significant changes in the analysis of consumer choices. In the first place, as Boulding emphasized in his *Reconstruction of Economics*,[13] it is necessary to distinguish between purchases and consumption, the two being separated by a stock of consumer capital. This distinction leads in a number of directions. In cycle theory, it points to the possibility of consumer inventory cycles, and to the possible importance of consumers' price expectations in the mechanism of conventional business cycles. In national income theory, it raises the fundamental question of what the national income as conventionally calculated really means: a country which is producing a stable output a substantial proportion of which consists of new consumer durables is really enjoying a rising standard of living; and a country which has a large stock of consumer durables has a war potential greater than its national income figures would indicate, since consumer capital permits both goods and labour time to be diverted from household consumption in time of emergency.

In the second place, the existence of consumer capital makes it necessary to distinguish in conventional demand theory between short-run and long-run adjustment, thus reintroducing a distinction between the short-run and long-run demand curve which was rejected by Marshall in spite of the attractive parallel with his treatment of supply.[14] The distinction between the short-run and long-run demand curve is necessary in two connections. First, the use of consumer durables involves a lumpy investment expenditure followed by a flow of maintenance expenditure which is determined by the durable's length of life, which is itself dependent on the price of the commodity. Consequently a change in the price of the good will have both a short-run effect on demand through altering the optimal length of life of the existing stock, and a long-run effect on demand through altering the stock of capital of this type that is desired. Second, the use of services of consumer durables in the consumer's consumption pattern implies that the consumer has the same problem of short-run fixity of capital equipment as the producer, so that the response of demand to a fall in the price of a currently consumed good (which may be either complementary with the services of consumer capital or an input into the capital-using

[13] K. E. Boulding, *A Reconstruction of Economics* (New York: Wiley, 1950), especially Chap. 8, 135–54.

[14] Marshall, in a letter to Edgeworth dated April 26, 1928, explains that he 'deliberately decided that temporary demand curves . . . would not be of any practical use'.

consumption process, such as fuel or power) will not be complete until the capital stock is adjusted to permit full advantage to be taken of the price reduction.[15]

In the third place, the prevalence of consumer capital makes the rate of interest, and the terms of credit which surround it, a much more significant determinant of consumer purchases, both in pattern and in total, than it is conventionally considered to be—the rate of interest may well be more important, as a determinant of the relative costs of substitutes and complements, than the prices of the goods themselves. In this connection, incidentally, the conception of consumption as using the services of capital goods provides a rationale for instalment buying, a practice often still condemned as mortgaging the future: there is no reason why a rational consumer should pay for his consumption in advance, by paying cash for capital goods, rather than concurrently, as he enjoys the services of those capital goods.

As I have already mentioned, the more interesting problems of demand in the age of opulence are concerned with the evolution of demand as wealth increases. Here the assumption that consumption is typically the consumption of the services of capital seems particularly illuminating. Progress, whether the result of capital accumulation or of technical progress, tends to cheapen commodities, and particularly the more durable commodities, in terms of labour, and consequently to encourage the substitution of capital-intensive for labour-intensive methods of satisfying consumer wants. The technique of consumption consequently tends to become progressively more capital-intensive. This increase in capital-intensity of consumption manifests itself in two contrasting ways.[16] On the one hand, there is the shift of labour services out of the household into the factory or service enterprise, where they can be more efficiently armed with capital. The most outstanding example of this is probably the development of the preparation and cooking, and even service, of food outside the home. On the other hand, there is the

[15] For a fuller analysis of the theory of demand for consumers' durables, see, for example, J. S. Cramer, 'A Dynamic Approach to the Theory of Consumer Demand', *Review of Economic Studies*, XXIV(2), no. 64, February 1957, 73–86; Richard Stone and D. A. Rowe, 'The Market Demand for Durable Goods', *Econometrica*, 25, no. 3, July 1957, 423–43; Hans Neisser, 'The Pricing of Consumers' Durables', *Econometrica*, 27, no. 4, October 1959, 547–74; Arnold C. Harberger (ed.), *The Demand for Durable Goods* (Chicago: University of Chicago Press, 1960).

[16] I am indebted for this notion to G. A. Elliott, 'The Impersonal Market', *Canadian Journal of Economics and Political Science*, 24, no. 4, November 1958, 453–64, especially 461–2.

replacement of labour service inside and outside the home by capital equipment in the home operated by the consumer. The most outstanding examples of this are entertainment devices, cleaning equipment, and do-it-yourself repair and maintenance equipment. The household thus tends to become a fully automated utility factory (apart from the managerial services of the householders themselves), a tendency which is undoubtedly fostered by the influence of high income-taxation and the special tax advantages enjoyed by householders.

The tendency of the household to become an automated utility factory through the substitution of capital for labour is associated with, and reinforces, two other features of the modern consumption pattern—the suburbanization of living, and the tendency to earlier marriages and larger families. Suburbanization is dependent on private transport facilities, convenient domestic storage capacity, and the conversion of electricity into power inside the home, all of which assume substantial capital investment; the familial trend, in addition, exploits economies of scale in the use of household capital.

So far, I have been suggesting the desirability of treating consumption as typically meaning consumption of the services of durable equipment, rather than of perishable commodities. To do so, however, is to stick to the classical view of consumer's choice as being mostly concerned with choices among commodities and labour services. I would now like to suggest that an increasingly important consumption good in the age of opulence is not a commodity or a labour service, but the use of one's own time, which opulence makes increasingly valuable by comparison with commodities. Choice of the use of one's time has three aspects. The first is the choice of how to employ one's working time. Here increasing opulence tends to make the non-pecuniary aspects of employment—working conditions and social considerations—more important as compared with the monetary rewards, a tendency which affects the supply of labour services from the household. The second is the division of time between working and leisure time, which includes length of working life as well as days and hours per week. Here the fact that the enjoyment of commodities and the availability of leisure in which to enjoy them are complementary, once basic physical maintenance is assured, implies a relative reduction in working as contrasted with leisure time as opulence progresses. The third is the choice of leisure-time activities. Here, the cheapening of commodities in terms of labour which I have already mentioned implies an increasingly capital-intensive use of leisure; this trend is exemplified in the growth of domestic and foreign travel, holiday resorts, and sports requiring expensive capital equipment.

Let me now turn from the theory of demand to another branch of economic principles, the theory of production and the firm. Despite the rise to dominance of the corporate form of enterprise, the theory of production still generally takes as its central unit of analysis the Marshallian firm. This is a small and essentially anonymous enterprise in which decisions are centralized in the hands of an 'entrepreneur'; and its main problem is conceived to be the choice of the optimum combination of factors to insert into a given production function to produce a given product. This conception is not fundamentally altered by Chamberlin's extension of it to include choice of the most profitable combination of product quality and advertising expenditure,[17] and more recent elaborations of the theory of multiple production. I suggest that both the unit of analysis and the conception of the decision-problem it faces need to be adapted to conform more closely to the facts of the corporation economy.

As to the unit of analysis: the Marshallian firm, it will be recalled, was likened by its author to a tree in the forest, each tree growing and dying in due course while the forest—which represented the industry in the analogy—retained its same outline.[18] The forest analogy will still serve for the corporation economy, provided, first, that the analogy is drawn for the economy as a whole and not the industry; and, second, that one thinks, not of a deciduous English forest, but of a California redwood forest, in which each tree is an individual distinct from the others, survives unless some disaster befalls it or the forest, and so long as it survives continues to grow in a competitive struggle to survive among its growing fellows. To drop the analogy, the corporation is not mortal, with a life cycle of vigour and senility which passes through a phase of maturity, but immortal and continually growing, provided that no disasters occur and its organization remains efficient.

This last proviso points to one of the key differences between the problems facing the corporation and those facing the firm as theoretically conceived. The corporation, in contrast to the single-minded Marshallian entrepreneur, is a large organization with a hierarchical administrative and decision-taking structure. One of its most important problems is to achieve and maintain an effective internal organization, which will secure both co-ordination and flexibility.[19] A second key difference is that, in contrast to the entre-

[17] E. H. Chamberlin, *The Theory of Monopolistic Competition* (Cambridge: Harvard University Press, 1933).

[18] Marshall, *op. cit.*, 315–17.

[19] Cf. A. G. Papandreou, 'Some Basic Problems in the Theory of the Firm', Chap. 5 in B. F. Haley (ed.), *A Survey of Contemporary Economics, Volume II* (Homewood: Richard D. Irwin, 1952).

preneur, who is assumed to be financially self-sufficient, the corporation is dependent on the capital market for finance, and this dependence imposes on it a built-in obligation to grow: as W. J. Baumol has argued in his recent book *Business Behaviour, Value and Growth*, the fact that success is immediately capitalized in a rise in the market value of a company's shares means that the company's executives cannot be content with one successful decision, but must go on making successful decisions to please the stockholders.[20] The need to grow points to a third key characteristic of the corporation as contrasted with the conceptual firm: in order to continue to grow, the corporation must both foster and adapt itself to the growth of the market, through the introduction of new products, the improvement of old products, and the extension of the range of products it offers; thus research, including both technological and marketing research, and selling activities, rather than physical production *per se*, are the vital activities of the corporation. Effective organization, satisfactory growth, and profitable change, rather than minimization of cost for a given production function and maximization of profit for a given demand, are the key problems of the productive unit in the opulent society. Correspondingly, the technique of organization it adopts in the pursuit of satisfactory growth through profitable change, rather than the technological or market characteristics of the products it produces, is the fundamental distinguishing characteristic of the corporate enterprise.

Let me now turn from the theory of value to the theory of distribution. The classical theory of distribution originated by Ricardo ran in terms of categories of income earned by factors which contributed recognizably distinct types of service to the production process and shared in the output in proportion to the values of their contributions to it, factors which, moreover, could be identified in the real world with definite social groups.[21] Initially three factors were distinguished, land, labour, and capital, receiving for their services incomes in the form of rent, wages and profits; later, the capital factor was separated into two components, pure capital and entrepreneurship (the management of capital embodied in specific real form), a corresponding distinction being drawn between interest and profits. The resulting picture of distribution was logical, simple, and conformable to common-sense observation; but it began to

[20] W. J. Baumol, *Business Behavior, Value and Growth* (New York: Macmillan, 1959), Chap. 10, 88–100, especially sec. 4, 93–5.

[21] For a critique of modern theory stressing this aspect of the Ricardian system, see M. H. Dobb, *Political Economy and Capitalism* (New York: International Publishers, 1945).

dissolve under closer theoretical scrutiny even as it was being perfected. Marshall began the rot, and inaugurated neo-classical distribution theory, by elaborating the principle that rent is not peculiar to land, but is the ubiquitous consequence of specificity and immobility of factors of production.[22] Fisher showed that interest, properly considered, is not a category of income but a means of relating the time-stream of income earned by a factor's services to the capital value of the factor, which is applicable to all factors and not simply to capital as generally understood.[23] Schumpeter and Knight showed that true profit is not an income earned by rendering productive services, but a capital gain resulting from the successful undertaking of contractual obligations in the face of uncertainty about the future.[24] Thus three of the four concepts of income distribution theory no longer match the categories of income distribution; and consequently the theory of distribution is, to put it mildly, in a rather unsatisfactory state.

Apart from the force of intellectual tradition, the main reason why the classical categories remain embedded in the theory of distribution seems to be that economists accept the classical notion of labour as a unique original factor of production, distinct on the one hand from other original factors in the shape of natural resources, and on the other hand from produced means of production in the shape of capital goods. This acceptance is explainable by the institutional fact that democracies expressly prohibit markets in human capital (so that only the services of labour are marketed whereas capital goods themselves rather than their services are typically bought and sold) and also by the liberal anthropocentricity of social science and the stereotyped concept of 'labour' employed in socialist political philosophy. But the notion of labour as an original factor of production is not necessarily economically sensible; on the contrary, the progress of opulence makes the concept less and less acceptable as a reasonable theoretical approximation. In the England of the Industrial Revolution, as in the underdeveloped countries today, labour could be reasonably be thought of predominantly as the application of crude human force, with which individual labourers

[22] Marshall, *op. cit.*, Book V, Chaps. 8–12.

[23] Irving Fisher, *The Nature of Capital and Income* (New York and London: Macmillan, 1906).

[24] J. Schumpeter, *The Theory of Economic Development*, translated from the German by Redvers Opie (Cambridge: Harvard University Press, 1934); F. H. Knight, *Risk, Uncertainty and Profit* (Boston and New York: Houghton Mifflin, 1921). For an interesting reformulation of the theory of profit on Schumpeterian lines, see R. Triffin, *Monopolistic Competition and General Equilibrium Theory* (Cambridge: Harvard University Press, 1940), esp. Chap. V, 158–87.

could be assumed to be roughly equally endowed, together with some decision-taking of a rather trivial kind. But in an advancing industrial society both the provision of force and the elementary decision-taking are increasingly taken over by machinery, while what the worker brings to his task are the knowledge and skill required to use machinery effectively. His knowledge and skill in turn are the product of a capital investment in his education in the general capacities of communication and calculation required for participation in the productive process, and the specific capacities required for the individual job, a capital investment which is variously financed by the state, the worker himself, and the employer. Thus the labourer is himself a produced means of production, an item of capital equipment. As capital equipment, labour differs from non-human capital in that a human being is necessarily present when his services are used in production; this means, on the one hand, that labour is inherently a more flexible instrument of production than machinery, on the other that its supply to particular employments is influenced significantly—and likely to be increasingly influenced as opulence progresses—by non-pecuniary considerations.

I suggest, therefore, that the time has come to sever the link with the classical attempt to identify categories of income with distinctly different kinds of productive factors; and that a more useful approach would be to lump all factors together as items of capital equipment, created by past investment and rendering current services to production. The exceptions are not important: 'the original and indestructible properties of the soil'[25] are now a threadbare unscientific myth, and human genius is rare enough to be ignored in the broad picture. Such an approach does not require the sacrifice of the concepts of classical income-distribution theory; on the contrary, these concepts appear as illuminating ways of looking at the price of factor services. The current price of a factor's services can be divided conceptually into two elements: the payment necessary to keep the factor in existence (or in a particular employment)[26] corresponding to the classical notion of 'wages'; and a surplus above that necessary payment, arising from scarcity of the factor and corresponding to the classical notion of 'rent'. Considered as a return on the capital investment incurred in creating the factor, the current price can be resolved analytically into interest on the capital

[25] David Ricardo, *On the Principles of Political Economy and Taxation* (P. Sraffa (ed.), *The Works and Correspondence of David Ricardo*, Vol. I (Cambridge: Cambridge University Press, 1951)), 67.

[26] Cf. Joan Robinson, *The Economics of Imperfect Competition* (London: Macmillan, 1933), Chap. 8, 102–19.

invested, and a residual corresponding to the profit or loss resulting from the entrepreneurial decision to invest capital in the specific form represented by the factor. This formulation, incidentally, clarifies the difference between wages and rent, which are income concepts, and interest and profits, which are capital concepts.

The revised approach to the theory of distribution which I am suggesting has the advantages of greater generality and logical simplicity; it also has important substantive implications. In particular, the conception of labour as a produced rather than an original factor implies that much of modern macro-economic theory has been concerned with problems that are wrongly formulated, if not entirely spurious. I refer especially to the theory of economic growth, where a great deal of intellectual effort has been devoted to exploring the difficulties of reconciling the accumulation of capital with the growth of the labour force at a different, autonomously determined rate,[27] and explaining the constancy of the share of labour which apparently results from the growth process.[28] These problems are in large part created by the classical apparatus itself, with its treatment of labour as an original factor and its identification of capital with the stock of capital equipment;[29] they present an altogether different appearance once labour as well as capital equipment is recognized as a medium of investment.[30] A similar criticism applies to the prevailing economists' conception of the problem of promoting the economic development of underdeveloped countries, which rests on an extremely questionable identification of development with the accumulation of physical, and primarily industrial, capital.[31]

[27] E.g. R. F. Harrod, *Towards a Dynamic Economics* (London: Macmillan, 1948), and the voluminous journal literature which has grown from it; W. J. Fellner, *Trends and Cycles in Economic Activity* (New York: Henry Holt, 1956); Joan Robinson, *The Accumulation of Capital* (London: Macmillan, 1956).

[28] See M. Kalecki, 'The Determinants of Distribution of National Income', *Econometrica*, 6, no. 2, April 1938, 97–112; also N. Kaldor, 'Alternative Theories of Distribution', *Review of Economic Studies*, Vol. XXIII(2), no. 61, February 1956, 83–100. Whether the share is constant enough to pose a problem is a matter for legitimate scepticism: compare J. T. Dunlop, *Wage Determination Under Trade Unions* (New York: Macmillan, 1944), chap. VIII, 149–91, and R. M. Solow, 'A Skeptical Note on the Constancy of Relative Shares', *American Economic Review*, XLVIII, no. 4, September 1958, 618–31.

[29] This remark is not inconsistent with the fact that interest in both problems is an outgrowth of the Keynesian Revolution, since Keynes was extraordinarily classical in his treatment of production, as evidenced by his use of the wage unit.

[30] This point has been mentioned in connection with the constant share problem by Solow (*loc. cit.*, 630).

[31] The identification of development with capital accumulation permeates the folklore of development planning, with its emphasis on investment programming, capital : output ratios, 'infra-structure', industrialization, 'balanced growth', and the like.

In this paper I have been concerned with the question of how economic principles can most usefully be formulated to fit the facts of economic life in the age of opulence. The main suggestions I have made call for explicit recognition of the role of capital in two contexts—consumption, and the nature of labour—where its importance is growing in fact but tends to be ignored in contemporary theory. In concluding, I should like to comment briefly on a subject which lies outside the range of economic principles but still within the scope of political economy as I conceive it, the implications of the economic system of opulence for the political and social life of the opulent society. Application of Marx's general analytical method to the system of corporate industrial production suggests, not the polarization and eventual breakdown of capitalist society that he predicted, but the consolidation of a highly differentiated hierarchical society in which status is determined ultimately by educational attainment. The gloomier implications of this form of social organization have been elaborated in a number of contemporary works, ranging from Burnham's *Managerial Revolution* through Riesman's *Lonely Crowd* and Whyte's *Organization Man* to Young's *Rise of the Meritocracy*.[32] But it is possible to take a more favourable view. While it is not true, despite the efforts of the apologists of corporate enterprise to persuade us to the contrary by adroit use of stock ownership statistics, that the masses are becoming capitalists in the sense of owning and controlling the means of production they use, it is true that they are becoming capitalists on an increasing scale in two other ways—as owners of consumption capital, and as possessors of educated skills. Thus, though the productive structure remains hierarchical, the political and social systems may nevertheless move in the direction of the ideal democratic free society.[33]

[32] James Burnham, *The Managerial Revolution* (New York: John Day, 1941); David Riesman, *The Lonely Crowd* (New Haven: Yale University Press, 1950); W. H. Whyte, *op. cit.*; Michael Young, *The Rise of the Meritocracy, 1870–2033* (London: Thames and Hudson, 1958); see also Vance Packard, *The Status Seekers* (New York: D. McKay, 1959).

[33] The argument is that ownership of capital in these two forms, and also in the form of financial assets, promotes the independence necessary for effective democratic citizenship; also that participation in the capitalist system is pluralist. It can, however, be argued on the other side that wealth breeds indifference and self-indulgence, exemplified in the opulent society by the problems of alcoholism, obesity, divorce, and automobile accidents; compare the pessimistic views of Dennis Gabor, 'Inventing the Future', *Encounter*, XIV, no. 5, May 1960, 3–16, especially 14ff.

IX

THE SOCIAL POLICY OF AN OPULENT SOCIETY

In the past ten years or so our ideas about the nature of the society in which we live have been changing rapidly. We have become aware that we are an opulent society, by any comparative or historical standard, and that we are becoming progressively more opulent as time goes on, as a more or less automatic consequence of the way our economic institutions function. At the same time, we have become aware that the ultimate sources of our large and growing wealth are very different from what the conventional wisdom of our times would have us believe; that they are to be found not in the individual parsimony and hard labour of our public imagery but in the accumulation of capital and application of technical progress by corporate enterprises and the acquisition of increasing skill and knowledge by individuals—the accumulation of human capital.

Our ideas about social policy have not been adapted to the facts of life in the opulent society. In saying this I am not simply referring to the point made by J. K. Galbraith in his powerful and provocative book *The Affluent Society*,[1] that an opulent society can afford to spend liberally on social security and collective consumption, and to tolerate any inefficiencies that result from such liberality, though that is true enough. I want to make the more fundamental point that our approach to social policy is still dominated by an individualistic conception of our society that might have been appropriate, or at least the best that could be managed, in the early stages of development of modern industrial society, but is certainly not appropriate now. This individualistic conception of society is most in evidence in the opposition of various sections of public opinion, notably business groups, to the spending of public money for almost any social

[1] J. K. Galbraith, *The Affluent Society* (London: Hamish Hamilton, 1958).

purpose—what one might call the rugged individualism of the directors' dining room, the prestige advertisement, and the expense-account business convention. But it also permeates the social security and welfare services that have been built up in spite of the rugged individualists. It is implicit in the two main concepts of our social security system, the insurance principle and the social minimum—as is evident from the most elaborate rationalization of these concepts available, that contained in the Beveridge Report.[2] The insurance principle seeks to disguise something that is not insurance, but the imposition of a special kind of income tax earmarked to finance special kinds of income transfers, in words acceptable to an individualistic philosophy. Insofar as true insurance principles are applied, by proportioning benefits drawn to contributions made, the result is inadequate provision of social security, and a need for supplementary social assistance. The social minimum principle conforms to individualism in its implication that the minimum is the maximum the state should provide, the individual being responsible for anything above it. Both principles, and indeed the prevalent philosophy of social policy, see the role of social policy essentially as that of mopping up the milk spilt by the system of private decision-taking. In that respect, our philosophy of social policy is the same as that of the nineteenth century; the principal difference, and it is an important one, is that in this century we have become much more critical in deciding how much spilt milk it takes to make a mess.

Now, I want to make it perfectly clear at the outset that I am not arguing in any sense against the liberal democratic ideal of individual self-development in a free society. On the contrary, my arguments will rest on that ideal. What I am arguing against is the naïve and unrealistic view of the relation of the individual to society on which we attempt to base the expression of that ideal in our social policy. We assume, in effect, that ours is a simple, stable, and relatively unchanging society, in which the normal individual arrives at maturity equipped with the capacity and knowledge to make the most of himself. We do assist him to take a place in society by providing a free education up to the secondary level and forcing him to accept it up to a certain age; we have been forced grudgingly to recognize contingencies—unemployment, old age, large family size and most recently hospital expenses—for which the individual may be unable or unwilling to provide; and we recognize that some individuals may be incompetent or unlucky enough to need help. But we assume

[2] Sir William Beveridge, *Social Insurance and Allied Services* (London: HMSO, 1942), Part I, 5–20.

that, by and large, the individual can and should be expected to cope with the society in which he lives; and that the society will operate efficiently if he is left, and preferably forced, to do so.

The realities of life in the opulent society are, I suggest, far different from the simple model on which our social philosophy is based. Far from being simple and easily comprehensible to the average person, our society is one of tremendously complex interdependence between people each of whom is specialized on a small part of the process of production, distribution and exchange. It is this specialization that provides our high standard of living. Far from being stable and relatively unchanging, our society is characterized by irregular, unpredictable growth and change; indeed, its basic dynamic principle is growth through change, change introduced by any person or firm that sees a profit in it. It is this freedom to introduce change that keeps our standard of living rising.

Complexity and dynamic change are the characteristics of the opulent society and the source of its opulence. But it takes only a little thought to realize how seriously these characteristics undermine the assumption of individual responsibility and capacity to cope with society. At this point I should stop talking about the individual, who is a nineteenth-century political fiction elaborated when only *men* counted for anything in society, and start talking about the family, which is really our basic social unit. Now the family in our society originates as a biological unit and not an economic one; and the more opulent we have become, the more personal preferences and social considerations rather than economic calculation have come to determine the selection of marriage partners, and the more too has the family been stripped down to its central core of parents and children. Yet in our individualistic system the family is entrusted with economic responsibilities that are of crucial importance to the welfare and progress of the opulent society. It is the basic spending unit, whose decisions determine whether increasing opulence will raise the quality of life or debase it; the income it has to spend is obtained by selling the services of its members and their property, so that its decisions in this regard determine both its income and the efficiency with which its human and non-human capital is used; and it determines the amount and type of education acquired by its children, so that collectively it determines the size and quality of the stock of human capital bequeathed to the next generation.

In a complex, rich, growing and changing society these are all difficult decisions requiring a high degree of knowledge, intelligence and foresight, and also the ability to command capital. The capacity of the family to undertake these responsibilities effectively is limited to start with by its small size as an economic unit and by its mode of formation. Its capacity is further limited by the fact that our free society prohibits it from dealing in what is usually its most important asset, human capital, with the same freedom as it can deal in non-human capital: you cannot sell your daughter into slavery to keep the family from starving, and you cannot sell your son to someone who will invest in his education. The small economic size of the family also makes its welfare dependent to an important extent on the physical and social environment in which it lives, and over which it has little control. Finally, the narrow economic base of the family, its dependence for income on the sale of the services of its head or heads, renders its income and welfare extremely vulnerable to the human risks of illness, accident, and death, and the economic risks resulting from either the freedom for change that the opulent society allows, or the inability or incompetence of the government to stabilize the economic system.

Let me elaborate on these points. First, consider the family in its role as a consuming unit, adjusting to a high and rising standard of living. It is not all that easy to grow rich successfully; it requires a continual process of learning to improve one's tastes and standards, to budget one's income, to invest wisely in the complex consumer capital goods that constitute a modern high standard of living, and to manage one's property and oneself efficiently. The possibilities of failure are amply illustrated by the financial problems of spend-thriftiness and personal bankruptcy, the medical problems of over-indulgence in food, drink and tobacco, and the social problems of irresponsible parenthood, lax morality, and broken homes. Much of the criticism of the opulent society is concerned with the foolish things on which people spend their money, and the susceptibility of the public to the appeal of gadgetry and meretricious advertising. As a believer in a free society one must have faith that all these things are part of the process by which people learn eventually to manage wealth successfully. But there can be no doubt that the family needs, and can profit by, a great deal of expert help.

Now consider the family as an income-earning unit, selling the services of its human and non-human capital. To make the most of the opportunities of the opulent society requires knowledge of the opportunities and the capacity to move resources to the most profitable opportunity. Knowledge and movement both cost money —in the case of geographical or occupational movement of human resources, often a great deal of money, more than the family with its limited borrowing power can raise. Now knowledge has the peculiarity that once it is there any number of people can use it; for that reason it can be profitable for society to collect it and place it at the disposal of families, even though no individual family would find it worthwhile to collect it. Again, the limitation of family borrowing power may mean that people do not move to higher-paying employment, even though the higher earnings would pay an ample return on the cost of movement. In both respects, the capacity of the family to exploit its opportunities may be seriously restricted by its small economic size.

Now consider the family as the source of the future stock of human capital. In the opulent society, the family typically does not provide on-the-job training for children destined to inherit a family craft, business or profession. Instead, it must prepare its children to seek employment in a specialized economy where their value will depend on the skills and talents they have to offer—which in turn depends on their education. Now, education entails an investment of family resources, even when schools and tuition are provided free, because it requires the family to support the child and forgo the money it could earn for the family if it did not go to school. The ways in which the character and attitudes of the family can affect the use the child makes of its educational opportunities are well known, and I need not elaborate on them. Instead, I want to make two points about the economics of investment in human capital. The first is that even for the best-intentioned and most thoughtful family the planning of a child's education is a terribly difficult problem which can only be solved by the most rudimentary kind of guesswork or rule of thumb. The product of this kind of investment is a more or less specific item of human capital, the returns on which will be realized by the owner by selling his services in the market over the next forty or fifty years. How much information would a professional investor want before he invested the cost of an education in a plant lasting fifty years? By contrast, how much relevant information does the typical parent acquire—and how much could be obtained if he tried—before he decides how much to invest in educating his children and what type of education to invest in? How can anyone—except a college president beating the bushes for endowments—be sure that 'an education', of any kind for anybody, is a good investment? My second point is that because our laws prohibit slavery, even if voluntarily entered into, investment in human capital tends to be very inefficient by comparison with investment in non-human capital. On the one hand, the bright child of poor parents cannot be sold to a capitalist who wants to invest in his talents, nor can his future earning capacity be tied up as security for a loan; the result is that his talents must go undeveloped unless a university or the state is willing to make him a present of an education. On the other hand, family pride coupled with money can result in expenditure on education yielding a low or negative rate of return—especially as education is a consumption good as well as a production good, and educational investment is a foolproof way of beating the inheritance tax.

I have been discussing the difficulties under which the family labours in carrying out the economic functions assigned to it by an individualistic economic system in the opulent society. I want now to discuss the ways in which the limited economic size of the family unit restricts its power to assume full responsibility for providing for its own welfare.

As a consuming unit, the power of the family to govern its own welfare is limited by the fact that, to participate in the benefits of the opulent society, it must live in a community, and its welfare and the quality of its life must accordingly depend in part on the nature of its community environment. One of the demographic effects of the progress of opulence is the concentration of the human population in metropolitan agglomerations of urban and suburban communities. Efficient living in such agglomerations demands the collective provision of a wide variety of services and amenities—water, roads, sewage and garbage disposal, parks, etcetera—and the quality of life depends on the quality of these services. But the family cannot itself choose the level and quality of the collective services it enjoys, except to the usually very limited extent that income and occupation permit it to choose between rival communities providing such services to different extents. Within the community, the level of collective services provided depends on the willingness of families collectively to finance such services by taxation. And there is an inherent tendency in an individualistic and mobile society for such services to be underprovided, because the sacrifice of family income entailed in paying taxes is direct and easily appreciated, while the contribution to family welfare of better community services is indirect, and generally not closely related to the family's tax contribution or proportioned to its current desires for such services. Aside from collective services, the welfare of a family living in a community inevitably depends in countless ways on how the other members of the community—families and business enterprises—conduct their affairs. Such dependence ranges from trivial matters like the irritation of having noisy and untidy neighbours to such serious matters as the threat to health from the pollution of air by smoke and chemicals and of water by sewage and industrial waste, and the threat to security of person and property from the existence of slum neighbourhoods. The welfare of the family is influenced by such things, but the family itself cannot control them—it can only move away if it can afford to. Like the provision of collective services, control of these things requires collective action. And as opulence progresses, it seems likely both that it will appear efficient to undertake the provision of more services collectively, and that increased scientific and social knowledge will reveal more and more cases in which the activities of some members of the community have adverse effects on others requiring social control.

The most serious limitations on the power of the family to support itself, however, result from the narrowness of its economic base—its dependence on the sale of the services of its human capital—and the personal and economic risks to which this subjects it. The personal risks—sickness, accident, incapacitation or death, and survival of self or dependents beyond the end of working life—can in principle be covered by private insurance, annuities or pension plans; the need for social provision for these contingencies arises from lack of sufficient family earning power or foresight to provide for them, or from the inability of commercial insurance to provide adequate coverage of the risks at a profit. The economic risks are uninsurable, because their incidence is unpredictable. They are especially serious for the family in the opulent society, both because its high income is obtained by specializing on a tiny part of the economic process, and because to enjoy that income to the full it must plan its expenditures on the expectation that income will continue to be earned. And these risks are an integral part of the opulent society itself, built into its structure.

There are in fact two sorts of economic risk to family income inherent in the structure of the opulent society. The first is due to the fact I have already noted, that the opulent society is built on the principle of freedom to introduce change if it seems profitable to do so, regardless of the effect on the value of other people's sources of income. The second arises from the fact that such a system is subject to fluctuations in aggregate income, prices, and employment that are difficult for the government to manage, and that may be aggravated by incompetence or wrong-headedness on the part of the managers. It seems to be asking a great deal too much to expect the family to bear the consequences of these kinds of risks, and to assume that it is capable of guessing when it selects occupations for its children what the probability is that twenty or thirty years later automation will be invented, the Japanese will learn to use modern technology, or the governor of the central bank will decide that it is more important to stop inflation than to maintain an adequate level of employment. Nor is unemployment insurance by itself an adequate form of protection of family income against these risks, since it amounts to little more than forcing the worker to save a part of his income to fall back on when he becomes unemployed.

I have spent a considerable amount of time on the problems of the family in the opulent society, because I think it is necessary to appreciate these problems in designing an appropriate social policy. My main point can be summarized in the following very oversimplified model of the opulent economy. In this society there are two basic economic units. On the production side there is the big, well-financed, scientifically managed corporate enterprise; on the consumption side there is the little, precariously financed, not scientifically managed family household. The enterprise is responsible for introducing the new, improved, or cheapened products and services that raise the standard of living; the household has to learn how to use them. The corporation is responsible for the replacement, accumulation and improvement of non-human capital; the household is responsible for the replacement, accumulation and improvement of human capital. The corporate enterprise has come to dominate the productive processes of our economy because it is peculiarly efficient in handling the problems of growth through technical change and capital accumulation; exactly parallel problems arise in the consumption processes of the economy, but our culture confines us to the family partnership. The household and not the corporation is supposed to be the beneficiary of the system; but the knowledge, intelligence and resources it can itself muster to the task of making the most of its opportunities are grossly inadequate by comparison with those of the corporation. The starting point of social policy in an opulent society should be to recognize these limitations and their sources; its objective should be to overcome them by social action consistent with the ideals of a free democratic society.

Before I go on to discuss what I think social policy in the opulent society should be, I want to say more about the notion of human beings as capital, which I have touched on at various points in my argument. The general idea is familiar enough, if only because politicians are so fond of declaiming to labour audiences that 'our greatest natural resource is the skill and adaptability of our people'. But we rarely carry it any further, because in a democratic society our thoughts—even those of economists—rebel at the idea of seriously considering people as pieces of capital equipment equivalent to inanimate objects. It is only recently that economists have begun to appreciate the importance of human skill and training as a cause of opulence, and to work seriously on the value of human capital and the returns to investment in it. There is, I think, nothing inhuman or undemocratic in looking at human ability and skill in this way, providing one knows where to stop. And serious application of the idea could provide a very useful guide to social policy and a yardstick for assessing its efficiency. By serious application I mean that we do not simply say 'education is an investment in human capital' or 'human beings are valuable assets' and conclude that any expenditure on education or conserving human life must be worth while. I mean instead that having recognized that various private activities in our society are concerned with investment in increasing the value of human capital or preventing loss of it—education, medical care, mobility of labour and so forth—we should, first, think seriously about the efficiency of these activities and whether it can be improved by social action; and secondly, calculate whether the investment of public money in carrying these activities further would pay a worthwhile rate of return or not. Similarly, one could check the return on activities now being undertaken, to see if the money could be better spent.

I have suggested the calculation of rates of return on investments in human capital as a guide to social policy; but I would point out that they could never be the final arbiter of our social policy, given our political and social attitudes and our legal restrictions on the sale or pledging of human capital. For one thing, our social and religious beliefs do not permit us to contemplate the scrapping of human capital; yet it is evident that some people, such as the mentally subnormal or ill and the old age pensioners, are economic liabilities, whose value as liabilities we in fact do much to increase by caring for them—in the interests of common humanity we are prepared to make investments with negative yields. For another thing, though this is something on which we might change our minds, our legal and political tradition is against the state charging interest or taking the profits on its investments in human capital; thus the returns on such investment accrue to the person invested in, and the question may legitimately be raised why the taxpayer should be burdened for such investments. This is an important source of discord over educational policy; for example, it is one thing to argue that poor bright boys ought to be invested in, quite another to insist that this be done by free scholarships, so that the boy and not the taxpayer who pays for it gets the return on the investment. Thirdly, the rates of return on investments in human capital can only serve as guides because both the costs and the returns are extremely difficult to measure, and once you have measured them you still have to decide what rate of return makes a profitable investment.

Before I leave the subject of human beings as capital, I should say something about the orders of magnitude involved. I have no figures for Canada, though one can obtain a rough idea of the importance of human capital in this country from the fact that about three quarters of Canadian national income is earned by work and only one quarter by property. For the United States, Dr Burton Weisbrod has calculated the value of the average male at $17,000, if one discounts his prospective earnings at a 10 per cent rate of interest, or $33,000, if one discounts them at a 4 per cent interest rate. He estimates the aggregate value of the male population in 1950 at $1,335 billions (using the 10 per cent rate); this figure may be compared with an estimate of $881 billion for the aggregate value of tangible non-human assets. Dr Weisbrod reckons, incidentally, that the social profit from preventing the death from tuberculosis of a man as old as fifty is in excess of 700 per cent.[3] My senior colleague at the University of Chicago, Professor T. W. Schultz, who is interested in the economics of education, has calculated that the value of the stock of education embodied in the United States labour force in 1957 was $535 billion, equal to 42 per cent of the stock of reproducible wealth (that is, tangible non-human wealth excluding natural resources). Professor Schultz has also calculated the ratio of additional lifetime earnings associated with education to the costs of the education (including both the cost of schools and teachers and the earnings foregone by students); for 1958 his ratios work out at eleven for a college education, twelve for high school, and forty for a completed elementary school education.[4] These results, however, do not necessarily mean that investment in education is more profitable than other investment. Dr Gary Becker, who has carried out a major study of the economics of education for the National Bureau of Economic Research, has concluded that the rate of return on college education is about the same as that on business capital.[5]

After this digression on human beings as capital, I return to the question of social policy in the opulent society. The argument I have

[3] Burton Weisbrod, 'The Valuation of Human Capital', *Journal of Political Economy*, LXIX, no. 5, October 1961, 425–36.

[4] T. W. Schultz, 'Education and Economic Growth', Chap. III, 46–88 in *Social Forces Influencing American Education 1961*, Sixtieth Yearbook of the National Society for the Study of Education, Part II.

[5] Gary S. Becker, 'Underinvestment in College Education?', *American Economic Review*, L, no. 2, May 1960, 346–54.

been presenting seems to me to lead to some general principles of social policy. Let me state these principles, and elaborate a little—I have no time for more than a few suggestions—on what concrete measures they might lead to.

The first principle is that the complexity and changefulness of the opulent society are such that the individual citizen may need, and ought to be provided with, assistance of a variety of kinds if he is to make the most of the opportunities it provides him. The first need is for as good an elementary and secondary education as the individual can absorb. The free provision of such education is our accepted way both of equipping the child to take a place in our complex economic system and of compensating, in part at least, for the inequalities of family circumstance into which children are born. But it needs to be recognized that in the opulent society an increasing part of the real cost of education is the earnings foregone by going to school instead of to work, a cost which may put severe pressure on poor children to drop out of school even though the advantages to themselves and society of further education are great; accordingly society should be ready to assume the financial burden of maintaining school children, as well as of paying the costs of teaching them. The second need is for social provision of a wide variety of expert informational, welfare, and counselling services to help the individual and family to manage their affairs as intelligently and successfully as possible; in this connection it needs to be recognized that a rising standard of living entails increasing use of consumer durables, and demands increasingly the ability to understand and manage credit. A third need is for appreciation of the severity of the demands that life in the opulent society makes on those who participate in it, and recognition that those who for one reason or another are unable to meet these demands ought not to be treated simply as contemptible failures, but should instead be treated as casualties of the struggle for progress.

The second principle is that in an urbanized industrial society an important part of the process of raising the standard of living consists in the progressive improvement of the standards of services and amenities provided collectively, and of the quality of the environment. A community in which the schools look like factories used to look and the factories like schools ought to look, in which the decay and squalour of city centres forces people to risk their lives and blood pressures commuting miles from and to cosy homes in cheerlessly regimented suburbs, and in which the pollution of local beaches forces them to drive hundreds of miles in search of water fit for people and fish to swim in, can hardly be said to be employing its opulence wisely. Nor can anyone seriously believe that urban and rural slums are an appropriate training ground for responsible citizens of the opulent society. The opulent economy concentrates people in metropolitan agglomerations and gives them increasing leisure for enjoyment. The welfare of the opulent society requires the social provision of the collective requirements of decent living, restraint on the private propensity to poison one's neighbour's pleasure, and progressive improvement of the social environment of private living through town planning, slum clearance, and imaginative public works.

The third principle is that since the society is founded on the belief that individual freedom to introduce change serves the social good, the society and not the individual member should assume the costs that this freedom may impose on other members when these costs become unreasonably high. Beyond a certain point, the society collectively should bear the economic risks imposed on the family by dependence on the sale of its services, because society itself creates those risks. The same principle should extend to the personal risks, though there the reason is that these risks are the only major remaining risks to family welfare in a properly functioning opulent society. What I am arguing for here is the reversal of the social insurance principle. In the opulent society, the average family should be able to bear the costs of short-term unemployment or minor illness and accident, by drawing on family savings or borrowing against future earning power. It is the prolonged loss of earnings from technological or structural unemployment or unemployment due to depressed business conditions, and the combined high expense and loss of earnings from severe illness or accident, that is disastrous to family finance. And these are precisely the contingencies that cannot be covered by insurance, whether private or social. Instead of providing unemployment benefits for a limited period after the individual has become unemployed, and eventually casting him off to depend on his own resources and public assistance, social policy should provide benefits beginning after the individual has been unemployed for some time, and increasing in amount towards the level of his normal income in employment as he remains unemployed. At some stage it should be recognized that the unemployed individual is a victim of anti-inflationary policy or of economic change; in the former case he should be supported until the government is prepared to restore full employment, in the latter he should be compensated by being retrained or provided with an adequate pension on which to retire. Instead of leaving the individual to bear the risks of unlimited medical expenses, social policy should hold him responsible for a first slice of the costs proportioned to his ability to pay, and bear the remaining costs of providing the medical care he needs up to a socially-determined standard. In addition, social provision should extend to replacing the income lost by prolonged illness or incapacitation, on the same plan as I have suggested for loss of income by unemployment.

The fourth principle is that the opulent society ought to apply to its social policy the same principles of rational calculation, innovation and exploitation of technical progress as it applies in its productive system. Let me illustrate what I mean by three examples. First, take education: this is by far our most important capital-goods-producing industry, yet it is very doubtful that it is carried on with anything like the efficiency of a commercial enterprise. Its selection of material for processing is strongly influenced by the irrelevant consideration of family capacity to pay, though it should be possible to design some form of enforceable long-term education loan to support poor but promising students, or at least to take some notice of the fact that an educated man generally will produce substantially more future tax revenue for the state than an uneducated man. Its standards of pay are set by political decision, its methods of teaching by academic tradition, and the proportion of the student's year devoted to it is an inheritance from our agricultural past; very little attention is paid to the fact that an opulent society progressively raises the value of labour—including students' time—and cheapens the cost of capital equipment. And it is very doubtful indeed that it allocates its output among products on the basis of sufficiently detailed and long-range forecasts of demand for them, or builds enough flexibility into its products to make them as adaptable to an uncertain future as they should be.[6]

Second, take medical care. The rising cost of medical care has created the chief threat to family security in the opulent society, and constitutes one of the main obstacles to generous social provision of medical care. One cause of the high cost of medical care is the high cost of doctors' services. This in turn is the consequence of allowing the medical profession to govern the standards and duration of medical training. The progressive raising of standards has had the effect of greatly increasing the investment of money and foregone earnings required by a medical education, an investment the returns on which must be recouped from the fees the doctor charges his patients; further, the great cost of the investment and the uncertainty of the returns has restricted the supply of doctors, so that the average rate of return on a medical education is appreciably higher

[6] T. W. Schultz, *op. cit.*, 82–4.

than that on almost any other comparable educational investment.[7] A rational approach to investment in medical training would aim at reducing the cost of the investment by specializing doctors at an earlier stage and fixing the standard of basic training at what society could afford to pay for, and by carrying investment in medical educations to the point at which the rate of return was brought down to the average for the economy. It would also remove the conflict between the doctor's professional responsibility and his private interest inherent in the fee system, by putting doctors on salary or fixing standard prices for standard treatments.[8,9]

Third, take the problem of relief of depressed areas, an activity Canada has been engaged in, one way or another, since Confederation. Sentiment strongly favours methods that leave the people in the area, and that aim at creating employment opportunities that otherwise would not exist there, to avoid the social and human problems of moving the people elsewhere and to reconcile aid with the ethic of self-respecting independence. The trouble with this type of policy is that it generally results in creating self-perpetuating pockets of low-quality living that continue to require public support. It would frequently be much cheaper over the long run to invest very large sums in moving people out of such areas and establishing them in more prosperous areas where they, or at least their children, could become full participants in the opulent society.

Those are the principles that I believe should govern social policy in the opulent society. Before concluding, I should comment briefly on two objections that will doubtless be raised to any and all applications of them.

The first objection is that such a poilcy costs money, and taxes are too high already. High taxes are often blamed on social security and welfare expenditure, though in fact the present level of taxes is accounted for to a great extent by defence expenditure and by our habit of financing wars by borrowing rather than taxation—two

[7] Cf. M. Friedman and S. Kuznets, *Income from Independent Professional Practice* (New York: National Bureau of Economic Research, 1945), Chap. 4, 95–173, and Chap. 9, sec. 3, 393–5. These authors found, on the basis of pre-war data for the United States, that the average income of doctors was 32 per cent higher than that of dentists; of this difference, 17 per cent could be accounted for by the cost of the three years additional education required of doctors; the remainder is attributed to the greater difficulty of entry into medicine.

[8] See Reuben Kessel, 'Price Discrimination in Medicine', *The Journal of Law and Economics*, 1, October 1958, 20–53.

[9] For an analysis of the influence of the Canadian medical profession on Canadian public policy regarding health and related matters, see Malcolm G. Taylor, 'The Medical Profession and Public Policy', *The Canadian Journal of Economics and Political Science*, XXVI, no. 1, February 1960, 108–27.

activities that probably contribute more to the security of the upper classes than they cost them in taxes. But more expenditure on social policy would undoubtedly require more tax revenue.

The main economic objection to high taxes is the incentive they give to tax avoidance. This problem and the revenue problem could to a significant extent be solved simultaneously by tightening up on business expense allowances and treating capital gains as income subject to tax; and additional taxes, including a tax on advertising and heavier taxes on gifts and inheritances between generations, could be easily justified. But the dilemma that more extensive social measures require more taxation is fundamentally a consequence of our antiquated way of financing governmental activity. Though government plays an important role in creating and maintaining the conditions under which wealth is created and income is earned, we allow the wealth and income to accrue as private property, and finance the government by taxing back the money after it has passed into private hands. I suggest that a more sensible way of conducting public finance in an opulent society would be to give the government a direct participation in the income of the economy, rather than a tax claim on it. One way of moving in this direction would be to accumulate the proceeds of inheritance taxes in the form of a government portfolio of ordinary shares and industrial bonds, instead of spending them as current income.

The second objection is the allegation that any extension of social security will sap the initiative and enterprise on which the competitive system depends. To that there are two answers. One is that an opulent society can afford to tolerate some inefficiency and waste in its social policy just as it does in its household consumption. The other is that there are good reasons for thinking that increased social security will increase and not reduce the initiative and enterprise of the individual in our society. One such reason is the characteristic ethos of the opulent society itself—an ethos of professional expertise and responsibility, of pride in applying intelligence and ingenuity to the solution of problems, of doing one's job well, of looking for opportunities to assume more responsibility. Educated people are not driven by the fear of failure but by the challenge of accomplishment, and they work best when they have the security to concentrate on the job they are qualified to do. Another, and to me more cogent, reason is that if social policy does not provide people with the security they want they will not simply do without it. They will try to provide it by whatever means they can, and usually the means they choose reduce the efficiency, flexibility, and progressiveness of the economy. Trade unions enforce restrictive practices; companies form price agreements; workers and executives alike demand that their company provide health and pension plans, thus tying themselves to that company; industries unable to meet foreign competition demand tariff protection; depressed areas demand discriminatory treatment. The result is an inefficient social security system and an inefficient economy. And whatever one thinks of an inefficient social security system, an inefficient economy is undesirable. In the first place, we face a challenge to our high standard of living from the spread of industrialization and modern technology around the world. In the second place, we have an obligation to share the fruits and techniques of our opulence with the underdeveloped nations. And finally, we are nowhere near the point of satiation with the good things that enrich and civilize life.

INDEX

For Product Safety Concerns and Information please contact our EU representative GPSR@taylorandfrancis.com
Taylor & Francis Verlag GmbH, Kaufingerstraße 24, 80331 München, Germany

www.ingramcontent.com/pod-product-compliance
Ingram Content Group UK Ltd.
Pitfield, Milton Keynes, MK11 3LW, UK
UKHW011013180926
475701UK00004B/723

* 9 7 8 1 0 3 2 0 2 9 4 6 7 *